A VITAL NATIONAL SEMINAR

The Supreme Court
in
American Political Life

☆

by
Richard Funston
Professor of Political Science
San Diego State University

The discussion of problems and the declaration of broad principles by the courts is a vital element in the community experience through which American policy is made. The Supreme Court is, among other things, an educational body, and the Justices are inevitably teachers in a vital national seminar.

—EUGENE V. ROSTOW
The Sovereign Prerogative

Mayfield Publishing Company

KF
8742
.F86

Copyright © 1978 by Mayfield Publishing Company
First edition 1978

All rights reserved. No portion of this book may be reproduced in any form or by any means without written permission of the publisher.

Library of Congress Catalog Card Number: 78-51944
International Standard Book Number: 0-87484-409-6

Manufactured in the United States of America
Mayfield Publishing Company
285 Hamilton Avenue
Palo Alto, California 94301

This book was set in Century Medium by Trend Western Technical Corporation and was printed and bound by the George Banta Company. Sponsoring editor was Alden C. Paine, Carole Norton supervised editing, and Zipporah Collins was manuscript editor. Michelle Hogan supervised production, and the book was designed by Nancy Sears. Acknowledgment is made to the following publishers: Yale University Press for permission to quote from Eugene Rostow, *The Sovereign Prerogative*, pp. 167-68; The University of Chicago Press for permission to quote (on p. 56) from Philip B. Kurland, *Politics, the Constitution, and the Warren Court*, pp. 17-18, 22; Harvard University Press for permission to quote (on p. 218) from Robert H. Jackson, *The Supreme Court in the American System of Government*, p. 81; The Association of American Law Schools for permission to quote (on p. 146) from Roscoe Pound, "The Still Small Voice of the Commerce Clause," in Vol. 3, *Selected Essays on Constitutional Law*, p. 932; *American Political Science Review* for permission to use material from "The Supreme Court and Critical Elections," v. 69 (September 1975), pp. 795-811; and *Political Science Quarterly* for permission to use material from "The Double Standard of Constitutional Protection in the Era of the Welfare State," v. 90 (Summer 1975), pp. 261-287.

This book is dedicated to

YORK

(without whose help it would have been finished
a lot sooner)

and

HIS MOTHER

(without whose love it would never have been
finished at all)

CONTENTS

PREFACE
xiii

CHAPTER 1
THE COURT AND THE CONSTITUTION

The Court as Policy Maker   1
The Power of Constitutional Interpretation   2
    The Importance of Discretionary Judgment   3
    The Importance of Authority over Coordinate Branches   3
The Source of the Court's Power   4
    The Rationale of *Marbury*   5
    The Failure of *Marbury* as a Source   6
    Constitutional Bases of the Power   7

        Historical Precedents for the Power   12
        The Structural-Cultural Bases of Judicial Review   13
        The Philosophic Rationale for Judicial Review   14
The Scope of Judicial Review   17
        Restraints Imposed by Congress   18
        Restraints Imposed by the President   19
        The Power of Appointment   20
        Limits Imposed by the Court Itself   21
        The Pros and Cons of Self-Restraint   29
Summary   30

CHAPTER 2
THE COURT AND POLITICAL CHANGE

The Court as Protector of Minorities   33
The Court as Agent of the Majority   34
        Patterns of Electoral Behavior   35
        Patterns of Party Behavior   37
        Patterns of Court Behavior   41
        Comparison of Court and Party Patterns   45
The Court's Roles in American Politics   46
        The Court as Legitimator   46
        The Court as Republican Schoolmaster   48
        Objections to the View of the Court as Educator   49
A Model of the Court's Role   52
        The Court's Role in Realignment Periods   53
        Criticisms of the Model   54
The Judicial Dialogue   54
Summary   56

CHAPTER 3
THE COURT AND THE PRESIDENCY

Conflict or Alliance?   63
Theories of Presidential Power   65
The Growth of Presidential Power   66
The Court's View of Presidential Power   66
    The Power to Protect the Peace   66
    The Power to Discharge Federal Officials   69
    The Power to Conduct Foreign Relations   71
    The Power to Make War   75
    Domestic Aspects of the War Power   78
    Executive Privilege   86
The Impact of the Court on Presidential Power   90
Summary   91

CHAPTER 4
THE COURT AND CONGRESS

Congressional Delegation of Power   96
    The Court's View of Delegation   97
    Delegation to Administrative Agencies   100
Congressional Investigatory Power   102
    The Requirement of Legislative Purpose   103
    The Presumption of Legislative Purpose   103
    The Scope Requirement   104
    The Fifth Amendment Privilege   105
    The Pertinence Requirement   105
    Shortcomings of the Legislative Purpose Doctrine   107
Congressional Immunity   108
    Obtaining Information   109
    Publishing and Distributing Information   110
Membership of the House   111
    Congressionally Imposed Qualifications   111
    The *Powell* Case   112

Apportionment   115
Congress's Regulatory Powers   117
    The Implied Power   117
    The Power to Tax   118
    The Commerce Power   120
    The Power to Enforce the Reconstruction Amendments   123
Restrictions on Congressional Power   127
    Fifth Amendment "Equal Protection"   128
    Unenumerated Substantive Rights   130
The Court's Current Stance   130
    Congressional Response   132
Summary   133

CHAPTER 5
THE COURT AND THE STATES

The Federal System   138
    The Federal-State Division of Power   139
The Court's Authority over State Courts   140
    The *Martin* Case   140
    The *Cohens* Case   141
The Court's Division of Power   143
    The Tenth Amendment   144
    The Marshall Court's View   145
    Developments under the Taney Court   145
    The Post-Civil War Policy   147
    The New Deal Court and After   148
    The Burger Court and the New Federalism   150
Expansions of Federal Power   152
    The Treaty Power   153
    Federal Reapportionment Mandates   157
    Nationalization of the Bill of Rights   161
Criticism of the Court's Policies   166
Summary   167

CHAPTER 6
THE COURT AND THE INDIVIDUAL

First Amendment Freedoms   173
    The Religion Clauses   173
    Freedom of Expression   177
The Rights of the Accused   183
    Search and Seizure   184
    Custodial Interrogation   186
    Burger Court Developments in Criminal Procedure   189
Equal Protection   190
    Judicial Response to the Fourteenth Amendment   191
    The Separate But Equal Doctrine   191
    Educational Equality   192
    "Benign" Racial Classifications   195
    Other Classifications   195
The Double Standard: "Human" Rights versus "Property" Rights   199
    Justifications of the Policy   200
    Modern Consequences of the Double Standard   205
Summary   206

CHAPTER 7
THE COURT AND AMERICAN SOCIETY

Constitutional Interpretation   213
    The Court as Reflection of Society   214
    The Error of Absolute Jurisprudence   214
    Limits on the Court's Flexibility   215
The Educational Dialogue   216
The Court as Symbol of Nationhood   218

INDEX
221

PREFACE

This book attempts to do two things: (1) summarize and survey Supreme Court decision making on a wide variety of significant issues, and (2) analyze that decision making in terms of an explicit theoretical framework concerning the Court's essential functions within the political system. The late Clinton Rossiter asserted that "the true study of our system of government begins with these points of contact—between President and Congress, Congress and Supreme Court, and Supreme Court and President—rather than with the powers . . . of any one of the three branches."[1] Adhering to this sage advice, the pages that follow discuss the Court's interfaces with other elements in the political process: the Constitution, the executive branch, Congress, the state governments, the political parties, and the American people, both as individuals and collectively.

This is not exclusively a treatise on constitutional law, though a discussion of that subject can hardly be divorced from an analysis of the judicial function. It is, after all, impossible to talk about the Supreme Court without talking about its decisions, and constitutional interpretation is intimately related to the Court's role in the American polity. But material is also included discussing the Court's construction of federal statutes, particularly as it affects the administrative agencies and congressional enforcement of civil rights. Nor is this a history of the Court, though some subjects have been treated historically where appropriate.

As such, the book should prove to be most useful in upper-division, undergraduate courses on constitutional law, the Supreme Court, and the judicial process generally. Because it does not emphasize civil liberties issues to the exclusion of other matters, the volume will be especially worthwhile for instructors who are teaching about the principles of federalism and the separation of powers. Also, unlike many other texts on the Court and constitutional law, this book does not discuss the Court's decisions as just a collection of cases; rather, it seeks to present the decisions within a coherent model of the Court's role in the policy-making process. Students, therefore, are discouraged from seeing the Court and the law as entities separate from and unrelated to politics.

I also hope that the book will find a market among survey courses in American government. The Supreme Court of the United States is a major component in the American political process and the most powerful court the world has ever seen. Yet this unique judicial agency is often the unwanted stepchild of the American government survey course. An all too common approach is to acknowledge that there is a third, judicial branch of the national government, assign for reading a simple case study of a single, landmark decision, and let it go at that. The students are given to understand that the Court plays some role in the political system, but, at best, they are left to wonder exactly what that role might be. At worst, they are taught strict—and unrealistic—separation of powers theory: Congress makes the laws; the president enforces the laws; the Court decides individual cases according to the law. This book tries to fill a gap in the texts available to survey course instructors who are not themselves expert in public law. Its aim is to explain the Court and constitutional decision making in nontechnical, understandable terms and to relate them to the overall political process. More sophisticated jurimetric materials, such as those dealing with the group dynamics of the Court's decision-making processes or psychometric analyses of the justices' voting behaviors, have been left to more advanced instruction.

However, the present volume departs from the traditional model of a text in that it takes a position. It is argumentative—and arguable. Judge Learned Hand admonished (an admonition I paraphrase in the concluding chapter) that criticism of the judiciary, while entirely proper, should be undertaken in a spirit of humility by those who will honestly seek to understand the courts and recognize the difficulties of their task. Bearing that in mind, I have throughout, sometimes more explicitly than others, advanced an evaluation of the wisdom and desirability of the Court's performance. It is my hope that this point of view, will stimulate readers to think and react, rather than merely absorb the information offered.

The writing of this book was assisted in part by a San Diego State University Summer Faculty Fellowship and by smaller grants from the San Diego State University Foundation, which I gratefully acknowledge. It was also encouraged by Dean Frank Marini of San Diego State, who made available to me released time and library space that greatly facilitated my research. While I labored as a visiting professor at U.C.L.A., my rough draft was transformed into typescript by Ms. Nancy Gusten, Ms. Becky Herrera, Ms. Teddi Maldonado, Ms. Clare Suen, and Ms. Clare Walker. Mrs. Veva Link of San Diego State University also provided valuable secretarial assistance. For all of their efforts, I am most appreciative.

The *American Political Science Review* and the *Political Science Quarterly* were kind enough to permit me to revise and incorporate essays I had previously published in those journals. On short notice and at long range, Zipporah Collins—muse of the blue pencil—performed herculean editorial tasks. Alden Paine, Carole Norton, and the rest at Mayfield were the kind of publishers any academic author would covet. And Harry Balfe (Montclair State College) provided small but critical contributions.

Most importantly, several scholars reviewed this work at various stages of its completion. Their suggestions, comments, and criticisms were sometimes infuriating, sometimes deflating, but invariably valuable and enlightening. Whether they believe it or not, I owe thanks to: David Adamany (University of Wisconsin, Madison), Gayle Binion (University of California, Santa Barbara), Keith O. Boyum (California State University, Fullerton), Richard Cortner (University of Arizona), Susan Heike (University of Nevada, Reno), John D. Kay (Santa Barbara City College), John R. Schmidhauser (University of Southern California), and Martin Shapiro (University of California, Berkeley).

My saddest duty is to acknowledge the help of the late Joel Ish (U.C.L.A.) whose untimely passing deprived us of a keen mind and a promising student of the Court.

It goes without saying that all of the above are to be absolved of blame for any errors, deficiencies, or other defects that may persist in the finished work. It is, however, my hope that most of those will have been eliminated and that this little book succeeds at least partially in following Justice Frankfurter's advice to another author about to write on the Court:

> I said that it seemed to me that the important thing for a man like himself to do was to educate the American people as to the nature and function of the Court and the nature of the duties of the judges; more particularly that the framers of the Constitution had decided not to make the Court another branch of the legislature.[2]

NOTES

1 Clinton Rossiter, *The Supreme Court and the Commander in Chief,* expanded ed. with an introductory note and additional text by Richard P. Longaker. (Ithaca, N.Y.: Cornell University Press, 1976), p. v.

2 Felix Frankfurter, *From the Diaries of Felix Frankfurter, with a Biographical Essay and Notes,* ed. Joseph P. Lash (New York: W. W. Norton & Co., 1975), p. 276.

THE COURT AND THE CONSTITUTION

CHAPTER 1

THE COURT AS POLICY MAKER

The Supreme Court of the United States is a political agency. Unless this is fully appreciated at the outset, attempts at understanding the Court will be in vain. Among judicial bodies throughout the world, past as well as present, the Court stands out as a uniquely powerful political institution. No other court has ever been so continuously, consistently, and intimately involved in the policy-making processes of government. On the other hand, the Supreme Court is also a court of law, and its policy making is *judicial* policy making. Its policy-making power resembles that of the legislature or the bureaucracy, but, precisely because it is a court, it labors under certain handicaps and restrictions that legislative and executive agencies do not experience. This double nature—being both political and legal—makes the Court one of the most fascinating institutions for study in American politics, yet at the same time one of the most difficult to understand. Overemphasis of either the political or the legal aspect of the Court to the exclusion of the other obscures its essential reality.

The Supreme Court has achieved its political eminence largely because it is, by design, independent from yet coordinate with the national executive and legislative branches and because it has been entrusted, perhaps by accident, with the ultimate authority to interpret the Constitution. Because the Constitution is written but imprecise, its interpretation requires the exercise of discretionary judgment. Rather than apply legal doctrines with well-determined meanings, the Court must choose between competing interpretations that arise basically from differing economic, social, or political values. Historically, the exercise of this power by the Court has had important consequences for the direction of American public policy.

THE POWER OF CONSTITUTIONAL INTERPRETATION

Foremost among the Court's interpretive powers is its power of judicial review. The concept of judicial review has a unique and specific meaning in the United States. It goes beyond the Supreme Court's exercise of its appellate jurisdiction, correcting errors of law made in lower courts. That judicial function is performed by appellate courts in other countries. It also goes beyond the Supreme Court's judging of the acts of *subordinate* governmental agencies within a federal system. This, too, is done by other courts in other federally organized countries, such as Canada. The distinguishing feature of judicial review in the United States is the power of the federal judiciary and ultimately of the Supreme Court to judge the constitutionality of the acts of *coordinate* branches of the federal government—Congress and the president—and, if necessary, to declare those acts unconstitutional, nullifying them with finality.

Actually, this finality does not mean that the Court's constitutional pronouncements are irreversible. The Constitution can be amended. Statutes may be redrafted to produce a desired policy while avoiding constitutional difficulties. Political pressures may be applied to the Court to bring about a change of mind. Or the inevitable processes of death and retirement may allow the appointment of new justices of a different persuasion who will vote to overrule a previous decision. What the fact of finality does mean is that, according to American political tradition, the coordinate branch whose act has been declared unconstitutional does not have the power to reverse the Court immediately. Americans accept the Court's interpretation of the Constitution as binding, even though they may disagree with it. Thus, the power to interpret the fundamental law authoritatively is lodged with a very small, highly secretive elite. This little band of unelected, life-tenured judges may thwart the will of the people's elected representatives by invoking its power of constitutional interpretation.

The Importance of Discretionary Judgment

This would not be a particularly important power, if the Constitution were a clear, precise, and all-inclusive legal code. In that case, the justices would merely discover the law. Many Americans appear to believe that this is in fact what happens, and the Court has on occasion fostered this conception. In *United States v. Butler*, for example, a 1936 decision declaring the New Deal's Agricultural Adjustment Act unconstitutional, Justice Owen J. Roberts, who actually knew better, wrote:

> There should be no misunderstanding as to the function of this court in such a case. It is sometimes said that the court assumes a power to overrule or control the action of the people's representatives. This is a misconception. The Constitution is the supreme law of the land ordained and established by the people. All legislation must conform to the principles it lays down. When an act of Congress is appropriately challenged in the courts as not conforming to the constitutional mandate the judicial branch of the Government has only one duty,—to lay the article of the Constitution which is invoked beside the statute which is challenged and to decide whether the latter squares with the former.[1]

This may be what happens in a trial court. Indeed, most trials involve the application of established law to unclear facts. The law of murder, for example, is reasonably clear. In a murder trial it is the facts that must be determined. But the Supreme Court is asked to render judgment when the law itself is unclear.

The Constitution's greatest strength has been its flexibility. That observation has become a cliché of American political discourse. Like most clichés, it contains more than a grain of truth. But the Constitution is flexible because it is vague and imprecise. Its lack of precision calls for an authoritative interpreter and demands the exercise of broad discretion in deciding its meaning and, thus, deciding questions of government power and public policy. Constitutional law, if it is to remain law, must retain some element of stability and predictability; but, if it is to be constitutional, at least for an evolving society, it cannot remain static. The Supreme Court, then, must play a creative role, and constitutional law becomes a political instrument.

The Importance of Authority over Coordinate Branches

The Court, of course, decides cases other than those concerning the constitutionality of a congressional statute or a presidential action. Obviously, the Court makes public policy when judging the constitutionality of state actions.

For an example one need look no further than *Brown v. Board of Education*, the 1954 decision outlawing racial segregation and setting the country on the long and difficult road to equal educational opportunity.[2] Similarly, the Court's power to interpret statutes is of great significance. When, for example, the Court interpreted the classification of conscientious objectors (who are exempt from the draft) to include those whose opposition to war is not based on traditional religious belief in a Supreme Being, it created a policy with important consequences for the lives of thousands of Americans. In fact, the power of judicial review has historically been the least used of the Supreme Court's policy-making powers, and the Court has seldom succeeded in having the last word with Congress on a major policy matter, though it has fought some fairly successful delaying actions.[3] However, the function that makes the United States Supreme Court a uniquely political court, unlike any other in the world, is this power to interpret the Constitution with respect to the acts of the president and Congress and to set them aside if it determines that they violate the supreme law of the land.

This power has significant implications for the democratic character, or lack of it, of the American system of government. As the English Bishop Hoadly observed, though speaking of other circumstances:

> Whoever hath an absolute authority to interpret any written or spoken
> laws, it is he who is truly the lawgiver to all intents and purposes,
> and not the person who first wrote or spoke them.[4]

THE SOURCE OF THE COURT'S POWER

How, then, did the Supreme Court obtain this unique, indeed incredible, power? A good lawyer's answer would be simply to cite *Marbury v. Madison*, the first case enunciating the doctrine.[5] Following its crushing defeat in the election of 1800, the Federalist Party retreated into the judiciary, as Thomas Jefferson put it. The lame duck Federalist Congress created dozens of new federal judgeships, to which the defeated President Adams appointed deserving Federalists who would otherwise have been unemployed once the Jefferson administration took office. Indeed, so numerous were the appointments that (at least, so legend has it) Adams stayed up until midnight of his last day in office signing the commissions. One of these "midnight appointees" was William Marbury, named a justice of the peace for the District of Columbia. But, although his commission had been signed by the president and the Great Seal of the United States had been affixed to it, due to an oversight Marbury never received the commission. Once the Jeffersonians were in the executive, they refused to deliver it. Marbury, therefore, brought an action for a writ of mandamus—a court order to compel the secretary of state, James Madison, to deliver his commission to him. Because it involved a public minister, the case was filed in the Supreme Court under its original jurisdiction; that is the Supreme Court would be the trial court, the first court to hear the case.

Marbury put Chief Justice John Marshall in a most difficult situation. He, ironically enough, had been the secretary of state under Adams who had failed to deliver Marbury's commission. It is perhaps not too much to say that Marshall was between the proverbial rock and the hard place. If he held in favor of his fellow Federalist's claim, the Jefferson administration had made it perfectly clear that it would ignore the writ of mandamus. The administration would be supported by its majority in Congress, and the Court would be revealed as a weak and ineffectual organ. On the other hand, if he simply capitulated to the administration's claim of absolute power to withhold Marbury's commission, Marshall himself would expose the Court's impotence. His solution to this problem exhibited nothing short of genius.

The Rationale of *Marbury*

Dividing his opinion into three parts, the Great Chief Justice inquired first whether Marbury had a legal right to his commission. This Marshall answered in the affirmative. When a commission is signed and sealed, he argued, it is complete; the appointment need not depend on its delivery. To withhold the commission was illegal. Denying any intention of involving the Court in the political affairs of the cabinet, Marshall nevertheless held that, when a cabinet officer's duties involve the rights of private persons, that officer is responsible to the law.

Having resolved the first question in Marbury's favor, the chief justice proceeded to his second inquiry: Marbury had a right to the commission, but did the law afford him a remedy? This, too, Marshall answered affirmatively. At this point Marshall's opinion seemed to be marching resolutely toward a logically inescapable conclusion—and a political disaster. But, as Marshall confronted his third question, the decision took a sudden and acute turn. If Marbury does have a remedy at law, asked Marshall, is it a writ of mandamus issuing from the Supreme Court? Marshall's answer, destined to ring down through the decades of American constitutional development, was an unexpected and resounding "No."

Why? Because, wrote Marshall, section 13 of the Judiciary Act of 1789, extending to the Supreme Court the power to issue writs of mandamus, is unconstitutional. Here is his reasoning: The Supreme Court's *appellate* jurisdiction is, under the Constitution, subject to "such Exceptions . . . as Congress shall make."[6] But the grant of its *original* jurisdiction contained no such qualification. Thus, Congress has no power to alter the Court's original jurisdiction. The Court's power to issue writs of mandamus was not prescribed by the Constitution as part of the grant of original jurisdiction. That power must therefore be excluded, and Congress cannot confer it on the Court by statute.

As virtually every commentator on *Marbury* has pointed out, this is very strained logic indeed. Marshall's interpretation of "original jurisdiction" is unreasonably narrow. It violates a basic canon of Supreme Court interpretation: that a law ought not to be held unconstitutional if by some other reasonable interpretation it may be held valid. Section 13 of the Judiciary Act of 1789 did not increase the Court's original jurisdiction in the sense of increasing the number of cases the Court might hear. It merely provided the Court with yet another tool, the power to issue writs of mandamus, for use in cases that the Constitution had already put under the Court's original jurisdiction. Moreover, even if Marshall's resolution of the jurisdictional question is correct, he should not have begun with his first two questions and answers. Rather he should have denied the Court's jurisdiction in the case and avoided any statement on the question of Marbury's right to the commission. After all, if the Court doesn't have jurisdiction, it doesn't have jurisdiction, and any other remarks it may choose to utter are irrelevant.

As a political document, however, the opinion in *Marbury* is a masterpiece of indirection. By avoiding the question of jurisdiction until the end, Marshall was able to deliver a lecture in an aside to Madison and, by extension, to Madison's superior and Marshall's chief foe, Jefferson. Yet, by deciding against Marbury, Marshall gave the executive branch no opportunity to defy the Court. Marshall's "logic" placed him in the enviable position of being able to assume and reject power all in the same breath. On the one hand, he is the soul of judicial modesty in denying that the Court may accept even the relatively trivial power of being able to issue writs of mandamus. On the other hand, he claims, by both precept and example, that the Court can nullify acts of Congress as unconstitutional.

The Failure of *Marbury* as a Source

Not the least interesting aspect of *Marbury*, in terms of the origins of the Supreme Court's power of judicial review, is that it rather seriously begs the question. Marshall chose to decide whether an act of Congress that does not conform to the Constitution can be valid. But the chief question in *Marbury* was: Who should be empowered to decide whether a given statute violates the Constitution? No one has ever claimed that a statute that runs afoul of the Constitution can be considered a valid law. The Constitution, both theoretically and according to its own terms, is the supreme law of the land, and a statute that violates any of its provisions must be null and void. However, whether a statute goes against the Constitution is usually something less than self-evident. The real question is: Who should have the power to interpret the Constitution and decide which statutes are and are not constitutional?

Marshall argued that Congress could not have the power to interpret the Constitution; this would allow an agency whose power is supposed to be limited by the Constitution to set the limits of its own power. This, he asserted, would be absurd. But Marshall neglected the fact that the Constitution was designed to limit the power of government generally, including the power of the judiciary. So it may be just as absurd to allow the courts to set the limits of their own power. In fact, it may be even more absurd: It could always be argued that giving the power of constitutional interpretation to the elected members of Congress would ultimately give the power to the people of the United States in their collective capacity, whereas the Supreme Court is not subject to electoral control.

Why, then, has this power been lodged with the Court? The answer that *Marbury* established it begs the question; for, if the Court's power to act as final arbiter is found in *Marbury*, it is not too much to ask, Where did the *Marbury* Court find this power? Reliance on precedent obscures rather than answers the question of the origins of judicial review.

Constitutional Bases of the Power

It is not inappropriate to turn to the text of the Constitution itself. In fact, in *Marbury*, Marshall briefly canvassed most of the arguments that have been advanced since to show that judicial review is found, at least implicitly, in the Constitution.[7]

Article III, Section 2
First, Marshall turned to article III, section 2, which provides that "the judicial Power shall extend to all Cases ... arising under this Constitution." How could the courts decide cases arising under the Constitution without examining the Constitution itself, Marshall asked. But note that the Constitution extends to cases arising under it only the "judicial power." The real question is whether the judicial power includes the power to decide the constitutionality of congressional statutes. What is the nature and extent of the judicial power? That is the question, and again it is the question that *Marbury* does not confront.

The Supremacy Clause
The supremacy clause provides that the "Constitution, and all of the Laws of the United States which shall be made in pursuance thereof ... shall be the supreme Law of the Land; and the Judges

in every State shall be bound thereby, any Thing in the Constitution or Laws of any State to the Contrary notwithstanding."[8] Marshall also relied on this provision, and some modern scholars have contended that it is the most persuasive textual support for the power of judicial review. If it is, it is not a very strong argument. First of all, the supremacy clause is addressed to state judges not to federal judges. The phrase "Judges in every State" might be stretched to include most lower federal judges, on the ground that they sit in the states. But that will not support the Supreme Court's power of judicial review, since it does not sit in a state. Actually, what the supremacy clause does, and all that it does, is to go over the heads of state governments and speak to state judges directly, telling them that the federal Constitution and federal statutes are superior to any state acts and that it is their duty to enforce the supreme federal law against any contrary state law.

But, then, doesn't the supremacy clause authorize state judges to declare congressional acts unconstitutional? And doesn't the Supreme Court therefore have the power of judicial review? This argument rests on the following syllogism: The supremacy clause entrusts state judges with the power to declare federal statutes unconstitutional, for only those laws that are made "in pursuance" of the Constitution are supreme; therefore, state judges must determine whether a law has been made in pursuance of the Constitution, that is, whether it is constitutional. If there were no central appellate agency, the exercise of this power by state judges would create confusion; a federal statute might be ruled constitutional in Maine and unconstitutional in Alabama. Therefore, if state courts are entrusted with the power to declare federal legislation unconstitutional, the Supreme Court must have a similar power when it reviews state court decisions.

But does the supremacy clause grant to state judges the power to nullify congressional acts? In other words, is the initial premise of the syllogism valid? Probably not, for this particular interpretation of the supremacy clause would actually achieve the exact opposite of what the clause was written to achieve. It is clear that the clause was intended to make federal authority supreme over state authority. Yet, if state judges had the power to overturn federal law, the opposite effect would be produced.

The clause simply states that state judges are to be bound by federal statutes made in pursuance of the Constitution. The term *a statute made in pursuance of the Constitution* may easily be interpreted to mean simply a statute properly enacted according to constitutionally specified procedure: a bill passed by Congress and signed by the president or passed over presidential veto by the required majorities in Congress. The responsibility for determining the constitutionality of a federal law would then rest with the president and the Congress that enacted the statute. Once the law is enacted, state court judges would take it as given that the law was made in pursuance of the Constitution. The question of its constitutionality would not be open for their examination.

If state courts do have the power of interpreting the Constitution in relation to federal statutes, it is true that the Supreme Court must have a similar power under its appellate jurisdiction in order to maintain uniformity of law. But, if state courts do not have such power under the supremacy clause, that section of the Constitution will not support the Supreme Court's exercise of the power of judicial review.

The Treason Clause   A third textual argument advanced by Marshall proceeds from the treason clause, which provides that "No Person shall be convicted of Treason unless on the Testimony of two Witnesses to the same overt Act."[9] Suppose Congress attempted to change this rule, declaring by statute that the testimony of only one witness would be sufficient to convict for treason. Would the federal courts have to accept such a statute, in spite of the Constitution? Surely not, Marshall asserts, for it is the particular duty of the courts to interpret the laws and give effect to the superior law of the Constitution over mere statutory law.

Marshall's reliance on the treason clause, however, is doubly interesting. For one thing, that clause is one of the few provisions of the Constitution that can be characterized as specific. Reasonable and intelligent individuals may differ in good faith over the meaning of many constitutional clauses—what procedures are required to comply with the mandate of due process, or what is a cruel and unusual punishment, or what constitutes an unreasonable search and seizure. But the question of how many is two is not subject to rational debate. Thus, all that Marshall's treason clause argument may support is the proposition that the judiciary must not defer to legislative or executive judgment *when the Constitution is clear.* This is not a particularly forceful assertion of judicial power.

Moreover, the argument predicated on the treason clause may say no more than that the Supreme Court has the duty and power to interpret constitutional provisions dealing with the judiciary. In other words, the Court has the responsibility for interpreting article III because that article is specifically addressed to Courts. This would accord perfectly with Thomas Jefferson's theory of constitutional review. Jefferson held that each of the three branches was to construe for itself the constitutional terms concerning its own powers. The interpretation of one branch would not be subject to review by the other branches. To do otherwise, Jefferson thought, would violate the principle of separation of powers.

The fact that such an arrangement would be constitutionally permissible, however, does not mean that it would be workable or should be adopted. Indeed, Jefferson's theory of departmental review is a formula for chaos.

Such a system would inevitably lead to disputes among the three branches over the boundaries of their respective powers—in other words, over the meaning of the Constitution. Some method would then be required for resolving these disputes. Almost surely that method would be an appeal to the people. But that would defeat the very purpose of a written constitution, particularly a constitution seeking to establish a mixed regime of limited powers.

Thus, the Jeffersonian scheme would stand the Constitution on its head; yet Marshall's reliance on the treason clause of article III simply supports Jefferson's departmental theory of constitutional review. We know, however, that Marshall did not agree with that theory but held a broader conception of judicial power.

The Article VI Oath   The last piece of textual evidence adduced by Marshall to sustain his claim that it is the Court's duty to exercise the power of constitutional review against the actions of the coordinate branches of the federal government was the oath prescribed by article VI, which requires that all judges "shall be bound by Oath or Affirmation, to support this Constitution." Would it not be immoral, Marshall asked rhetorically, to impose this oath on judges and then expect them to uphold laws that they considered to violate the Constitution? Surely it would. But, as even friendly critics of *Marbury* have long pointed out, the same oath is also required of "Senators and Representatives . . . , and the Members of the several State Legislatures, and all executive and judicial Officers . . . of the several States." Marshall's logic would require that all these officers interpret the Constitution for themselves. Surely it would be as immoral for them to accept a Supreme Court decision that they considered to violate the Constitution as it would be for the justices to uphold laws that they thought to be unconstitutional.

In short, the Constitution nowhere *explicitly* provides for the Supreme Court's power of judicial review, and arguments such as those advanced in *Marbury* to demonstrate that it *implicitly* provides for this power, when analyzed carefully, will support only very modest claims of judicial power. This is not to say that the power of judicial review cannot be squared with the Constitution, only that it cannot be found there.

Evidence of the Framers' Intent   Some have contended that, although the Framers of the Constitution failed to provide for judicial review in the text itself, the evidence of their deliberations and statements made by Alexander Hamilton in the *Federalist Papers* demonstrate that they foresaw that the Court would assume this power and, indeed, invited the Court to do so. Stripped to its essentials, this is a conspiracy theory. It maintains that the

Framers desired judicial review but were aware that, if it were spelled out, the Constitution would not be ratified. They therefore left the matter open but phrased the Constitution so that at the first possible opportunity the Court would be able to assert this power.

Naturally enough, the best exposition of this thesis was provided by the greatest of conspiratorial historians, Charles Austin Beard. In *The Supreme Court and the Constitution*, Beard used public statements and private letters of the Founding Fathers to argue that they had indeed intended to establish judicial review as one of the nation's constitutional institutions. But, as in his later classic *An Economic Interpretation of the Constitution of the United States*, Beard's evidence is weak and suffers from unsupported inference. At best, he shows merely that the Framers wanted judicial review. But they also wanted many other things that never finally made it into the Constitution.

On the other hand, no one can argue, nor has anyone tried to argue, that the Framers opposed judicial review. At worst, it can only be said that their intentions cannot be accurately ascertained. They were a brilliant and contentious group. Some thought this; others that; and it will never be entirely clear where the final, collective judgment came to rest.

Nonetheless, it is clear that the Congress of the United States, a Congress including a good many members of the constitutional convention, very shortly assumed that the Court was the appropriate agency for rendering final interpretations of the Constitution. This was made evident by the 1796 case of *Hylton v. United States*, arising out of a tax on carriages.[10] Congress had enacted the tax and was concerned about whether it was constitutional. Article I, section 2, of the Constitution states that direct taxes shall be apportioned according to population. Article I, section 8, however, provides that excise taxes shall be uniform throughout the nation. Congress had passed the carriage tax as an excise tax, but, according to the practice of the time, it might also be construed as a direct tax, since it was levied directly on the taxpayer, as distinguished from the central government's requisition of revenues from the states under the Articles of Confederation.

The Court had already indicated that it would not render advisory opinions, so Congress contrived a suit, in which Hylton was prosecuted for refusal to pay the tax. With the government paying for counsel on both sides of the litigation, Hylton raised as his defense that the tax was a direct tax and was unconstitutional, since it was not apportioned throughout the states according to population. Hylton was convicted and appealed to the Supreme Court on the ground that the statute was null and void.

The Court held that the direct tax provision applied only to those taxes, such as capitation taxes, that could be fairly apportioned according to population. The carriage tax was, thus, constitutional, and Hylton's conviction was allowed to stand. But the more important point of the *Hylton* case is that Congress, in contriving the suit and paying for the litigation, had assumed that the Court was the agency vested with the power to rule on the unconstitutionality of Congress's own enactments. Yet *Hylton* does not explain why the power of judicial review was assumed any more than *Marbury* does.

Historical Precedents for the Power

If the existence of judicial review in the United States cannot be explained by resort to the Constitution or to decisions of the Supreme Court, an examination of early American history may provide an answer. In fact, some argue that a practice analogous to judicial review was familiar before the framing of the Constitution, and the doctrine enunciated in *Marbury* amounted to little more than the reaffirmation of accepted principles.

The difficulty with this approach lies in the fact that the colonial institutions or events that provide precedents for judicial review are either not exactly analogous or were not well known or both. For example, there are some judicial decisions rendered before adoption of the Constitution in which state supreme courts appeared to assert the power to nullify actions of their coordinate legislative bodies on the ground that those acts violated the states' fundamental charters.[11] Upon closer examination, however, the exact bases for some of these decisions are not as solid as they seem. The reasons for the declarations of statutory invalidity are less than clear, and any assertions of a judicial power to negate statutes on constitutional grounds reduce themselves to mere dicta (statements outside the scope of the decision, which do not have the legal significance of the court's holding). Moreover, even if the precedents amounted to unequivocal assertions of a power of judicial review, it is extremely doubtful that most members of the constitutional convention or of the ratifying conventions knew of these scattered examples, let alone approved of their philosophy.

Another example cited is the power of disallowance of colonial legislation exercised by the British Privy Council. This is hardly analogous, however, because the colonial legislatures were not coordinate in power with the Privy Council. This practice may provide a historical precedent for the Court's power to scrutinize the constitutionality of state acts, but it will not support the Court's exercise of that power against congressional acts.

The councils of revision that existed in some colonies are also seen by some as examples of early American experience with a practice analogous to judicial review. But they are not truly similar, because, unlike Supreme Court justices, most members of the councils of revision were responsible to the electorate.

The Structural-Cultural Bases of Judicial Review

While none of the legal, textual, or historical explanations is sufficient to account for the existence of judicial review in the United States, this does not mean that its existence cannot be explained. A combination of structural necessities and cultural factors may answer how it became established. Such a structural-cultural explanation is certainly not as neat as a precise factual reason why the nation adopted this institution; it is, consequently, much less susceptible of proof. Indeed, those who require elegant, demonstrable proofs will feel most uncomfortable with such an argument. Nevertheless, the cumulative effect of certain American political institutions and the historical existence of certain characteristics of the American mind suggest why the ultimate power of constitutional interpretation has been lodged in the Supreme Court.

In the first place, Americans have always entertained a "higher law" tradition. They have believed that there is a higher law, whether of natural or divine origin, with which mere statutory enactments must accord if they are to be legitimate. In 1789, the Founding Fathers carried this tradition yet a step further, taking what was then a novel action by reducing the higher law to writing, placing limits on the government, and guaranteeing certain rights to the individual. The existence of a written higher law presupposes a final arbiter, although there is no reason why it must be a court of law.

Secondly, the device of sovereignty chosen by this country is federalism, and federalism implies a need for legalism. Some agency must determine where the powers of one jurisdiction end and those of another begin. Here again, however, this final arbiter need not be a court composed of nonelected, life-tenured judges.

Thirdly, the constitutional system of separation of powers also requires an institution able to judge the nature and extent of each department's powers. Still, there is no reason why that agency must be the Supreme Court.

Finally, however, Americans have shown a traditional, peculiar, and largely irrational reverence for the legal profession. They particularly venerate judges, who seem to represent the ultimate achievers in that profession. Almost a century and a half ago, that sharp-eyed critic of American manners, Alexis de Tocqueville, noted that Americans had an "aristocracy of the bar" and a "cult of the robe,"[12] and neither of these customs appears to have diminished over time.

None of these elements alone is sufficient to explain the existence of judicial review in the United States. But their combined effect has impelled the country toward the adoption of that institution.

The Philosophic Rationale for Judicial Review

While the structural-cultural explanation may empirically account for the existence of judicial review, it offers no justification for the practice. But a philosophic rationale for judicial review can be rather easily constructed.[13] The argument proceeds from the premise that the Constitution, both theoretically and by its own terms, is fundamental law. In political theory, the Constitution must be fundamental law, for it establishes the very character of the government that will make all subsequent laws. The supremacy clause clearly envisions the existence of two types of federal law: the Constitution itself, which is unqualifiedly supreme, and the laws and treaties of the United States, which are supreme only insofar as they are consonant with the Constitution.

Since the Constitution is fundamental law, it follows that it is to be permanent law. This does not mean that the Constitution is not flexible, that it does not change. Indeed, the document itself allows for constitutional change by both *legal* and *practical* means. Formal amendments may modify the written Constitution, and social changes may increase or diminish the force of certain constitutional principles. In addition, the Constitution may be changed by judicial interpretation. But the flexibility of the Constitution does not contemplate any change in the basic form of government. For example, the method of electing members of Congress may be changed or their terms of office altered by amendment, but the Constitution does not anticipate an amendment that would abolish Congress altogether. Such an amendment would do mortal damage to the principle of the separation of powers and the system of checks and balances. It would not simply amend the Constitution; it would destroy it. One can conclude, therefore, that the Constitution is absolutely permanent in essence but only relatively permanent in fact; and, indeed, this rather nicely summarizes the Supreme Court's function—reconciling permanence with change.

If the Constitution is both fundamental and permanent, it requires a final and relatively stable authority to resolve its meaning. To understand why, one must reconsider the departmental theory of constitutional review and contemplate the consequences of such a system. If each branch of government interpreted the Constitution for itself, the meaning of the Constitution might change with each succeeding election. Change, of course, is inevitable, and the Constitution does change through judicial interpretation. But rapid and abrupt change undermines constitutional law's claim to be *constitutional*. Under a system of departmental review, just as the statutes of one legislature may be diametrically opposed to those of the previous legislature, so one Congress might interpret its powers differently from its immediate predecessor's interpretation. The United States would then be presented with the spectacle of legislators, executive officers, and judges, both federal and state, solemnly taking an oath to support a Constitution that might mean one thing today, another thing tomorrow, and yet a third thing the day after. The Constitution would mean anything and everything and, therefore, nothing.

Another scheme of constitutional interpretation once very much in vogue in some sections of the country was John C. Calhoun's theory that the states should be the final arbiters of the Constitution. This scheme would result in very much the same sort of constitutional anarchy as departmental review, with the Constitution meaning one thing in one place and another in another. Some states would soon be seceding or threatening to secede. This scheme has been rejected and for good reason.

Clearly, either of these systems would be a political monstrosity. Equally clearly, a single, final arbiter is necessary, and for practical if not logical reasons this arbiter must be one of the branches of the federal government. The problem, thus, is reduced to this: Which branch of the federal government should exercise the authority of interpreting the Constitution with at least relative finality?

There are a number of persuasive reasons, all of them in one way or another related to the electoral principle, why Congress should be that branch. There are even more why Congress should not. Its membership is too large, as well as too changeable. More than either of the other two branches, the legislature is prone to partisan division, factionalism, and the influence of outside interests. The opinions of members of the House and Senate are too closely tied to their own personal interests as elected officials. Their sentiments are bound up with the immediate passions and interests of their constituents. Congress, in short, lacks the detachment needed for a just and wise interpretation of a fundamental, essentially permanent law.

Much the same may be said of the president. The presidential office is too subject to change. The president, especially in the age of nuclear war, is too preoccupied with foreign matters to acquire a thorough understanding of the fundamental law of the land. The president must perform too many other duties to devote steady and considered judgment to policy questions involving the Constitution. Because he is elected, his judgment may be swayed either by his passion for office or by the immediate interests of his party. Finally, if the President were the final judge of constitutionality, the system of checks and balances would be abolished in favor of absolute authority. The president already possesses the veto power, but presidential vetoes may be overridden by extraordinary majorities in both houses of Congress. If the presidency were invested with final authority on issues of constitutional interpretation, the president would have in effect an absolute veto.

The power to interpret the Constitution with finality, therefore, must fall to the Supreme Court by default. Not only are its justices devoid of immediate personal interest in the resolution of constitutional questions, but they also are without the power to coerce others to do their will. To be sure, Supreme Court justices make value choices influenced consciously and unconsciously by their policy preferences. But this is far different from making a particular decision in order to advance their own personal fortunes. The Court's impartiality, then, is a relative, not an absolute, condition. While the justices may not be psychologically neutral, they are personally neutral. Moreover, even an extremely partial Court would still be, in Alexander Hamilton's words, "the least dangerous" branch [14] It has neither the power of the purse nor the power of the sword. If the Court's actions pose a danger to constitutional government or the rights of the people, those actions are likely to be ineffective because of the Court's place in the constitutional system. Thus, it is prudent to give the Supreme Court the power of constitutional interpretation.

But there are other grounds for giving the power to the Court. Judicial review is also based upon justice. As already noted, the justices do not serve their immediate personal interests and ambitions in the exercise of this public function. Given life tenure, they are removed, at least to a certain degree, from the concerns of daily life. They are thus able to lead a scholarly life *as public officials*, devoting themselves to researching wise and just interpretations of the fundamental law. The Supreme Court is unique not simply in that it allows the justices to consider social issues removed from the immediacy of practical politics but also in that its detachment affords them the opportunity to think about these problems and then express their conclusions in more or less well-reasoned opinions.

The very character of the Constitution, therefore, requires a final, authoritative constitutional interpreter, and both prudence and justice suggest that this interpreter should be the Supreme Court. While such a philosophic justification of judicial review may not have been consciously intended by any of the Founding Fathers, it is not inconsistent with their ends and purposes in framing the Constitution.

THE SCOPE OF JUDICIAL REVIEW

Today the task of accounting for or justifying the Supreme Court's power of constitutional interpretation seems largely irrelevant. Americans accept the Court's exercise of this power because it has passed the essential, pragmatic American test: It works. It has stood the test of time. Over nearly two centuries, it has proved functional. The crucial question, then, is not whether the power of constitutional construction should be given to the Court. It has been, and, short of a true catastrophe, it is most unlikely that the power will ever be taken away. Franklin Roosevelt's experience in 1937 seems to bear this out. The New Deal's ability to cope with the Great Depression had been seriously hampered by several Supreme Court decisions declaring key features of the president's economic program unconstitutional. Roosevelt's response, however, was not to attack the power of judicial review but rather to propose that the Court's membership be enlarged, enabling him to appoint six new justices who would be more in tune with the New Deal's philosophy. And even this failed to pass Congress. The critical contemporary issue, therefore, is not should the court have this power, but how vigorously should the Court exercise it? What is the proper scope of judicial review? How actively should the Court intervene in the policy-making process?

In considering what should be the proper role of the Supreme Court in American government, the central problem one must keep in mind is that the Court is electorally irresponsible and potentially opposed to the majority of the population. It is not necessarily an "undemocratic" institution, depending on one's understanding of the term *democracy*. Nevertheless, a small, unelected group authoritatively interprets the charter that establishes the very framework of government, the document that grants, defines, and limits governmental power.

Does this give the justices unchecked authority? Bishop Hoadly maintained that whoever has absolute authority to interpret the law is really the lawgiver, more so than the body that originally framed the law. The good bishop's observation is not entirely applicable to the Supreme Court, however. The Court's power is not absolute. Hamilton is more nearly correct: The Court is the least dangerous branch. The Constitution incorporates a series of democratic checks on the oligarchic elements of the federal government (as well as a variety of oligarchic checks on its democratic tendencies). The other two branches have several means of curbing an overambitious or thoroughly wrongheaded Court. And the Court itself has developed a number of canons of self-restraint that conserve its power, limit its policy making, and protect it from the politically more powerful branches of government.

Restraints Imposed by Congress

Short of its power to propose a constitutional amendment in order to reverse a particular Supreme Court decision, Congress can employ a variety of devices to exercise some control over the Court's decision making. Among these is Congress's power to control the size of the Court. Nowhere in the constitution is the number of Supreme Court justices specified. Article III provides merely that there shall be one Supreme Court. The number of justices may be increased or decreased at the discretion of Congress. For example, following Justice Catron's death in 1865, Congress reduced the size of the Court from ten to eight in order to deny Andrew Johnson a Supreme Court nomination. When Justice Grier retired in 1870, Congress returned the size of the Court to nine. This enabled President Grant to appoint *two* justices, Bradley and Strong, and create a new majority on the Court. The new majority promptly reversed a significant monetary decision reached only the year before.[15] Similarly, Franklin Roosevelt's attempt to "pack" the Court, even though defeated in Congress, succeeded in winning the Court's acceptance of his recovery program by influencing at least one justice to rethink his position on government economic regulation.

Congress may also exert power over the Court's jurisdiction in an effort to control judicial decision making. The Court's original jurisdiction, that is, the cases the Court hears as a trial court, rather than on appeal, is specified in the Constitution and is very limited. Moreover, according to *Marbury*, it cannot be expanded. The Court's appellate jurisdiction, however, which has historically proved much more important, is not exclusive. It can be expanded by Congress, and it can be contracted or even entirely curtailed.

This device, too, was used by the Radical Republican Congress during Reconstruction to effect a desired result. William McCardle, a Mississippi journalist, had written editorials not pleasing to the commanders of the Union occupying forces. Consequently, he was tried and convicted by a military commission for publishing "incendiary and libellous articles." He appealed, contending that the military court, which had been established by the Reconstruction Acts, had no lawful authority to try him. The case, therefore, questioned the constitutionality of the Reconstruction Acts. The Supreme Court heard the appeal and appeared on the verge of issuing a decision declaring Reconstruction unconstitutional. Fearing this outcome, Congress rescinded the statute that gave the Court jurisdiction over such appeals. President Johnson vetoed the rescission bill, but his veto was overridden. Despite the fact that the case had already been heard, that an opinion had apparently been written, and that the statute could have been construed as applying only to future cases, the Court then dismissed McCardle's appeal on the ground that Congress had constitutionally exercised its power to rescind the Court's jurisdiction over the case.[16] Though it is not a masterpiece of legal logic, the *McCardle* decision is explainable and even commendable in terms of political prudence.

Restraints Imposed by the President

While Congress may control the Court's appellate jurisdiction, the president has an even more direct mechanism for influencing judicial policy making. The Court lacks the power to enforce its decisions; this is the responsibility of the president. Most governmental acts within the American system require at least two branches to act before a declaration of public policy is effectively implemented. The Court's acts are no exception. Just as Congress may appropriate funds for a program and the president may fail to spend them, or the president may initiate a program that Congress then will not adequately fund, so the Supreme Court must depend on presidential enforcement for its will to become law.

According to constitutional legend, Andrew Jackson explicitly refused to execute a Supreme Court mandate. The case arose from the attempt by Georgia to remove the Cherokee Nation from the western portion of the state. The status of the Indian tribes had been left ambiguous by the Constitution. By implication they were outside the constitutional system, and from the beginning the Indians were dealt with by the federal government as if they were foreign nations. During the confederation period, Georgia along with several other states laying claim to vast tracts of land beyond the Appalachians had been persuaded to cede these western lands to the central government. In exchange, the central government agreed to obtain for the state all Indian lands lying within the state.

The Cherokees, determined to remain on their land, proved extremely skillful negotiators, and their evacuation proceeded slowly. By the 1820s Georgia was exasperated and decided to take matters into its own hands. The state extended its laws over the Indian territory, annulled all Indian law, and directed the seizure of Cherokee land by its militia. In the process, a Methodist missionary named Worcester was arrested, tried, and convicted for residing on the Indian lands without a license from the state.

Worcester appealed to the Supreme Court and secured a favorable decision. Chief Justice Marshall ruled that the Indian tribes were "domestic, dependent nations" and, as such, distinct political communities over which state law could have no force.[17] Georgia openly refused to honor the decision; and, although Marshall implied in his opinion that the president had a duty to uphold the Court's judgment, Jackson, who was no friend of the red man, is reported to have responded, "John Marshall has made his decision. Now let him enforce it." While the story may not be true, it illustrates the Court's lack of implementation power.

Whatever Andrew Jackson may have said, it is certain that Abraham Lincoln did ignore a direct order of the chief justice of the United States that Lincoln considered contrary to the best interests of the Republic.[18] Despite a ruling by Chief Justice Taney that the president had exceeded his constitutional authority, Lincoln directed Union military commanders to hold suspected Confederate sympathizers and saboteurs without benefit of the writ of habeas corpus. (The case is discussed more fully in chapter 3.)

Fortunately, such dramatic presidential defiance has been rare and has occurred only under the most extraordinary circumstances. But direct defiance is not necessary for the president to blunt Supreme Court policy making significantly. Reluctant or half-hearted enforcement is usually enough, as the Eisenhower administration's implementation of the desegregation decisions demonstrates.

The Power of Appointment

The *primary* mechanism for congressional and presidential control over the Court's policy making has historically been the power of appointment—and its corollary, the power of removal. Congress's power to impeach is a drastic tool for rectifying judicial error. To be sure, only eight federal judges have ever been impeached, and only one of these, Justice Samuel Chase, was a member of the Supreme Court. Moreover, only four were actually convicted and removed. But, as events of the 1970s have demonstrated, it would be foolhardy to ignore this ultimate power that the Constitution has lodged in the legislature.

More significant, however, as a device for influencing the content of the Court's decisions, has been the process of judicial appointment. This is a frankly and openly political matter and probably should be. The Supreme Court is a unique judicial agency, and criteria relevant for service on other courts are not applicable to its potential justices. Since the Constitution does not specify even minimal qualifications for appointment to the Court, critics have sometimes suggested that Congress should set stringent requirements by statute. For example, some have proposed that presidential nominations be approved by the American Bar Association, that all nominees be required to have law degrees, or that no one without prior judicial experience be considered for nomination.

The adoption of such rules would be unfortunate. Officially incorporating the ABA into the recruitment process would set an undesirable precedent for other areas. Could the American Medical Association then demand veto power over nominations for the surgeon general or the secretary of health, education, and welfare? Requiring nominees to have law degrees would be superfluous (most justices have them anyway) and irrelevant, because the questions with which the Supreme Court deals require political judgment rather than proficiency in the technicalities of private law. Nor has prior judicial experience proved indicative of greatness on the Court. Of twelve justices generally recognized as the greatest in the history of the Supreme Court, nine (Marshall, Story, Taney, Hughes, Brandeis, Stone, Black, Frankfurter, and Warren) would have been disqualified by such a requirement.[19] Nomination by the president, who is elected, usually by a majority of the voters, insures that a prospective justice will be, in general terms, representative. Presidents, after all, seldom appoint their political enemies to the Court. Confirmation by the Senate further assures not only competence but also that the political views of the nominee will be within the mainstream of current American values. (I return to this point at greater length in Chapter 2.)

Limits Imposed by the Court Itself

Recognizing its political limitations, the Court itself has developed certain general doctrines on the timing and scope of its judicial functions.[20] As Justice Jackson once put it, the Supreme Court "has a philosophy that, while it has a duty to decide constitutional questions, it must escape that duty if possible."[21] The self-imposed doctrines by which that duty is escaped are sometimes dismissed as mere "technicalities," but their function is far from technical. They are part of the court's political armor. They serve to protect its public prestige, ultimately the source of the Court's power, by ensuring that it does not expend its energies on cases that are either unimportant or of too immediate political importance. Each of these rules proceeds from a common premise: The Court's power is limited. It must not use that power in vain gestures, no matter how noble, that will antagonize the public or its elected representatives.

These rules of decision are of two sorts. There are, first, doctrines that allow the Court to refuse to hear a case. Secondly, if it hears a case (and if it follows the rules), the Court has a set of rules, that enable it to reach a decision on the narrowest possible grounds.

Case and Controversy Rule Foremost among the first group of doctrines is the "case and controversy" rule. Article III of the Constitution extends the judicial power only to "cases and controversies." The Court, in other words, must confine itself to real issues, in a real controversy, between real parties. This does not, however, mean that *all* cases that could be decided must be heard. Each term's business must be limited to what nine judges and their law clerks can fruitfully deal with as a practical matter. Given this necessity, the Court can use the case and controversy rule to evade difficult cases.

What is a case and controversy? Not every issue that can be framed in the form of a lawsuit will qualify for a hearing by the Supreme Court. To have a case and controversy, in the constitutional sense, there must be (a) opposing parties (b) who have a substantial legal interest (c) in a dispute arising out of real, not hypothetical, facts and in which (d) there can be an enforceable determination of the rights of the parties. No "friendly" or collusive suits in which both parties are actually seeking the same result will be heard.

Certainly, there have been exceptions to this rule, cases decided that should have been denied a hearing. *Hylton v. United States*, the 1796 carriage tax case discussed above, was one, and there have been others. In *Carter v. Carter Coal Co.*,[22] for example, Carter sued his family's coal company, in which he was a major stockholder, seeking to enjoin it from complying with the Bituminous Coal Act of 1935, a New Deal measure. He argued that the statute exceeded Congress's powers under the interstate commerce clause and invaded areas of regulation reserved to the states by the Constitution. The Carter Coal Company, which actually opposed the act, was placed in the position of defending its constitutionality in the suit. Naturally enough, it did not do a very good job for the defense, and the Court struck the statute down.

But such exceptions merely prove that the rule is flexible enough to allow the Court to interpret it with discretion. Each of the exceptions was a case that the Court was eager to decide at the time. On the other hand, if the Court wishes to avoid an issue, for whatever reason, it can insist on a strict interpretation of the doctrine. In *United Public Workers v. Mitchell*.[23] for example, the 1947 Court invoked the case and controversy rule to dodge ruling on the constitutionality of the Hatch Act, a law intended to prevent political influence in the civil service. A public employees' union sought a ruling against the act so that in the future its members could engage in various political activities that it argued were protected by the First Amendment but apparently forbidden by the act. None of the public workers had yet violated the act, however, and thus their claim was based on conjecture. The Court, seeking to avoid a decision on the constitutional merits of the statute, replied that no justiciable case and controversy was presented. The civil servants should violate the act, and then, if penalties were imposed on them, they would have a case that the Court *might* hear.

Rule against Advisory Opinions   Related to the case and controversy doctrine is the Court's rule against issuing advisory opinions. This rule originated in 1793 with George Washington's effort to secure legal counsel on a contemplated treaty. The president sent a copy of the treaty to the members of the Court and asked them to render legal advice on a few technical points. Chief Justice John Jay returned the treaty with the curt reply that the Court was not in the business of issuing opinions in the abstract. Since that time, the Court has adhered to the rule that it will not issue advisory opinions, even for presidents.

Requirement of Standing   The requirement of standing to sue is yet another hurdle a case must negotiate before the Court will decide it. To maintain a suit in the federal courts, a litigant must have a personal and substantial interest in the outcome that differentiates him or her from the general mass of the citizenry. This constitute's the party's standing. In *Tileston v. Ullman*, for example, in 1943, the Court was able to avoid, at least for the moment, deciding the constitutionality of a Connecticut statute prohibiting the *use* (not just sale or distribution) of contraceptive drugs or devices.[24] Dr. Tileston, a Yale Medical School faculty member, filed suit on behalf of three of his female patients whose lives, he claimed, would be endangered by pregnancy. He alleged that the Connecticut anti-birth-control statute threatened these women with the deprivation of life without due process of law, in violation of the Fourteenth Amendment. Tileston's suit was rejected for a very elemental reason: He had no standing to assert the constitutional claim. Wrote the Court:

> There is no allegation or proof that appellant's life is in danger. His patients are not party to this proceeding and there is no basis on which we can say that he has standing to secure an adjudication of his patient's right to life, which they do not assert on their own behalf.[25]

Perhaps the most significant impact of the standing doctrine for Supreme Court policy making has been its restriction of taxpayers' suits challenging federal spending programs. The general rule was stated in 1923, when the Court held in *Frothingham v. Mellon* that a federal taxpayer lacked standing to maintain an action in the federal courts as simply a taxpayer.[26] The Court reasoned that the individual taxpayer's relationship with the challenged program was shared with millions of others, was comparatively minute and indeterminate, and was too remote, fluctuating, and uncertain to satisfy the standing requirement. If one taxpayer were allowed to maintain such a suit, the floodgates would be open to every taxpayer, and the efficient administration of federal programs would be seriously impaired. Therefore, the party invoking the judicial power of the United States must be able to show that he or she has suffered or is in danger of suffering some direct, personal injury. An injury that affects interests shared by all citizens in common is not fit for judicial correction. In such situations, the appropriate resort is to the political, not the judicial, process.

The *Frothingham* rule was somewhat modified by *Flast v. Cohen*,[27] a 1965 decision permitting a taxpayer's suit against a statute authorizing the use of federal funds to purchase textbooks that could be used in parochial schools. The plaintiffs argued that the law violated the establishment clause of the First Amendment. Noting that the standing rule was necessary to assure the genuine clash of interests to be adjudicated in an adversary system, the Court created a two-step test to determine whether a taxpayer had a sufficient personal stake to create that clash. According to *Flast*, a federal taxpayer does have standing to maintain a suit if (1) he or she can demonstrate a direct link between taxes paid and a particular program, and (2) the particular program is challenged as violating a specific constitutional limitation.

While *Flast* lowered the standing barrier slightly, the Court has since refused to lower it further. *United States v. Richardson*[28] in 1974 denied standing to a taxpayer who claimed that failure to reveal the expenditures of the CIA violated the statement and account clause of the Constitution, and a companion case, *Schlesinger v. Reservists Committee to Stop the War*,[29] refused standing to an antiwar group of taxpayers who contending that the incompatibility clause was being violated by the Pentagon policy of allowing members of Congress to retain their status in the military reserve. Strictly construing the two-step requirement of *Flast*, the Court found that neither the statement and account clause nor the incompatibility clause was a specific limit on congressional spending power.

At first glance, these results seem at odds with the Court's own relaxation of the standing requirement in reviewing actions taken by regulatory agencies. But the differences between the administrative agency cases, on the one hand, and *Richardson* and *Schlesinger*, on the other, may be traced to differences in the Court's roles. As Chapter 4 discusses more fully, judicial review of administrative actions seldom raises issues of constitutionality. Rather, these cases usually involve questions of interpretation of the statutes creating and empowering an agency, interpretations that Congress can overturn subsequently. Citizens' suits to enforce provisions of the Constitution, however, may involve the Court in confrontations with its coordinate branches of the federal government or the governing institutions of the states. While the Court has engaged in such confrontations throughout its history, it is desirable that they be minimized for reasons of prudence and principle. Rigorous application of the rule of standing serves that purpose.

Ripeness Rule   A litigant with standing must present his or her case in a "timely" manner. Once more, the history of the Connecticut anti-contraception law is illustrative. Having failed in *Tileston*, opponents of that law tried again in *Poe v. Ullman* (1961).[30] They again received a lesson in the complexities of Supreme Court procedure when the case foundered on the reef of "ripeness."

In *Poe* a doctor sought an injunction to stop enforcement of the Connecticut statute, alleging that it inhibited conscientious exercise of his profession. In addition, two of his patients, suing under fictitious names, claimed that their health would be impaired unless they could prevent conception. During oral argument, however, counsel for these parties was forced to acknowledge that the law had never been enforced against people who used contraceptives. The entire history of enforcement of the Connecticut statute amounted to only three prosecutions: two for vending machine sales and a third for operation of a birth control clinic. Counsel for Connecticut, moreover, produced a letter from the state's commissioner of food and drugs to the effect that, since diaphragms might have therapeutic, as distinguished from contraceptive, value, there was no legal reason why a doctor might not presecribe them or a woman use them. At this point, the Court dismissed the case on the ground that it was not "ripe"; it raised an issue that was merely academic.

Constitutional challenges may come too late as well as too early. Marco DeFunis, for example, challenged the admission procedures of the University of Washington School of Law. DeFunis claimed and the law school admitted that it employed differential admission procedures that tended to favor applicants from certain ethnic minorities. This, DeFunis argued, amounted to denying him equal educational opportunity solely on the basis of his race, in violation of the mandate of *Brown v. Board of Education*.[31] While his suit was pending DeFunis was admitted to the law school. By 1974, when the case had wound its way through the appeal process to the Supreme Court, DeFunis was within a few weeks of graduation. The Court then refused him a hearing, because it considered that his case had become moot (was no longer in controversy).[32] The Court thus temporarily avoided deciding an issue of the greatest contemporary importance, the constitutionality of affirmative action programs, benign quotas, and remedial discrimination.

Rule of Exhaustion of Remedies   Related to the doctrines of ripeness and mootness is the rule of exhaustion of remedy. No case will be considered by the Court unless all other appeals allowed for by law have been taken. Even a real case and controversy that is perfectly ripe and brought by litigants having standing to pose the issues cannot be taken directly from the court of first instance to the Supreme Court; all intermediate appeals must be exhausted before the Court can be asked to hear the case, and even then the Court may not consent to hear it.

Requirement of a Substantial Federal Question   Since the Judges Bill of 1925, the Court's control over its own docket—that is, its power to choose the cases it will hear—has been virtually complete. Most cases are appealed to the Court by a legal process known as a petition for certiorari. The granting of certiorari is wholly discretionary. Even cases that, in the strict legal sense of the word, are appealed—cases that come to the Court on a writ of appeal, and thus theoretically have a legal right to be heard—may, nevertheless, be dismissed by the Court for want of a substantial federal question. Each term literally thousands of cases that conform to all the rules are summarily dismissed, because in the opinion of six or more justices they do not present issues of sufficient importance for the country, no matter how significant they may be for the immediate parties. In short, even in a perfectly real, concrete, timely, fully developed case and controversy, the Supreme Court does not owe litigants an adjudication.

Requirement of Narrow Decision Making   If and when the Court does accept a case, there is yet a second set of rules of self-restraint, those doctrines that guide the Court in arriving at its judgment. These rules have been devised and refined over the years by justices concerned with the appropriate role of the Court within the American political system, seeking to protect both the public and the Court. They limit the scope of the Court's decisions, but they are purely self-imposed, if imposed at all.

One rule is that the Court will not decide a constitutional question, if there exists some nonconstitutional ground on which the case may be resolved. Thus, if a case can be decided on either of two bases, one involving a constitutional question, the other a question of statutory construction, this rule demands a decision based on the statutory ground. If a case correctly challenges a state law as violating both the Fourteenth Amendment and a federal statute, the state law would be struck down only on the latter basis, according to this rule. However, if a state court judgment is based on an adequate and independent state ground, the Supreme Court will not overturn it, even though the state court may have misconstrued the Constitution. Related to this rule is the canon that the Supreme Court will accept as authoritative the construction of state law rendered by the highest court in the state, no matter how foolish or irrational that interpretation may be.

The Court will construe federal law. But here again the canons of judicial construction encourage decision on the narrowest possible grounds. If the constitutionality of an act of Congress is challenged, the Court will seek to save the statute, if at all possible. Suppose, for example, that two interpretations of a challenged congressional statute are possible: according to one, the act would be constitutional, though meaningless; according to the other the act would be unconstitutional. The Court should adopt the construction that avoids a declaration of unconstitutionality.

Finally, if a constitutional question must be faced, the Court should not formulate a rule of constitutional law broader than is required by the precise facts to which it is to be applied. In voiding the New York Regents' Prayer, for example, in 1962, the Court explicitly noted that its holding was confined to prayer in the public schools and did not apply to other possible manifestations of public piety, such as the inscription "In God We Trust" on American coins.[33] Much of the rancor that the school prayer decisions occasioned might have been muted if the public had understood this simple rule of judicial decision making.

If all else fails, the Supreme Court's widest and most radical avenue of escape from deciding constitutional questions is to invoke the "political question" doctrine. All issues brought before the Court are "political" in a sense, but this doctrine uses the term in a unique sense. If the Court cannot avoid a highly controversial case or if it wishes to indicate that it will not adjudicate a certain category of cases, it may label the issue a "political question," meaning a question that judicial power cannot resolve satisfactorily.

One of the best examples of the use of this doctrine is still the case in which it originated, *Luther v. Borden* (1849).[34] It arose out of the Dorr Rebellion in Rhode Island. When chartered in 1663, Rhode Island established a relatively democratic political system by the standards of the time. Following the Revolution the colonial charter was adopted as the new state constitution. The charter, however, contained no provision for amendment, and, by 1842, Rhode Island had become one of the least democratic states, surely offering a classic example of the need for constitutional adaptability. Dissidents demanded a long overdue expansion of the right to vote and, when their demands were not met, took matters into their own hands by proclaiming their leader, Thomas Dorr, the new governor. The established governor, however, called out the militia, and, with the help of some federal troops dispatched by President Tyler, quashed the "Dorr Rebellion."

During the brief hostilities, Borden, a member of the militia, had entered the home of Luther, a Dorr supporter, to arrest him. After the failure of the "rebellion," Luther sued Borden for trespass. Realizing that he stood no chance to recover in a Rhode Island court, Luther moved to Massachusetts and filed the action in a federal district court on the basis of diversity of citizenship. Borden responded that he could not be held personally liable, since he had been acting as an agent of the state. Luther countered that the Dorr government had been the legitimate government of Rhode Island and that Borden could not rely on the orders of an illegitimate government to protect himself.

The case, thus, asked the federal courts to decide which faction had been the legitimate government of Rhode Island. The Supreme Court declined this invitation to decide, by holding that the question of the legitimacy of a state government was not susceptible of judicial resolution. Such an issue was, according to Chief Justice Taney, nonjusticiable because it presented a "political question."

Taney's formulation of this new doctrine turned on several considerations; the primary one was perhaps the fact that a finding against the charter government would have created chaos. Although the rebellion had occurred in 1842, *Luther v. Borden* did not reach the Court until 1849. If the Court then decided in favor of Luther, it would have been declaring with one stroke of the judicial pen that all actions taken under the authority of the Rhode Island government for the past seven years had no legal validity.

Moreover, there were no standards of law to apply to the question, since the Rhode Island courts had never accepted responsibility for determining questions of governmental legitimacy, and the federal Constitution committed the matter to Congress. According to Chief Justice Taney, the only constitutional authority for determining the legitimacy of a state government was article IV, section 4, which guarantees to each state a republican form of government. This determination is made, Taney argued, by Congress when it admits or refuses to admit a state's representatives to their seats.

The Constitution, then, had committed the question to a coordinate branch of the federal government, and Congress had, since 1842, routinely admitted Rhode Island's representatives. Moreover, the executive branch had indicated its view of the matter when President Tyler sent troops to put down the Dorr Rebellion. There is a need for finality in executive decisions, noted Taney. Confronting this necessity was a total absence of judicially discoverable or manageable criteria for reaching a judgment on the question. These factors obviously influenced Taney in declaring the case a "political question," but he was less than clear about how the "political question" doctrine should be applied in future cases. Rather, it is apparent that the most significant factor influencing Taney's decision was the impossibility of resolving the matter satisfactorily; thus he chose not to resolve it at all.

Since 1849 the "political question" doctrine has been invoked to extricate the Court from several difficult situations. It proved extremely helpful during Reconstruction and was used for many years to avoid the thorny problem of legislative apportionment. Some students of the Court have attempted to define the doctrine with greater precision, arguing that certain categories of cases always present "political questions." But these efforts have invariably proved futile. The doctrine simply cannot be confined. It is a rule of prudence rather than of construction and, as such, is as expandable (and contractible) as an accordion. The Court, not legal scholars, declares questions "political," and it does so by the case, not by the category.

The Pros and Cons of Self-Restraint

Sometimes these Court's self-imposed limits are criticized for introducing irrelevant considerations into constitutional interpretation. By obstructing concerned citizens from challenging government programs, it is argued, these various rules contribute to civic frustration and create public distrust of the judiciary. But the basic policies underlying these doctrines are unquestionably sound. If the Supreme Court is to remain a court, it cannot be open to every person who is unhappy in some indefinite way about some government action or inaction. The alleged frustration created by these rules of procedure is, moreover, peculiarly American. If it exists at all, it rests on the assumption that someone somewhere *must* be able to challenge every government policy in a court of law; the only question is: Who? That is an assumption that very few legal or political philosophers outside the United States in this century would be willing to grant without argument.

Rightly understood, the doctrines of self-restraint should be applauded, because insistence on their applications has a number of benefits. Because of these rules, matters of great importance are raised before the Court by parties whose interests are sufficiently adverse so that they will vigorously present all relevant issues. The Court, then, derives the benefit of well-briefed, well-argued cases and is better informed in its policy making. These doctrines discourage frivolous actions, thereby saving the defendant the costs of litigation when the plaintiff has no substantial personal stake in the outcome. (In constitutional cases, moreover, the defendant is usually the public.) These rules diminish the number of issues that may be presented to the Court, thus reducing its enormous caseload. Finally, these rules, if followed, permit the Court to avoid unnecessary confrontations with the other branches of government.

Of course, the justices have discretion in applying the doctrines, and how strictly they are followed varies according to the political tenor of the times and the wisdom of the justices. These rules are born of a sense of prudence and of institutional self-preservation, and some justices are more prudent or have a greater commitment to the institution of the Supreme Court than others.

Disregard of the rules will enlarge the Court's potential as a policy maker. If the Court modifies, qualifies, or overlooks the rules that limit the number of cases it will hear, its opportunities to make policy will increase. If the Court qualifies or ignores the rules that guide its decision making, the scope of its policy making will expand. But, to the extent that the Court fails to apply these rules, it will increase its political visibility and invite partisan response to its policy making.

SUMMARY

The Supreme Court is a political as well as a legal institution. Its independent, unelected, and life-tenured justices often play a role in the formulation of public policy in the United States. Its power is the power of choice, choice between competing interpretations of the law. In particular, through its constitutional interpretation, the Court enjoys a discretion to limit the two popularly elected branches of government. This power was lodged in the Court because of certain institutional imperatives and because of the civic culture of the United States. The arrangement has then been sanctified by time.

Although the legitimacy of judicial review is now generally acknowledged, the Court must still exercise this power with restraint. The Constitution makes available to Congress and the president a variety of devices to influence the direction of judicial decision making, should that direction become sufficiently disturbing. Recognizing this, the Court itself has created a body of rules that encourage judicial restraint. The paradox is that these rules further increase the Court's discretion and, thus, enhance its power.

How should that power be used? How has it been used? What is the Supreme Court's purpose in the policy process? These questions are discussed next.

NOTES

1 297 U.S. 1, 62-63 (1936).

2 347 U.S. 483 (1954).

3 See Robert A. Dahl, "Decision-Making in a Democracy: The Supreme Court as a National Policy-Maker," *Journal of Public Law,* 6 (fall 1957), 279-95; David Adamany, "Legitimacy, Realigning Elections, and the Supreme Court," *Wisconsin Law Review* (September 1973), 790-846; Jonathan D. Casper, "The Supreme Court and National Policy Making," *American Political Science Review,* 70 (March 1976), 50-63.

4 Bishop Hoadly's sermon "The Nature of the Kingdom or Church of Christ," preached before the king, March 31, 1717, quoted in James Bradley Thayer, "The Origin

and Scope of the American Doctrine of Constitutional Law," *Harvard Law Review*, 7 (October 1893), 152.

5 5 U.S. (1 Cranch) 137 (1803).

6 U.S. Const. art. III, sec. 2.

7 This discussion of the textual bases for judicial review relies heavily on Bickel's outstanding critique. For a more extensive treatment, consult Alexander M. Bickel, *The Least Dangerous Branch: The Supreme Court at the Bar of Politics* (Indianapolis: Bobbs-Merrill Co., 1962), pp. 1-12.

8 U.S. Const. art. VI, sec. 2.

9 U.S. Const. art. III, sec. 3.

10 3 U.S. (3 Dal.) 171 (1796).

11 Holmes v. Walton, New Jersey (1780); Trevett v. Weeden, Rhode Island (1786); Bayard v. Singleton, 1 Martin (N.C.) 5 (1787). See generally Alfred H. Kelly and Winfred A. Harbison, *The American Constitution: Its Origins and Development*, 4th ed. (New York: W. W. Norton & Co., 1970), p. 99.

12 Alexis de Tocqueville, *Democracy in America*, ed. Phillips Bradley, 2 vols. (New York: Vintage Books, 1954), vol. I, pp. 283-86.

13 The discussion of the philosophy of judicial review summarizes and draws from the excellent analysis in Paul Eidelberg, *The Philosophy of the American Constitution* (New York: Free Press, 1968), pp. 202-46.

14 *The Federalist* No. 78.

15 Knox v. Lee, 79 U.S. (12 Wall.) 457 (1871), *reversing* Hepburn v. Griswold, 75 U.S. (8 Wall.) 603 (1870).

16 *Ex parte* McCardle, 74 U.S. (7 Wall.) 506 (1869).

17 Worcester v. Georgia, 31 U.S. (6 Pet.) 515 (1832).

18 *Ex parte* Merryman, 17 F. Cas. 144 (No. 9487) (1861).

19 See *Life*, October 15, 1971, pp. 53-59. The three "greats" who had prior judicial experience, and thus would not have been disqualified, are the first Harlan, Holmes, and Cardozo. See also Albert P. Blaustein and Roy M. Mersky, "Rating Supreme Court Justices," *American Bar Association Journal*, 58 (November 1972), 1183-89.

20 The finest analysis of these doctrines remains Alexander M. Bickel, "The Supreme Court, 1960 Term—Foreword: The Passive Virtues," *Harvard Law Review*, 75 (November 1961), 40-79. The present discussion has been much influenced by Professor Bickel's treatment. But see Gerald Gunther, "The Subtle Vices of the 'Passive Virtues'—a Comment on Principle and Expediency in Judicial Review," *Columbia Law Review*, 64 (January 1964), 1-25.

21 Robert Jackson, *The Struggle for Judicial Supremacy* (New York: Alfred A. Knopf, 1941), pp. 305-6.

22 298 U.S. 238 (1936).

23 330 U.S. 75 (1947).

24 318 U.S. 55 (1943).

25 318 U.S. at 46.

26 262 U.S. 447 (1923).

27 392 U.S. 83 (1965).

28 418 U.S. 166 (1974), construing U.S. Const. art. I, sec. 9, cl. 7.

29 418 U.S. 208 (1974), construing U.S. Const. art. I, sec. 6, cl. 2.

30 367 U.S. 497 (1961).

31 347 U.S. 483 (1954).

32 DeFunis v. Odegaard, 416 U.S. 312 (1974).

33 Engel v. Vitale, 370 U.S. 421, 435 n. 21 (1962).

34 48 U.S. (7 How.) 1 (1849).

SUGGESTED ADDITIONAL READING

Berger, Raoul. *Congress v. the Supreme Court*. Cambridge, Mass.: Harvard University Press, 1969.

Bickel, Alexander M. *The Least Dangerous Branch: The Supreme Court at the Bar of Politics*. Indianapolis: Bobbs-Merrill Co. 1962.

Corwin, Edward S. *The Doctrine of Judicial Review*. Princeton, N.J.: Princeton University Press, 1914.

Freund, Paul A. *The Supreme Court of the United States: Its Business, Purposes, and Performance*. Cleveland: World Publishing Co., 1961.

Eidelberg, Paul. *The Philosophy of the American Constitution: A Reinterpretation of the Intentions of the Founding Fathers*. New York: Free Press, 1968.

Spaeth, Harold J. *An Introduction to Supreme Court Decision Making*. Rev. ed. San Francisco: Chandler Publishing Co., 1972.

Stern, Robert L., and Eugene Grossman. *Supreme Court Practice*. 4th ed. Washington, D.C.: Bureau of National Affairs, 1969.

Strum, Phillipa. *The Supreme Court and "Political Questions": A Study in Judicial Evasion*. University, Ala: University of Alabama Press, 1974.

THE COURT AND POLITICAL CHANGE

CHAPTER 2

THE COURT AS PROTECTOR OF MINORITIES

The Supreme Court's power to participate in making public policy has for decades created disquiet among American legal and political theorists. Sensitive to the problems of democratic theory posed by placing the authority for constitutional interpretation in the hands of a small group of unelected individuals, these scholars have produced a voluminous body of literature, largely impressionistic and prescriptive, seeking to account for the existence of judicial review in the United States and to create a consistent theory of its appropriate scope. In admittedly oversimplified terms, these analysts of judicial policy making have tended to divide into two camps, the proponents of judicial activism and the advocates of judicial self-restraint. Those who urge restraint believe that the Court should normally defer to the elected branches of government, while those who favor activism argue that the Court should vigorously intervene in the policy-making process.

It is important to recognize, however, that activists and restraintists basically share the same conception of the Supreme Court's function in the American political system. The Court is seen by both groups as the protector of minority rights against a majority tyranny. Even James Bradley Thayer, a leading advocate of judicial restraint and the intellectual forebear of two others—Holmes and Frankfurter—believed that at times the popular majority, through its elected representatives, would act irrationally—and in Thayer's scheme of analysis this meant to act unconstitutionally.[1] At such times, the Court would have to step in and exercise its power of constitutional review. The problem, then, is: When should the Court interfere with the popular will? Or, put differently, what constitutes unconstitutional action?

The advocates of judicial restraint believe that "unconstitutional" must be defined narrowly. In their view, the Constitution is a vague, imprecise charter that allows great leeway to the dominant political forces. If "unconstitutional" is narrowly defined, the Court will not often interfere with the popular will through the exercise of judicial review. It must on occasion move to protect a minority, whether an ethnic minority, a religious minority, or a minority of wealthy capitalists irrationally persecuted by a hostile proletariat. For reasons of democratic principle or political prudence, however, these instances must be infrequent and well justified. The Court, in other words, will rarely exercise its power to strike down legislation.

Activists, on the other hand, believe the Constitution to be a more precise document than do the restraintists, and, therefore, they define "unconstitutional" more broadly. As a consequence, they believe that the Court must interfere with the popular will more frequently. They are also more optimistic about the Court's political strength than are the restraintists, and so they believe not only that the Court should interfere more frequently but also that it can.

It bears emphasis, however, that both schools believe that the Court's function is to protect minority rights. They differ over how frequently this should be done and why, but both share a similar view of the Court's purpose within the political process.

THE COURT AS AGENT OF THE MAJORITY

Some years ago in a famous article Professor Robert Dahl argued that the traditional concern over the Supreme Court's power of judicial review was largely unfounded.[2] The Court cannot and does not function to protect minorities, Dahl contended. With admirable rigor, he demonstrated that seldom, if ever, had the Court been successful in blocking the will of a law-making majority on an important policy issue.

Dahl persuasively demonstrated that the Court could not block the desires of a dominant political coalition for long. Even more importantly, he suggested that the Court would not often even wish to attempt to block the majority will. National politics in the United States has been dominated by relatively cohesive alliances that endure over long periods of time. Because the Court is a political institution whose members are recruited with their political preferences and prejudices in mind, it is inevitably part of the dominant political alliance, except for transitional periods during which the old alliance is crumbling and a new one is rising to take its place. During these periods, the Court will presumably be out of step with the political times, since the justices have lifetime appointments. When the Court strikes down legislation as unconstitutional, Dahl demonstrated, it is seldom successful in the long run in thwarting the majority policy. But the crucial point is that most of the time the Court is not out of line with the dominant political values.

Professor Dahl did not examine this point at length, having arrived at his conclusion by simple logical deduction. He did not, therefore, consider when the Court would be most likely to act counter to the popular majority's values. But, in light of the tremendous scholarly time and effort devoted to analyzing the Supreme Court's policy-making powers generally and the institution of judicial review in particular, Dahl's suggestions were relatively shattering.

Essentially Dahl's thesis was the same as that advanced by Finley Peter Dunne's turn-of-the-century cartoon character, Mr. Dooley: "The Supreme Court follows the election returns." This is true not in the sense that the Court examines the newspapers on the morning after an election and adjusts its decision-making behavior accordingly, but in the sense that over long periods the Court's decisions tend to reflect the will of the dominant political forces. During transitional periods, however, when the Court is composed of holdovers from the old coalition, it is more likely to perform the function ascribed to it by traditional theory: opposing the will of the elected, lawmaking majority.

Patterns of Electoral Behavior

To examine the Dahl-Dooley thesis that the Supreme Court follows the election returns, the first evidence to turn to is the election returns. A look at political history, reveals that American electoral behavior has been relatively stable, with one party or another dominating national politics for long periods of time. What explains such behavior?

Many modern polticial scientists have emphasized the fact that party identity strongly influences a voter's choice of presidential candidates.[3] A great deal of research on voting behavior has concluded that the single most important factor in determing how a person will vote is his or her identification with or loyalty to one of the competing political parties. Elections, according to this view, are essentially reaffirmations of party allegiance. The study of electoral behavior, then, becomes the study of the flow of party allegiances rather than the study of a single election or candidate.

Central to this theory is the concept of the "normal vote." Simply stated, the normal vote is the expected division of voter strength between the competing parties. In any given election, short-term forces (candidates' images, transitory issues) affect this vote according to their intensity and direction. The net influence of the short-term forces on the electorate's existing party allegiances determines the election outcome. Thus, according to this theory, any election result is composed of two factors: (1) the normal vote division to be expected, and (2) the deviation from the norm that occurs because of the immediate circumstances of the election. The outcome is the result of short-term forces acting on the underlying distribution of party loyalties.

Classifications of Elections Elections can then be classified based on the concept of the normal vote and deviations from it. For the recent past, survey measurements are available to calculate the normal vote and assess the meaning of electoral changes. But, even for earlier American political history, where normal vote divisions can only be estimated, the *concept* of the normal vote may be used in formulating an electoral classification scheme. Under this scheme each American presidential election may be classified as (1) maintaining, (2) deviating, or (3) realigning.[4]

In a maintaining election, the current pattern of party allegiances is maintained, and the candidate of the majority party is elected. In a deviating election, the net short-term forces work to the advantage of the minority party and are strong enough to cause its presidential candidate to win, but the electorate's underlying pattern of party loyalties is unaffected. In a realigning election, the electorate's political feeling is so intense that the basic underlying patterns of party allegiance are changed, and a new party balance is created, which will endure for several decades.

Such fundamental shifts in national political alignments, usually associated with national crises, are not actually accomplished in a single election. Instead, there are realignment phases or realigning electoral eras. For example, the partisan realignment that produced New Deal Democracy was begun by Al Smith in 1928, when he changed the image that the Democratic Party had been given by William Jennings Bryan and captured small pluralities in the populous, Catholic, urban Northeast; that realignment was completed by Franklin Roosevelt's sweep in 1936. During such realignment phases, large numbers of new voters are influenced by events with widespread and powerful impact, such as war or depression. Rather than simply accept the political attitudes of their parents, as is usually the case, these new voters are socialized by events. Naturally enough, there have been very few realigning phases in American political history.[5]

This classification scheme is helpful in gauging voter preferences over time. The behavior of the Court can then be compared with the ebb and flow of electoral patterns to test the thesis that Supreme Court decision making normally agrees with the values of the dominant political coalition, except during transitional phases of electoral realignment.

Patterns of Party Behavior

Such a comparison has been facilitated by the work of Professors William Nisbet Chambers and Walter Dean Burnham, who have already employed the electoral classication scheme to study the development of American political parties.[6] Their findings cast light on the substantive preferences of American voters throughout history and on the values of the law-making majorities that they have elected. It will be useful to summarize those findings briefly before turning to a consideration of the Court.[7]

The First Party System

Based upon their study of voting alignments, Chambers and Burnham identify five major eras of stable party competition or, as they call them, five national party systems in American political history. The first of these national party systems existed from 1789 to 1820. This really was a transitional phase between the establishment of the United States and the regularization of its political patterns. As in any new nation, political life at this time was very experimental. The political parties, like other institutions in the new society, were seeking to define their role in the American political system.

Because the roles or functions that political parties could or should play were not yet well defined, understood, or accepted, the party system in the 1790s exhibited certain peculiarities that set it apart from all succeeding party systems. First, both parties—the Federalists and the Republicans—were organized at the center of the national government; the organizational structure filtered from there down to the states. In contrast, today the national parties are little more than loose coalitions of state parties that come together every four years to attempt to elect a president. The state party organizations in this first American party system were much more centrally controlled than are contemporary state parties, which are virtually autonomous. Secondly, because of the new nation's heavy economic dependence on Europe and involvement in the European diplomatic and military struggles that followed the French Revolution, foreign policy was an enormously partisan issue. Thirdly, because the idea of political opposition as a legitimate part of the governing process was not yet firmly entrenched, each political coalition viewed the opposing party as subversive. This outlook gave rise to such excesses as the Alien and Sedition Acts. The result was ideological behavior by both parties that would be abnormal in later American politics.

Nevertheless, the Republican and Federalist parties shared certain values in common. Despite his liberal, laissez-faire statements, Thomas Jefferson's election in 1800 did not noticeably change national policy. Neomercantilism continued to be the order of the day. The national government continued to claim broad powers, imposing a total embargo on trade with Europe, rechartering the Bank of the United States, and purchasing the Louisiana Territory from France. And, though democratic in sentiment, the Republican leadership was hardly less elitist in practice than were the Federalists.

These similarities between the two parties, coupled with the fact that elections, particularly at the national level and especially for president, remained undemocratized, may account for the collapse of the first party system. By 1820, when Monroe ran unopposed for the presidency, there evidently were insufficient points of political conflict to sustain competition between national parties.

The Second Party System   Recognizably modern parties emerged during the second American party system, following a party realignment in response to the election of John Quincy Adams. The presidential election of 1824 was the major event in a chain that brought significant electoral changes. The realignment produced would endure until 1860. The growing popular demand for expanding the right to vote coincided with popular revulsion at the "deal" by which Adams was elected from within the House of Representatives. Dissent soon coalesced around the charismatic figure of Andrew Jackson.

This second American party system was significant for a number of interrelated reasons. First, it contributed to the decentralization of political power in the United States. The period, for example, saw the rise of the convention and the decline of the centralized congressional caucus as a mechanism for selecting presidential candidates. Under Jackson and his successors, the federal government progressively declined in power in relation to the states, and eventually withdrew completely from intervention in the economic sector. This was due largely to the rise of slavery as a political issue. Any active federal economic policy would have necessarily worsened the emerging conflict on this issue.

The presidency also experienced a decline in prestige in relation to the locally elected Congress. After Jackson, with the exception of Polk, the office was occupied by a succession of nonentities whose chief virtue was their acceptability to both the North and the South. A further consequence of the democratization and decentralization of politics was that both major parties developed a nonideological character. The Democratic party was an extremely mixed group that had grown up around Jackson; the Whig party was an even more diverse collection of individuals who gathered in opposition to "King Andrew," as they called Jackson. Neither party was united by any political program other than a desire for office and its spoils. Both lacked a positive commitment to anything.

Because the two national parties were so nonideological and decentralized, the second American party system was extremely unstable. Both parties were motley collections of contradictory elements incapable of reconciling within themselves the conflict over slavery.

The Third Party System   The result was that between 1852 and 1860 an explicitly sectional party appeared on the political scene. The central reality of the realignment that produced the Republican party was the restructuring of all political relationships along sectional lines. This was the only institutional arrangement possible to limit the cancer of slavery so that it might eventually be removed from the body politic and the social system built on it be destroyed. The second party system might have endured and the Civil War might have been averted if slavery had not emerged as a political issue. But, in view of the social changes taking place in the North and West, it probably would have been impossible to suppress national debate on the "peculiar institution."

Indeed, a textbook example of a prerevolutionary situation had developed in the Unites States by the 1850s. New elites, representing the urban, industrial Northeast, were challenging the rule of the old, southern, agrarian elite that had dominated national policy making under the Jacksonian system. Old arrangements and institutions were proving inadequate to the needs of new realities. For the Union to survive, entirely new ways of doing things had to be adopted or invented. The Civil War and the political realignment that accompanied it were perhaps the only true revolution in American history.

Certainly the period immediately following the war was one of great ferment, experimentation, and change. Not only was slavery abolished but also the national government attempted for a time to elevate the freedman to a position of first-class citizenship, while simultaneously initiating measures to foster economic expansion.

By the 1870s, however, the radical phase of the third party system had collapsed. The infamous bargain of 1876 ratified this collapse: The Republican party abandoned its efforts to create a Republican stronghold in a reconstructed South, in exchange for southern votes for the Republican presidential candidate, who had failed to win a victory in the electoral college. For the next twenty years, partisan competition was so close that national political life was virtually stalemated. At the same time, political institutions generally were declining in significance, overshadowed by the changes wrought in society at large by the corporate-industrial revolution.

The Fourth Party System   These changes rendered the third party system obsolete. The old political structures were incapable of taking into account demographic and economic developments of major importance. As a result, they excluded certain groups by definition from participation in the political process. In particular, the western farmers and a growing, urban, immigrant proletariat were powerless. Rationally, these two groups should have joined forces against the conservative, industrial elite that had come to dominate both major parties during the third party system. This did not happen, however, for two reasons.

The first was simple ethnic hostility. For complex reasons of structural weakness, one of the excluded groups, the western farmers, managed to capture one of the two major parties, the Democrat, without the assistance of the immigrants in the Northeast. But the populism of the Democratic leader, William Jennings Bryan, based on opposition to industrial capital, also contained an element of hostility toward the "new immigration." The large voting of blocs of Slavic and Italian immigrants in the Northeast responded in kind by shunning a Democratic party that was openly prejudiced against them.

Secondly, in 1893 the country suffered its worst economic depression to that date, while a Democrat, Grover Cleveland, was president. The response of the industrial workers was electoral rejection of the party in power. The consequent political realignment produced a system of one-party states and reduced both competition and participation in politics, and provided the Republicans with an electoral majority that lasted until the late 1920s.

The Fifth Party System   The realignment that produced the winning coalition associated with Franklin Roosevelt—composed of the rural and urban underprivileged, labor, ethnic minorities, and the academic elite—actually was foreshadowed by Al Smith's campaign of 1928. The "Happy Warrior" was able to wrest control of the Democratic party from the old southern-rural-colonial forces that had dominated it since the realignment of 1888-96. As a big city Catholic, Smith attracted a huge bloc of new immigrant voters into the political system for the first time, precipitating a realignment in the urban Northeast. The stable sectionalism of the fourth party system was then shattered a year later by the force of the Great Depression.

The consequences of this realignment are well known. A bureaucratized, welfare-warfare state became the major reality in American politics. The Democrats replaced the GOP as the dominant party in a system of partisan competition based, at least outside the South, on appeals to economic self-interest and group identification. Economically, a mixed system of welfare capitalism emerged, within which the federal government was actively involved in the creation, promotion, and perpetuation of countervailing sources of power. In institutional terms, the presidency and the executive branch moved into the ascendancy as the center of policy planning and initiation.

These developments in American government and politics were occasioned by and have been continued by three major socioeconomic changes: urbanization, population migration, and the increased importance of ethnic minorities, particularly blacks, as a political factor. Whether these factors have diminished in importance and, consequently, whether American party politics has experienced yet another realignment are still unknown. Some evidence does support the thesis that the United States has recently passed through a new realignment phase.[8] But, because the electoral classification scheme developed by modern political scientists is not a predictive device, it is not now possible to say with any certainty whether such a realignment has occurred, let alone what its consequences might be.

Patterns of Court Behavior

The electoral classification scheme has been profitably used to study the development of American party politics; might it be applied with equal profit to a discussion of the development of American constitutional politics? Many students of the Court have remarked that its history has been divided into five fairly specific periods.[9] Moreover, these periods generally coincide with the dates of the party systems identified by Chambers and Burnham.[10] In each of these five periods certain legal doctrines have prevailed, only to be abandoned in a later period. In some periods of the history of constitutional law, the Court has tended to emphasize the affirmative aspects of the Constitution as a grant of power to the government, while in other periods it has placed greater stress on the constitutional limitations on governmental power. The Court seems always to have some special interest to protect or value to advance. Have these interests or primary legal norms been opposed to or in consonance with the primary values expressed within the larger political system?

The Marshall Court   The first and formative period of the Supreme Court's history is identified with the tenure of Chief Justice John Marshall. Under Marshall, the primary legal norms advanced by the Court were national supremacy, judicial power, and the protection of private property.[11] The Court labored to establish the supremacy of the national government over the states through broad interpretations of such constitutional provisions as the commerce clause and the necessary and proper clause. Similarly, it asserted its own power to review the validity of state legislative and judicial actions, thereby increasing the power of the federal government generally and the power of the federal judiciary in particular. Nationalism also proved a useful tool for the protection of property rights. Since most of the statutes that interfered with private property during this era were state laws, such as debtor relief legislation, interpretations that severely limited states' rights were frequently used to invalidate such statutes.

There would, indeed, seem to be a certain coincidence between the values asserted or advanced by the Court under Marshall and the dominant norms of the first American party system identified by Chambers and Burnham. That party system was characterized by strong, central organization. Both Republicans and Federalists were committed to the protection of aristocratic privilege, a part of which involved the protection of property rights. Both parties followed a neomercantilist economic policy, and that involved maintaining a strong national government. Thus, the harmony that developed between Marshall's Supreme Court and Jefferson's successors may have been no accident. It is true that great enmity existed between the Court headed by Marshall and the executive office headed by his cousin, Jefferson. But this may be attributed more to differences of personality and temperament than to differences of politics. When Jefferson left the White House and, thus, eliminated the personality factor, the Marshall Court and succeeding Republican presidents got along quite well. For example, when the Republican Congress rechartered the Bank of the United States, Marshall's Court quickly upheld the constitutionality of the bank on the basis of sweeping assertions of federal power.[12]

The Taney Court   The collapse of the first party system and the realignment of 1820-28 created a second party system in which Jacksonian Democrats expressed the dominant political values of the day. Not surprisingly, Marshall's successor was none other than Jackson's right-hand man, Roger Brooke Taney. Just as Jackson and his successors dismantled the neomercantilist system and withdrew the federal government from the economic sector, so the Taney Court was less inclined to invalidate state legislation and viewed corporate enterprise with a less hospitable eye than the Marshall Court.[13]

During this period, the federal government declined in power in relation to the states, and the presidency experienced a sharp drop in prestige. Although the Court under Taney did not suffer an equivalent decline, it did behave similarly, in that it took a position somewhat more like an impartial arbiter between states and nation, rather than acting as an active champion for the central government, as the Marshall Court had done. Finally, just as the second party system was characterized by extreme sectionalism in voting patterns, so the Court under Taney came to divide increasingly along sectional lines in its disposition of cases, with the southerners holding a slim but stable majority as in the other two branches.

The differences between the Taney and the Marshall Courts should not be exaggerated, however. The realignment that brought the Jacksonian Democrats to power did not represent a sharp break with the preceding party system, as did the realignment of 1928-36. Most historians and certainly most Democrats trace the history of that party back through Jackson to Jefferson. In other words, the dominant party of the second party system, the Jacksonian Democrats, was in large part the child of the Jeffersonian Republicans; the two parties had much in common.

Similarly, the Court under Taney deviated only somewhat from the Court under Marshall. The differences between the two Courts were often more of emphasis than of substance. For example, the property rights that were so dear to Marshall were not subjected to a wholesale attack by the Jacksonians or abandoned by the Taney Court. The Democratic party was largely composed of small farmers, especially in the South and Southwest, and the emerging urban proletariat in the Northeast. It is not surprising, then, that the Supreme Court of this era viewed the protection of corporate property with a jaundiced eye but was as quick as Marshall ever was to protect vested rights in land and slaves, two forms of property closer to the hearts of Jacksonians.

The Reconstruction Court   The infamous *Dred Scott* decision[14] and its subsequent repudiation on the battlefield brought about a decline in the Court's prestige that lasted throughout the 1860s. As a result, the Supreme Court did not participate in the radical phase of the third party system. This is not surprising, however; popular disregard of the judicial process is not uncommon in revolutionary situations.

The program initially followed by the Republican victors of the third realignment had two major thrusts: on the one hand, federal protection of civil rights, especially those of the newly freed blacks; on the other, federal intervention in the economy to encourage the development of commercial and corporate enterprise. By 1870, the first half of this program had been abandoned, and this abandonment of the black man by the Republican leadership was formalized in the bargain of 1876. The Tilden-Hayes Compromise produced a sectional deadlock between the parties that lasted for the next decade and a half. This solution came to be accepted by public opinion, and in the 1880s it was recognized as legitimate by the Supreme Court in a series of decisions that crippled most of the radical program for the protection of black Americans.[15]

Having regained its strength and prestige, however, the Court did its part in advancing the second half of the Republican program, federal encouragement of industrial capitalism.[16] Not only did the Court thus validate the practices of the dominant political coalition but it also laid the groundwork for new doctrines of constitutional limitation that could be used to protect corporate property if the dominant political values changed.

The Conservative Court   If anything, the Surpeme Court anticipated the electoral realignment that brought about the fourth party system. By 1893, the stage was set for a political coalition between western farmers and immigrant laborers. Many members of the corporate, industrial elite feared that such a coalition would occur and that it would overthrow their rule. Because the United States, unique among western democracies, had democratized its politics before industrialization occurred, such a popular attack would be constitutionally valid. The coalition, of course, did not occur. But, before it was clear that this would be the case, while the industrial elite still feared such a coalition, the Supreme Court handed down a series of decisions in 1894-95 that undermined the legitimacy of any massive assault on established elite rule.[17]

When it became apparent, however, that the feared coalition would not emerge and that the result of the realignment of 1888-96 was to elevate McKinley Republicanism to preeminence in the political system, the Court began a campaign completely in consonance with the values represented by the dominant party. Those values are best expressed in the popular slogans of the time: "Dollar Diplomacy," "The Gospel of Wealth," "A Return to Normalcy," "The Open Door Policy in China," and "The Business of America Is Business"—in short, laissez-faire at home and imperial dominance abroad. In a series of decisions at the turn of the century, the Court validated the nation's rise to imperial power, holding in essence that the Constitution need not follow the flag, or that the Constitution allowed Americans, in Kipling's phrase, to "take up the white man's burden."[18] With respect to domestic laissez-faire economics, the Court used the due process clause of the Fourteenth Amendment as a formidable weapon against an assortment of state laws that sought to protect consumers, unions, farmers, unorganized labor, women, and children against the abuses of business enterprises.[19]

It was no coincidence that the Supreme Court reached its greatest power as an economic policy maker in a period when Theodore Roosevelt became president only because an assassin's bullet found McKinley, and Woodrow Wilson became president only because of an abnormal, three-party election. In other words, this was a period in which the majority of the voters favored conservatives—William McKinley, William Howard Taft, Warren G. Harding, Calvin Coolidge, Herbert Hoover—and this conservatism was reflected on the Court. The high point of the judicial attempt to control economic policy was reached during seventeen months in 1935-36, when the Court launched a frontal attack on the New Deal.[20] But the country's mood had shifted. Public opinion, though opposed to Roosevelt's "packing" of the Court, was outraged at the Court's "veto" of the president's recovery program, and the Court beat a strategic, if belated, retreat. Thus, one of the inevitable institutional modifications that followed the realignment of 1928-36 was elimination of the Supreme Court's veto over economic regulatory legislation.[21]

The Liberal Court In the most recent period of the Court's history, constitutional law has been brought into accord with the norms of the New Deal Democrats. Obsolete doctrines, especially the precedents of economic due process, have been scuttled.[22] The authority of the government to intervene in the economy is almost undisputed. From the New Deal to the Great Society, the Court sustained the welfare state. At the same time, it liberalized the constitutional law of civil liberties and, in particular, advanced the ideology of egalitarianism, the doctrine of the "common man," on many fronts.[23]

Comparison of Court and Party Patterns

On the basis of this brief review, it certainly seems that the Supreme Court follows the election returns over time. Due to the life tenure of the justices, however, the Court is most likely to act against the will of the majority—the role ascribed to it by traditional theory—during transitional phases identified as critical periods of electoral realignment. Table I suggests that some of the Court's most notable collisions with elected agencies of government have indeed occurred during periods of party realignment. The Court then is likely to lag behind the evolution of political values that is taking place within the nation, and an interval is needed for the Court to catch up with the country. As time passes, the newly dominant political coalition appoints its own adherents to the supreme bench, and the Court returns to harmony with the new law-making majority. In recent years, this hypothesis has received increasing support from some of the most sophisticated students of the Court.[24]

THE COURT'S ROLES IN AMERICAN POLITICS

What significance do such findings have for understanding the Supreme Court's role within the American system of government? First of all, the traditional concept of the Court as the champion of minority rights against majority demands appears to be *largely* incorrect. Of course, many questions in American politics and certainly many that reach the Supreme Court do not resolve themselves into clear-cut issues of a majority versus a minority but instead involve conflict between two competing minorities.[25] In such situations, no matter which way the Court rules, it will advance the rights of a minority. But in resolving such conflicts the Court will be guided by the political, social, economic, and even moral values dominant at the time. If the dominant value system liberally favors recognition of the aspirations of at least certain minorities, the Court will tend to favor those claims; but it will do so because those values are dominant and not because something inherent in the nature or structure of the institution predisposes it to favor minority claims.

The traditional concept of the Court as an entity separate from and independent of the dominant political coalition, a bulwark against the potential tyranny of the majority of the moment, is not entirely incorrect, however, During and immediately following transitional phases of party realignment, the Court is likely to oppose the newly dominant values. Yet it is precisely at these periods that it is least likely to be effective. Most of the time, then, the debate between the judicial activists and the advocates of judicial restraint has little bearing on the actual distribution of political power in the American constitutional system.

The Court as Legitimator

If the Court is normally in line with the popular or, at least, the law-making majority of the day, what function does it serve? Traditional theory had a role for the Court to play—protector of minority rights. If the Court does not usually play that role, does it serve any function at all that is distinctive to it?

TABLE I AMERICAN PARTY SYSTEMS, ELECTORIAL REALIGNMENTS, AND SUPREME COURT DECISION MAKING

Date	Party System	Court Period (by Chief Justice)	Exemplary Cases of Realignment
1800	Jeffersonian Republican	Marshall	
1820 } Realignment phase			
1828	Jacksonian Democracy	Taney	Worcester v. Georgia, 31 U.S. (6 Pet.) 515 (1832)
1852 } Realignment phase			
1860	Radical Republican	Chase; Waite	Dred Scott v. Sandford, 60 U.S. (19 How.) 393 (1857)
1888 } Realignment phase			
1896	McKinley Republican	Fuller; White; Taft; Hughes	
1928 } Realignment Phase			
1936	New Deal Democracy	Stone; Vinson; Warren; Burger	Schechter v. United States, 295 U.S. 495 (1935); United States v. Butler, 297 U.S. 1 (1936)
Present Realignment Phase?			Lamont v. Postmaster Gen'l, 381 U.S. 301 (1965); Shapiro v. Thompson, 394 U.S. 618 (1969)

47

Professor Dahl and others have argued that it does.[26] For them, the Court's principal function in American government is to confer legitimacy on the specific policies of the dominant coalition by upholding their constitutionality. According to this analysis, an empirically correct view of the Court must emphasize its positive power to sustain legislation rather than its negative power to strike statutes down.

This argument can be cast in comparative, even metaphorical, terms. Louis Heren, Washington correspondent of the *London Times*, has likened the Court's relationship to Congress and the executive branch to the church's relationship to the medieval monarch.[27] It is the Court's function to legitimate contemporary public acts, if possible, by demonstrating their consonance with fundamental constitutional principles.

Other scholars have vigorously disputed the idea that the Supreme Court possesses any ability to legitimate particular policy actions.[28] Besides, they have pointed out that, if the Court can legitimate policy, during critical periods of party realignment it must work to delegitimate the policies of the newly emergent regime. Of course, these short-term aberrations may be offset for the nation by the long-term good the Court does during periods of political stability. But it is true that, while Dahl did have much data to support the argument that the Court does not function to protect minorities, he had no data to indicate that the Court could legitimate policies. He merely assumed that it could.

Both Dahl and his critics, however, may have taken too narrow a vision of legitimacy and the legitimating function. If Mr. Dooley was right about the Court, it still may function as a legitimator—but of the regime generally, not of specific policies. By making the Constitution fit the needs of the contemporary times, by finding power within it for the government to act, while not abandoning the transcendent values for which the Constitution stands, the Court may confer symbolic legitimacy on the dominant political coalition itself and on its values, although it only indirectly legitimizes particular policies. Perhaps Justice Oliver Wendell Holmes had this function in mind when he wrote:

> The past gives us our vocabulary and fixes the limits of our imagination; we cannot get away from it. There is, too, a peculiar logical pleasure in making manifest the continuity between what we are doing and what has been done before.[29]

The Court as Republican Schoolmaster

The general congruence over time between Supreme Court decision making and the main currents of American political thought suggests an alternative role that the Court may play in the constitutional system. The Court may be seen as an educational institution. While this educative function is not unrelated to its legitimating function, the two are also distinguishable.

The view of the Court as educator rests on the distinction between expediency and principle. It begins with the premise that all governmental actions have two kinds of effects. The first is their immediate, intended effect. The second is a public policy's bearing on principles or values that the nation holds to be fundamental.

The citizens can see the relation between their immediate needs or desires and a particular governmental action, and they transmit these perceptions to their representatives by the electoral process. But they do always perceive the relation between a given policy, program, or action and their long-term values.

Assuming that the United States wishes to have principled government, some agency must, in the normal operation of the policy process, be concerned with society's fundamental, underlying values. As chapter 1 argued, that agency should be the Supreme Court, and in fact, in American politics, it can only be the Court. Because of its position within the American constitutional system, the Court is able to deal with matters of principle, whereas Congress and the president, because they are responsible to the electoral whims of the moment, cannot. The justices "have, or should have, the leisure, the training, and the insulation to follow the ways of the scholar in pursuing the ends of government."[30]

This insulation and the mystique of the judicial process allow the Court to appeal to the country's principled good sense, which may be forgotten in the heat of the moment. It is true, as Dahl points out, that the Court cannot withstand the majority will when the majority is determined to enforce it, but through the exercise of its power of judicial review the Court may entreat the majority to take a sober second look at the course it has set for the nation. As Professor Eugene Rostow has put it, the justices "are inevitably teachers in a vital national seminar."[31] They are in a better position to conduct that seminar than any other officials in American government.

Objections to the View of the Court as Educator

Some social scientists would object that, if the Court is teaching a national seminar, "few Americans are enrolled in the course."[32] These scholars point to the results of so-called "impact" studies that have stressed the public's ignorance about the Court, the government's unresponsiveness to its decisions, and the variance between Supreme Court doctrine and local behavior.[33] They emphasize the degree to which lower court autonomy checks the Supreme Court's power, and they note the means available to avoid, evade, or delay the implementation of its rulings. Given such apparent lack of effect, these scholars argue, it is difficult to believe that the Court is able either to legitimate policy or to teach Americans about fundamental constitutional principles.[34]

The Inadequacy of the Evidence This argument misses the mark, however, because it confuses compliance with impact. Compliance, to be sure is one facet of impact. But the concept of the Supreme Court's impact embraces many other phenomena, such as attitudinal change. A ruling by the Supreme Court may affect many people's attitudes, even if it does not change them enough to gain their compliance.

Concentrating on compliance also oversimplifies the relationship between judicial decision making and social change. Researchers tend to investigate only the extent to which a single, specific decision is being obeyed. But an entire line of precedent, let alone a single decision, is only one factor among many that may be related to social change. How much of the change in American race relations has been attributable to economic forces? How much to population migration? How much to the rise of the Third World? How much to black protest? And how much to *Brown v. Board of Education*? To isolate the Supreme Court's contribution to a given situation may make it impossible to study anything other than cases of clear noncompliance. The result is a self-validating hypothesis.

Moreover, even if the Court is ineffective in commanding compliance with specific decisions that go against popular norms, this does not invalidate the thesis that the Court functions to confer a general legitimacy on changes in the governmental regime. At best, it supports that thesis. At worst, it is irrelevant. Nor does it say anything about the argument that the Court serves as an educator, as a positive catalyst, accelerating and channeling the direction of social change. The degree of compliance with Court decisions is no measure of the Court's teaching ability.

Positive Evidence of the Court's Impact Even on their own terms, the compliance studies have not shown the Supreme Court to be a consistent and total failure. "Schools have desegregated, legislatures have reapportioned, welfare residency rules have been eliminated . . . sometimes even before, in anticipation of decisions not yet handed down or before specific implementing directives are issued."[35] Where the population affected by the decision has been small and the Court's mandate has been clear and well publicized, as in the area of reapportionment or, more spectacularly, in *United States v. Nixon*[36] (the president *did* surrender the tapes—and resign!), the Court has been singularly effective.

Similarly, the efforts to debunk the idea that the Court plays a legitimating or educating function have tended to confuse public support for specific decisions with more general support for the Court itself. Yet the most thorough study to date of public attitudes toward the Court, though it casts some doubt on the Court's ability to legitimate specific policies, concluded that support for the Court

> dips far beneath the Court's attentive public into the more articulate layers of the less knowledgeable . . . . Despite the unpopularity of its decisions in recent years, the Court still maintains a substantial reservoir of . . . support . . . . Quite evidently, many people who are critical of the Court's specific decisions nontheless support the institution.[37]

This conclusion can only bolster the argument that the Supreme Court plays an important, if symbolic, role in the American political system—a role that is not tied to the substantive content of its particular decisions.

Beyond this, however, it is difficult to produce evidence to support the thesis that the Supreme Court performs either an educative or a legitimating function. The research just has not been done. Perhaps those areas where rapid compliance seems to have occurred should be more thoroughly studied. But, thus far, research interest has focused on noncompliance. Appalled by the degree to which the school desegregation decisions were ignored or defied, academics tended to study the factors influencing noncomplying behavior. This initial concern for noncompliance then led to the investigation of other areas where compliance seemed most lacking, such as the response to the school prayer decisions.[38] The result may have been to overstate the Supreme Court's impotence.

The less tangible roles of the Court are even more seriously in need of study. The compliance studies concentrate on the Court's influence on the populations involved in and immediately affected by judicial decisions. But the Court's impact may be indirect as well as direct. One must, therefore, look beyond the population immediately affected by a given decision. The impact of *Brown v. Board of Education*, for example, must be assessed not only from the behavior of segregating school boards but also from the values, expectations, and self-perceptions of black Americans.

In dealing with the Court's impact, moreover, one must allow for the passage of time. Legitimation and education may be long-term processes that gain strength from the Court's gradual building of constitutional doctrine. All impact may not be instantaneous or observable. In particular, this will be true of decisions that reinforce existing practices or thought patterns. Little, if anything, will happen after such a decision. Yet, as was the case with *Marbury*, the decision's long-range implications may be enormous. If nothing else, Supreme Court decisions help to determine the agenda for political actors.

Thus, "the impact of Supreme Court decisions [must be] measured not only in terms of its effects on the parties who actually win or lose the case, but by the manner in which it is reflected in the later conduct and thinking of society as a whole."[39]

A MODEL OF THE COURT'S ROLE

In all fairness, it would seem that the Scottish verdict, "Not Proven," must be awarded both to the thesis that the Supreme Court plays an educating or legitimating function (or both) and to the attacks on that thesis. One critical qualitative difference between the two positions exists, however. While the compliance studies and the arguments bases on them have remained largely atheoretical,[40] the view of the Court as legitimator and educator does proceed from a comprehensive and coherent model of the policy-making process, based on both communication theory and learning theory.

According to this model, government policy making may be seen as a case of successfully educating the public.[41] In order to function, government must develop new policies to meet new situations. These policies, in turn, must be effectively communicated to the population. In learning theory terms, government policies represent stimuli. The populace responds to them because sanctions or reinforcements are attached to each stimulus. The likelihood that effective public learning will take place and particular policies will be accepted is increased to the degree that the public views those policies or, at least, the government processes by which they were adopted as legitimate. To succeed in producing such learning, therefore, political regimes must develop symbols that define the criteria of legitimacy and the methods by which legitimacy may be conferred either on a particular administration or on its policies.

The mechanisms of legitimation in any complex society will be numerous. No single agent can be fully responsible. But, in the American system, the Constitution is an especially important collection of legitimacy symbols, a kind of metasymbol. As guardian of the Constitution, "the Supreme Court plays a major role not only in defining the contexts in which particular legitimacy symbols may be used, but also in substituting or generating new symbols for old . . . ."[42]

Again in terms of learning theory, a Court declaration of constitutionality may be viewed as a positive reinforcement. Ironically, although the range of sanctions available to the Court is limited, it can play a meaningful role in the process of legitimation because positive reinforcement is generally a more effective teaching strategy than negative reinforcement.

Single opinions are unlikely to affect strongly held beliefs. But each decision is not an isolated matter. As the reapportionment cases well illustrate, the Court's development of a line of precedent whose direction is reasonably clear and consistent can have great impact on the nation's political beliefs and practices.

The Court's Role in Realignment Periods

During and immediately after periods of party realignment, however, a life-tenured Court, out of sympathy with the emerging or newly dominant political coalition, either fails or refuses to manipulate the constitutional symbols to the advantage of that coalition. This creates a division between legitimacy symbols and actual government practice that is not conducive to the formation of effective public policy. To win the Court's support becomes critical for the new coalition in power. From one perspective, then, realignment periods "may be seen as the attempt by partisans to attach the available legitimacy symbols to [themselves and their policies] and to sever the relationship between these symbols and ... their opponents."[43]

Even after they have been elevated to positions of governmental power, the leaders of the newly dominant coalition may still be unable to convert popular demands into acceptable policy outputs, unless "certain changes are made in the boundaries customarily observed between sets of public officers or between public authority and individual liberty—in short, the rules under which politics is traditionally conducted."[44] The power of the federal government may have to be increased at the expense of the states, for example; or, a previously recognized personal right may have to be confined in its scope, as happened to personal rights in private property following the realignment of 1928-36. In the American system the task of adjusting constitutional boundary disputes has fallen to the Supreme Court. That task, in the face of periodic, major shifts in public sentiment and values, has been greatly eased by the fact that the boundaries specified by the Constitution are more than just a little vague.

In the years following a realigning period, through the normal processes of death and retirement of the justices, the Court returns to sympathy with the values represented in the popular branches; or it may be brought to such a position by presidential and congressional action changing the number of justices or threatening to do so. In either case, the result is the same: For several decades, until the next party realignment, the Court adapts constitutional principles to meet the needs of the dominant political coalition.

This task, however, is complicated by one, fundamental difficulty: the rule of precedent. The Court does not start with a clean slate, "free to invent what it will, but must function within an existing intellectual tradition."[45] In its verbal manipulation of that tradition in order to permit or support political change, the Supreme Court plays a truly creative role. Over the years, the Court has with great ingenuity devised a number of means "for reconciling new experiences and expectations with past values, while at the same time preserving at least the illusion that the law is consistent over time."[46] The Republic can have both desired political change *and* a sense of constitutional stability.

Adapting the legitimacy symbols to meet the felt needs of the time, however, has a second aspect. On the one hand, the Court helps to legitimate the political present in terms of traditional constitutional values. On the other hand, by enabling the Constitution to remain relevant to present values, the Court keeps the Constitution legitimate.

Criticisms of the Model

Some, no doubt, will object to the emphasis on rhetoric and symbolism in this view of the Court's function within American politics. "One possible response to a person who insists upon the importance of what he calls 'reality' over mere language is to say that a public system of discourse, such as the law is, is itself an important reality, a social and intellectual fact in the life of our society with independent force and significance."[47] Law making, especially judicial law making, is to a very large degree manipulation of language. Its ability to perform such manipulation, coupled with its great moral authority, enables the Court to mold its decisions into powerful political symbols.[48]

While there is little empirical evidence on the symbolic effects of the Court's decisions, the data that have been gathered suggest that the Court's virtuous image has a "halo effect"—for example, this image caused some people to support the decisions outlawing school prayers, even though they had previously approved of such religious exercises.[49] There is every reason to believe that the desegregation decisions radically accelerated changes in Americans' racial attitudes.[50] Even those who decry the Court's lack of "impact" concede that its "strength is in its symbols."[51]

THE JUDICIAL DIALOGUE

The relationships between the Supreme Court and the Constitution, between the Court and the American people, and between the Court and elected public officials are extremely dynamic. The preceding discussion should not obscure that fact. The Court is neither the cause of constitutional change nor solely its instrument. It is both.

Most of the time, the Court will be in line with the values that are dominant in American politics. But those values and, thus, the values dominant on the Court may be unclear or even contradictory; or they may prove inadequate when novel issues arise. In such situations the justices will enjoy a good deal of leeway in reaching their collective decision.

Even here, however, the Court does not have the last word. Politics is a process in which "no one has the last word because *there is no last word*."[52] Therefore, judicial interpretation, which is a political act, is seldom definitive.

For the Court to command, certain factors must be present.[53] First, it must be clear that the Court itself has spoken. Secondly, there must be no doubt about the Court's authority to deal with the subject matter. Thirdly, the Court must speak unambiguously. Fourthly, the decision must be communicated to the affected parties so that they are aware of their new responsibilities and of the new rules governing their behavior. Fifthly, the affected parties must have the necessary means to implement the decision. Since this combination of factors hardly ever exists, the Court seldom finds itself in a situation of command. Rather, it has only the power to persuade. But the Court can impose few sanctions and offer even fewer favors; virtually its only means of persuasion lies in the strength of the arguments it musters to support its decisions.

From this point of view, the Supreme Court is engaged in a dialogue with the American people and their representatives. A judicial decision is a political phenomenon to which the public or its officers respond; the Court reacts to their response; and so on. Since true education normally occurs through a process of dialogue, the Court may be seen as an educator performing a teaching function.

Like most teachers, however, the Court is not always effective. The notion of the court as a vital national seminar, instructing the American people in republican virtue, "flatly accepts the great probability of some significant political tension."[54] Like many students, the Court's pupils do not always accept their instructor's views as revealed truth.

Nevertheless, throughout American history, the Surpeme Court has done more than recognize and express the moral judgments of the time. It has done that, but it has also played a role in shaping and refining those judgments. It has stimulated thinking and debate about important and difficult philosophic issues in public life and has provided the conceptual tools with which that thinking and debate could proceed in an orderly and intelligent manner.

SUMMARY

A substantial body of research during the past generation advances the view, first, that Supreme Court decision making tends to be cyclical in nature and, secondly, that these cycles tend to coincide with larger patterns of political change and electoral realignment. These findings contradict the traditional view of the Court as a powerful body exercising a will independent of society and often contrary to executive and legislative policies.

Supreme Court justices, as well as other judges, bring certain preferences, known and unknown (sometimes unknown even to themselves), to the decisional process. Most of the time, these preferences reflect the value structures of the political coalition that is dominant in American society. As Professor Philip B. Kurland has expressed it:

> There is at least one lesson to be derived form the history of the [Court] . . . and that is that the equation cannot be drawn . . . between "activist" and "liberal" or between "judicial restraint" and "conservative." An "activist" Court is essentially one that is out of step with the legislative or executive branches of the government. It will thus be "liberal" or "conservative" depending upon which role its prime antagonist has adopted . . . .
>
> There is obviously little merit in rehearsing the arguments about whether it was intended to grant the Supreme Court the power of judicial review . . . . Even the question of the scope of that authority . . . puts undue emphasis on what has not been a central question. For the fact of the matter is—whatever the romance may be—that so far as the relations between the Court and [the popular branches] are concerned, [judicial review] has proved historically to be [not as] important . . . as law professors would make it.[55]

If this is so, then it would seem that, rather than protect minorities against the majority of the moment, the Court has usually functioned to confer legitimacy either on the particular policies of the dominant, law-making majority or generally on the coalition itself. Citizens obviously are not born with a sense that their political institutions, processes, or policies are legitimate. These attitudes are learned. One model of how law, especially American constitutional law, works is that it is part of this teaching process. According to this model, "legal institutions act as learning theorists, almost without knowing it. They induce reactions more or less like conditioned reflexes."[56]

The Supreme Court is not the only institution, and constitutional interpretation not the only process, for legitimation in American politics. The principal process for legitimation is still probably majority coalition building. One can, of course, argue that, because majorities are artificial constructs, majority rule is essentially a myth. Nonetheless, a number of formal procedures have been established in American law and government to ensure that decisions are in some way traceable to this artificial construct, the majority. Indeed, this is part of the country's problem during periods of party realignment: The "old" constitutional principles are pitted against appeals to majority rule. This conflict cannot be tolerated for long and normally is corrected by reinterpreting the principles. Usually, however, these two processes—majority rule and constitutional interpretation—reinforce one another.

Several objections may be raised to this model. But they say only that the model is wrong in some places. Complex reality necessarily mocks simple formulations. The important thing is to determine how often and to what extent the model is inaccurate. All models are presumably mistaken somewhere. The real question is whether this model is a better overall approximation of historical reality than are competing models.

A second body of contemporary, historical research has demonstrated that from the country's earliest days the Supreme Court was intended to function and has functioned as an educator.[57] Some justices have performed this role more consciously than others, but none has escaped it. "In the United States," Professor Theodore Lowi has observed, "the history of political theory since the founding of the Republic has resided in the Supreme Court."[58] The following chapters examine the lessons that the Court has taught regarding some of the most important theoretical issues in American politics: the scope of presidential and congressional powers, the relationship between the federal government and the states, and the definition of individual liberties.

NOTES

1 James Bradley Thayer, "The Origin and Scope of the American Doctrine of Constitutional Law," *Harvard Law Review*, 7 (October 1893), 129-56.

2 Robert A. Dahl, "Decision-Making in a Democracy: The Supreme Court as a National Policy-Maker,' *Journal of Public Law*, 6 (fall 1957), 279-95. See also Jonathan D. Casper. "The Supreme Court and National Policy Making," *American Political Science Review*, 70 (March 1976), 50-63.

3 See Angus Campbell, Philip E. Converse, Warren E. Miller, and Donald E. Stokes, *Elections and the Political Order* (New York: John Wiley & Sons, 1966).

4 Ibid., pp. 63-77. The seminal work on cyclical electoral patterns was V. O. Key, "A Theory of Critical Elections," *Journal of Politics*, 17 (February 1955), 3-18. For a sophisticated attempt to synthesize the work on political party systems, explaining election cycles in general theoretical terms, see Thomas P. Jahnige, "Critical Elections and Social Change: Towards a Dynamic Explanation of National Party Competition in the United States," *Polity*, 3 (June 1971), 465-500. See also Gerald Pomper,

"Classification of Presidential Elections," *Journal of Politics*, 29 (August 1967), 535-66, distinguishing between realigning and converting elections depending on whether the dominant party of the previous era continues in its dominant position though changed in composition.

5 Depending on whose count one uses, there have been three, four, or six. Compare Campbell et al., *Elections and the Political Order*, with William Nisbet Chambers and Walter Dean Burnham, eds., *The American Party Systems: Stages of Political Development*, 2d ed. (New York: Oxford University Press, 1975), James L. Sundquist, *Dynamics of the Party System: Alignment and Realignment of Political Parties in the United States* (Washington, D.C.: Brookings Institution, 1973), and Charles Sellers, "The Equilibrium Cycle in Two-Party Politics," *Public Opinion Quarterly*, 29 (spring 1965), 16-37.

6 Chambers and Burnham, *American Party Systems*. See also Sundquist, *Dynamics of the Party System*. But see Douglas Price, "Critical Elections and Party History: A Critical View," *Polity*, 4 (December 1971), 236-42.

7 The following summary of the findings reported in Chambers and Burnham, *American Party Systems*, relies heavily on Professor Burnham's next to last essay in that volume. For a more extensive treatment, consult Burnham, "Party Systems and the Political Process," in *American Party Systems*, pp. 277-307. See also Arthur Schlesinger, Jr., ed., *The Coming to Power: Critical Presidential Elections in American History* (New York: Chelsea House Publishers, 1971). The general patterns identified by Chambers and Burnham are essentially the same as those advanced by Jahnige, "Critical Elections and Social Change," p. 468.

8 See Richard Scammon and Benjamin Wattenberg, *The Real Majority* (New York: Coward, McCann & Geohogan, 1970); Kevin Phillips, *The Emerging Republican Majority* (New Rochelle, N.Y.: Arlington House, 1969); Samuel Lubell, *The Hidden Crisis in American Politics* (New York: W. W. Norton & Co., 1970); Herbert Weisberg and Jerrold Rusk, "Dimensions of Candidate Evaluation," *American Political Science Review*, 64 (December 1970), 1167-85; James L. Sundquist, "Whither the American Party System?" *Political Science Quarterly*, 88 (December 1973), 559-81. But see Walter Dean Burnham, "American Politics in the 1970s: Beyond Party?" in *American Party Systems*, ed. Chambers and Burnham, pp. 308-57.

9 See, e.g., Leonard Levy, ed., *American Constitutional Law: Historical Essays* (New York: Harper & Row, 1966), pp. 1-9; Robert Scigliano, *The Supreme Court and the Presidency* (New York: Free Press, 1971), p. viii. See also Glendon Schubert, *Judicial Policy Making: The Political Role of the Courts*, rev. ed. (Glenview, Ill.: Scott, Foresman & Co., 1974), pp. 184-213.

10 See Richard Funston, "The Supreme Court and Critical Elections," *American Political Science Review*, 69 (September 1975), 795-811; David Adamany, "Legitimacy, Realigning Elections, and the Supreme Court," *Wisconsin Law Review* September 1973), 790-846; Sheldon Goldman and Thomas P. Jahnige, *The Federal Courts as a Political System* (New York: Harper & Row, 1971), pp. 261-68.

11 See, e.g., Marbury v. Madison, 5 U.S. (1 Cranch) 137 (1803); Fletcher v. Peck, 10 U.S. (6 Cranch) 87 (1810); Martin v. Hunter's Lessee, 14 U.S. (1 Wheat.) 304 (1816); Sturges v. Crowninshield, 17 U.S. (4 Wheat.) 122 (1819); McCulloch v. Maryland, 17 U.S. (4 Wheat.) 316 (1819); Cohens v. Virginia, 19 U.S. (6 Wheat.) 264 (1821); Gibbons v. Ogden, 22 U.S. (9 Wheat.) 1 (1824); Brown v. Maryland, 25 U.S. (12 Wheat.) 419 (1827).

12 McCulloch v. Maryland, 17 U.S. (4 Wheat.) 316 (1819).

13 See, e.g., Mayor of New York v. Miln, 36 U.S. (11 Pet.) 102 (1837); Charles River Bridge Co. v. Warren Bridge Co., 36 U.S. (11 Pet.) 420 (1837); Bank of Augusta v. Earle, 38 U.S. (13 Pet.) 519 (1839).

14 Dred Scott v. Sandford, 60 U.S. (19 How.) 393 (1857).

15 E.g., The Civil Rights Cases, 109 U.S. 3 (1883).

16 E.g., Knox v. Lee, 79 U.S. (12 Wall.) 457 (1871); Chicago, M. & St. P. Ry. v. Minnesota, 134 U.S. 418 (1890).

17 E.g., United States v. E. C. Knight Co., 156 U.S. 1 (1895); Pollock v. Farmers' Loan & Trust Co., 157 U.S. 429 (1895); Pollock v. Farmers' Loan & Trust Co., 158 U.S. 601 (1895).

18 E.g., DeLima v. Bidwell, 182 U.S. 1 (1901); Downes v. Bidwell, 182 U.S. 244 (1901); Dorr v. United States, 195 U.S. 138 (1904); Rasmussen v. United States, 197 U.S. 516 (1905).

19 E.g., Smyth v. Ames, 169 U.S. 466 (1898); Lochner v. New York, 198 U.S. 45 (1905); Coppage v. Kansas, 236 U.S. 1 (1915).

20 E.g., Schechter Bros. Poultry Corp. v. United States, 295 U.S. 495 (1935); United States v. Butler, 297 U.S. 1 (1936); Carter v. Carter Coal Co., 298 U.S. 238 (1936).

21 E.g., West Coast Hotel Co. v. Parrish, 300 U.S. 379 (1937); NLRB v. Jones & Laughlin Steel Corp., 301 U.S. 1 (1937); United States v. Belmont, 301 U.S. 324 (1937); United States v. Darby, 312 U.S. 100 (1941); United States v. Pink, 315 U.S. 203 (1942); Wickard v. Filburn, 317 U.S. 111 (1942).

22 E.g., Ferguson v. Skrupa, 372 U.S. 726 (1963).

23 E.g., Gideon v. Wainwright, 372 U.S. 335 (1963); Reynolds v. Sims, 377 U.S. 533 (1964); Shapiro v. Thompson, 394 U.S. 618 (1969).

24 David Adamany, for example, has examined Supreme Court decision making during realignment periods; his analysis tends to substantiate the thesis. See Adamany, "Legitimacy." Sheldon Goldman and Thomas P. Jahnige, focusing not on the Court's behavior but on the reactions of others to it, have reported a distinct correlation between realigning election cycles and the "Court-curbing" periods identified by Stuart S. Nagel. Goldman and Jahnige, *The Federal Courts.* Nagel and Wallace Mendelson, though their work has not been guided by critical election theory, have discussed the effect of party differences between Congress and the Court on judicial policy making. Stuart S. Nagel, *The Legal Process from a Behavioral Perspective* (Homewood, Ill.: Dorsey Press, 1969), pp. 245-79; Wallace Mendelson, "Judicial Review and Party Politics," *Vanderbilt Law Review,* 12 (March 1959), 447-57. And Adamany has adduced evidence, though slight, that justices are more reluctant to resign after a realigning election.

Nevertheless, the attempts to use the voting behavior research to correlate the Court's behavior over time with the dynamics of the political system at large remain few, and those attempts are still in very beginning stages. But see Walter Dean Burnham, *Critical Elections and the Mainsprings of American Politics* (New York: W. W. Norton & Co., 1970), p. 10 n. 15, arguing that Supreme Court decision making provides "the most obviously plausible example of synchronization of institutional-role and policy-output change with critical realignment" in American politics.

Ultimately, the subject calls for an extended, systematic examination of Supreme Court decision making explicitly based on the electoral classification scheme—a treatment of the Court similar to the one that Chambers and Burnham have done for the parties. To date, efforts at statistical investigation of the relationship between the composition and behavior of the Court and electoral change have not proved entirely satisfactory. The precise definitions and operationalizations of concepts necessary for statistical study have proved too arguable, and the limited nature of the data permit only very modest conclusions to be drawn at best. See Bradley C. Canon and S. Sidney Ulmer, "The Supreme Court and Critical Elections: A Dissent," *American Political Science Review*, 70 (December 1976), 1215-18. But see Richard Funston, "Reply," *American Political Science Review*, 70 (December 1976), 1218-21. The subject, therefore, is probably more susceptible to traditional narrative and descriptive methods than to quantitative techniques. The politically dominant values of each period must be identified and compared with judicial opinions through in-depth content and dialectical analyses to determine if Mr. Dooley's speculative interpretation has actually coincided with historical fact.

25 See generally Robert A. Dahl, *A Preface to Democratic Theory* (Chicago: University of Chicago Press, 1956).

26 Dahl, "Decision-Making in a Democracy"; Charles L. Black, *The People and the Court: Judicial Review in a Democracy* (New York: Macmillan Publishing Co., 1960).

27 Louis Heren, *The New American Commonwealth* (New York: Harper & Row, 1968), p. 18.

28 See, e.g., Adamany, "Legitimacy."

29 Oliver Wendell Holmes, *Collected Legal Papers* (New York: Harcourt, Brace & Howe, 1920), p. 139.

30 Alexander M. Bickel, *The Least Dangerous Branch: The Supreme Court at the Bar of Politics* (Indianapolis: Bobbs-Merrill Co., 1972), pp. 25-26.

31 Eugene Rostow, *The Sovereign Prerogative: The Supreme Court and the Quest for Law* (New Haven, Conn.: Yale University Press, 1962), pp. 167-68.

32 James P. Levine and Theodore L. Becker, "Toward and Beyond a Theory of Supreme Court Impact," *American Behavioral Scientist*, 13 (March/April 1970), 567.

33 The literature on Supreme Court "impact" is far too voluminous to cite in full. Some of the leading examples are collected in Theodore L. Becker and Malcolm M. Feeley, eds., *The Impact of Supreme Court Decisions: Empirical Studies*, 2d ed. (New York: Oxford University Press, 1973). Far and away the best introduction to this social science subfield is Stephen L. Wasby, *The Impact of the United States Supreme Court: Some Perspectives* (Homewood, Ill.: Dorsey Press, 1970).

34 It is worth noting that most of those behavioral scientists engaged in conducting "impact" studies have not attacked the thesis that the Supreme Court performs a legitimation function, however defined. Rather, other scholars not involved in "impact" studies have used the "impact" findings to support their own objections to the validity of this thesis. See, e.g., Adamany, "Legitimacy."

35 Wasby, *Impact of the United States Supreme Court*, p. 10.

36 418 U.S. 683 (1974).

37 Walter F. Murphy and Joseph Tanenhaus, "Public Opinion and the United States Supreme Court: A Preliminary Mapping of Some Prerequisites for Court Legitimation of Regime Changes," in *Frontiers of Judicial Research*, ed. Joel B. Grossman and Joseph Tanenhaus (New York: John Wiley & Sons, 1969), pp. 290-91.

38 Studying the behavioral effects of the school prayer cases was an unfortunate choice for generating information about the impact of the Supreme Court. While the Court and the Constitution are powerful symbols, they do not rank with God in the value systems of millions of Americans. Decisions that appear to place the Court in opposition to the Deity seem peculiarly well-calculated to produce resistance and backlash.

39 Note, "*Dombrowski v. Eastland*—a Political Compromise and Its Impact," *Rutgers Law Review*, 22 (fall 1967), 164.

40 But see Don W. Brown and Robert V. Stover, "Court Directives and Compliance: A Utility Approach," *American Politics Quarterly*, 5 (October 1977), 465-80; id., "Understanding Compliance and Noncompliance with Law: The Contributions of Utility Theory," *Social Science Quarterly*, 56 (December 1975), 363-75.

41 For a much fuller and more technical examination of the theory of political legitimacy using the framework of psychological learning theory and the theory of cognitive dissonance, see Richard M. Merelman, "Learning and Legitimacy," *American Political Science Review*, 60 (September 1966), 548-61. See also Richard Schwartz, "A Learning Theory of Law," *Southern California Law Review*, 41 (spring 1968), 548-87.

42 Merelman, p. 555.

43 Ibid., p. 553.

44 Murphy and Tanenhaus, "Public Opinion," p. 273.

45 James B. White, "The Fourth Amendment as a Way of Talking about People: A Study of Robinson and Matlock," in *The Supreme Court Review: 1974*, ed. Philip B. Kurland (Chicago: University of Chicago Press, 1975), p. 168.

46 Austin Sarat and Joel B. Grossman, "Courts and Conflict Resolution: Problems in the Mobilization of Adjudication," *American Political Science Review*, 69 (December 1975), 1207.

47 White, "The Fourth Amendment," p. 168 n. 4.

48 See Leonard Berkowitz and Nigel Walker, "Laws and Moral Judgments," *Sociometry*, 30 (December 1967), 410-22.

49 Kenneth Dolbeare, "The Supreme Court and the States: From Abstract Doctrine to Local Behavioral Conformity," in *The Impact of Supreme Court Decisions*, ed. Becker and Feeley, pp. 202-9.

50 Herbert H. Hyman and Paul B. Sheatsley, "Attitudes toward Desegregation," *Scientific American*, 211 (July 1964), 16-23.

51 Levine and Becker, "Toward and Beyond a Theory," p. 572.

52 Hannah Pitkin, "Obligation and Consent—II," *American Political Science Review*, **60** (March 1966), 52 (emphasis added).

53 These factors resemble those identified by Professor Richard Neustadt as necessary for the president to command; see Richard Neustadt, *Presidential Power: The Politics of Leadership* (New York: John Wiley & Sons, 1960), pp. 9-32. For a most intelligent effort to put Neustadt in judicial terms, see Walter F. Murphy, *Elements of Judicial Strategy* (Chicago: University of Chicago Press, 1964).

54 Ralph Lerner, "The Supreme Court as Republican Schoolmaster," in *The Supreme Court Review: 1967*, ed. Philip B. Kurland (Chicago: University of Chicago Press, 1967), p. 177.

55 Philip B. Kurland, *Politics, the Constitution, and the Warren Court* (Chicago: University of Chicago Press, 1970), pp. 17-18, 22.

56 Lawrence M. Friedman, *The Legal System: A Social Science Perspective* (New York: Russell Sage Foundation, 1975), p. 125.

57 See Lerner, "Supreme Court as Republican Schoolmaster"; Russel Wheeler, "Extrajudicial Activities of the Early Supreme Court," in *The Supreme Court Review: 1973*, ed. Philip B. Kurland (Chicago: University of Chicago Press, 1974), pp. 123-58.

58 Theodore J. Lowi, *The End of Liberalism: Ideology, Policy, and the Crisis of Public Authority* (New York: W. W. Norton & Co., 1969), p. 314.

SUGGESTED ADDITIONAL READING

Black, Charles L. *The People and the Court: Judicial Review in a Democracy.* New York: Macmillan Co., 1960.

Chambers, William Nisbet, and Walter Dean Burnham, eds., *The American Party Systems: Stages of Political Development.* 2d ed. New York: Oxford University Press, 1975.

Forte, David F., ed. *The Supreme Court in American Politics: Judicial Activism vs. Judicial Restraint.* Lexington, Mass.: D. C. Heath Co., 1972.

Friedman, Lawrence M. *The Legal System: A Social Science Perspective.* New York: Russell Sage Foundation, 1975.

Levy, Leonard W., ed. *Judicial Review and the Supreme Court.* New York: Harper & Row, 1967

Harrell, Mary Ann. *Equal Justice under Law: The Supreme Court in American Life.* Rev. ed. Washington, D. C.: Foundation of the Federal Bar Association, 1975.

McCloskey, Robert G. *The American Supreme Court.* Chicago: University of Chicago Press, 1960.

Steamer, Robert J. *The Supreme Court in Crisis: A History of Conflict.* Boston: University of Massachusetts Press, 1971.

THE COURT AND THE PRESIDENCY

CHAPTER 3

CONFLICT OR ALLIANCE?

The Supreme Court, Justice Robert Jackson once observed,

> has been in angry collision with most dynamic and popular Presidents in our history. Jefferson retaliated with impeachment; Jackson denied its authority; Lincoln disobeyed a writ of the Chief Justice; Theodore Roosevelt, after his Presidency, proposed a recall of judicial decisions; Wilson tried to liberalize its membership; and Franklin Roosevelt proposed to "reorganize" it.[1]

In light of the patterns of interaction described in chapter 2 between the Court and political coalitions, it seems that Jackson over-stated the case. At least three of these presidents, if not more, were the products of realigning elections. Moreover, Theodore Roosevelt, while in office, confined his attacks on the Court to strictly verbal, though vigorous, assaults. Rather than a tale of angry confrontation, the preponderance of American constitutional development has been a story of a close, though informal, alliance between the Supreme Court and the presidency.

Perhaps the most rigorous survey done thus far estimates that "about three-fourths of those justices for whom an evaluation could be made conformed to the expectations of the Presidents who appointed them."[2] While this suggests a laudable degree of judicial independence (after all, one-fourth of the justices thus did not conform to the expectations of their nominators), it also indicates that most of the time the Court tends to reflect the general values of the political coalition capable of electing the president and, thus, the values of the president himself.

This affinity between the Supreme Court and the presidency is not coincidental. The Framers of the Constitution sought to create a mixed regime in which the executive and judicial branches, and to a lesser extent the Senate, would be aligned against the House of Representatives. The Framers were not necessarily antidemocratic, but they were mindful of the power of democratic rule. This rule was to be embodied in the House, and thus the House would present the greatest potential threat to individual liberty. In order to check democratic excesses, therefore, an institution wielding counterbalancing power was necessary.

The president, given a longer term of office than members of the House, and given a different constituency from that of the House, and given a veto power over legislation, was to serve as that counterbalance. Yet, so leery were the Framers of unrestrained majority rule that they feared, even so, the executive branch would ultimately be unable to resist legislative encroachment without additional assistance. Hence, one of the reasons for creation of the Supreme Court was to aid the president in checking the democratic rule of Congress; and, of course, the president, not Congress, was given the initiative for staffing the Court.[3]

Those members of the Constitutional Convention who feared that the presidency would inevitably succumb to an all-powerful legislature proved poor prophets indeed. The grand age of the legislature has passed, and in the twentieth century, American government, like the governments of other countries, has tended to concentrate power in the hands of the executive. Compared to a hundred years ago, Congress has unquestionably declined in both power and prestige, although perhaps less so than any other legislative body in the world. (Whether this decline has been reversed by the events of Watergate remains unknown and unknowable.) War, economic crises, and the complexity of social problems created by the Industrial Revolution have thrust on executive branches everywhere power and responsibilities not contemplated in an earlier age. The American presidency has been no exception.

THEORIES OF PRESIDENTIAL POWER

In the history of American political thought, three theories of the nature and scope of the president's constitutional power have been developed: the executive theory, the stewardship theory, and the executive prerogative theory. The minimum view of presidential power is taken by the executive theory. According to this, Congress makes the law; the President merely executes it. His power is expressly enumerated in article II and does not extend beyond that. To date, the best statement of this theory appears in William Howard Taft's book, *Our Chief Magistrate and His Powers.* "[T]he President," wrote ex-President Taft, "can exercise no power which cannot be fairly and reasonably traced to some specific grant of power or justly implied and included within such express grant as proper and necessary to its exercise.... There is no undefined residuum of power which he can exercise because it seems to him to be in the public interest."[4]

The stewardship theory is normally associated with Taft's predecessor, Theodore Roosevelt. Essentially this position holds that the president is the steward of the people and has the duty to take any action that the needs of the nation require, unless that action is expressly forbidden by the Constitution or the laws.

Franklin Roosevelt provides an example of the executive prerogative theory guiding the conduct of a president in office. But the best philosophic statement of this theory is contained in the writings of John Locke, who defined executive power as "the power to act according to discretion for the public good, without the prescription of law and sometimes even against it."[5] In searching for a constitutional basis for such a power, some proponents of the executive prerogative theory of presidential power have turned to the opening clause of article II. The statement, "The executive Power shall be vested in a President of the United States of America," they argue, should be interpreted as an independent grant of power rather than merely a definition.

A more recent formula has it that the executive power is an aggregate of the powers vested in the president by the Constitution, which combine to form a whole greater than the sum of its parts. In *Youngstown Sheet & Tube Co. v. Sawyer*, for example, at the federal district court level the government argued, "We base the President's power on sections 1, 2, and 3 of Article II of the Constitution and whatever inherent, implied, or residual powers may flow therefrom.... The President has the power to take such action as is necessary to meet an emergency. The only limitations on executive power are the ballot box and impeachment."[6]

THE GROWTH OF PRESIDENTIAL POWER

During the past three generations the executive theory of presidential power has passed into oblivion, and the other two theories have recruited empirical support from a succession of "strong" presidents, the Great Depression, the two world wars, the "cold war," hostilities in Asia, and complicated, occasionally bellicose diplomatic maneuvering. The number and scope of activities of the presidential office has greatly increased, and its power has expanded in turn, with consequences for constitutional interpretation. The complexity of the modern presidency is reflected in the number and range of functions that contemporary presidents are expected to perform. The late Professor Clinton Rossiter identified ten different, although interrelated, presidential roles: chief of state, chief executive, commander-in-chief, chief diplomat, chief legislator, chief of party, voice of the people, protector of the peace, manager of prosperity, and leader of the western world.[7]

THE COURT'S VIEW OF PRESIDENTIAL POWER

Because not all of these multiple, broad functions, are legally imposed burdens, some are not germane to an analysis of the relationship between the Supreme Court and the president, although all would be relevant to a discussion of the presidency. In fact, several constitutional issues related to the presidency, such as problems of presidential qualification, election, and succession, and reform of the Electoral College, have largely been dealt with outside the courts. In the main the Supreme Court has been concerned with defining the scope of the president's powers, and the history of the presidency at the Court's hands has been a tale of almost uninterrupted aggrandizement.

The Power to Protect the Peace

In one of its earliest utterances on the subject, the Court held that the clause providing that the president shall "take care that the laws be faithfully executed"[8] conferred an independent power of action on the president. The case, *In re Neagle*,[9] arose out of a highly romantic, even bizarre, set of facts.

David S. Terry came to California during the Gold Rush. He earned a deserved reputation as a proficient dueler and coincidentally became chief justice of the California Supreme Court. Feeling that his honor was more important than his judicial position, however, he resigned in 1859, in order to engage Senator David C. Broderick in a duel that ended Broderick's life and

Terry's political future. Several years later, Terry again appeared in the public eye as counsel for Sarah Althea Hill in her celebrated attempt to establish that she had been the wife of the late Senator William Sharon rather than simply his mistress. Terry, having married his client, perhaps in the anticipation of a rich settlement, argued the case on appeal before United States Supreme Court Justice Stephen J. Field, sitting as circuit judge to hear federal appeals in California.

Field had served with Terry on the California Supreme Court and had been Terry's successor as chief justice of the state court. Nevertheless, Field found against Mrs. Terry. Disappointed, her lawyer and husband delivered a serious courtroom outburst, which included threats on the life of Justice Field. For this Terry was held in contempt and sentenced to jail.

When Justice Field next returned to California to perform his duties as circuit judge, he was accompanied by a United States Marshal, David Neagle, who had been assigned by the attorney general to protect the justice. During breakfast at the Lathrop, California, railroad station, Field was approached by Terry and may or may not have been slapped by him. In any event, Neagle asked no questions. Claiming that he feared the justice's assassination, he shot Terry dead. Terry had been popular in California, and the incident aroused a good deal of public sentiment favorable to him. The United States marshal was arrested by the local sheriff for murder.

Neagle, however, sought a writ of habeas corpus from the federal district court. Habeas corpus is a legal process designed to safeguard against illegal imprisonment. It directs the person holding a named prisoner to appear before a court and show cause why the prisoner should not be released. The federal district judge found there was no good reason for keeping Neagle in custody and ordered him set free. The state authorities appealed.

On appeal, the Supreme Court affirmed the issuance of the writ. The Court found that Neagle could not be held in state custody for an act done in pursuance of the laws of the United States. Congress, however, had enacted no law authorizing the president to assign bodyguards for federal judges. Nevertheless, the Court held it was simply impossible that a sovereign government lacked the power to protect its own officers, including its judges. (Naturally the Court was not wholly disinterested in the matter, even with Justice Field absenting himself.)

This power must necessarily exist by virtue of the sovereignty of the United States; the only question was, who held the power? Congress might, the Court acknowledged; but so must the president. The president must have the power to protect all those who aid in the performance of his duties. There is, the Court held, a public peace, a peace of the United States, and by necessity and design the president is the principal protector of that peace.

Consequently, the duty of the president to ensure that the laws are faithfully executed is not limited to enforcement of the acts of Congress or treaties of the United States according to their express terms. The president's duty extends to all the obligations growing out of the Constitution itself and out of American international relations, and to all the protections implied by the nature of the government created by the Constitution. A personal attack on a federal judge in the discharge of his duties is a breach of the peace of the United States. Protection of that peace rests with the president. Thus, Neagle as a federal marshal had authority to prevent a breach of that peace. Under the supremacy clause of the Constitution, his act under that authority was immune from punishment by the laws of California. A person cannot be guilty of a crime under state law for doing what it was his duty to do as an officer of the United States.

At the time of its announcement, *Neagle* represented the "broadest interpretation yet given to the implied powers of the National Government under the Constitution."[10] But quite apart from its consequences for federalism, the decision was a major statement of presidential power. The Court examined a clause that seemed to impose only a duty—the duty to see that acts of Congress are faithfully executed— and it found also a grant of power— the power to prevent violations of the peace of the United States.

Within five years, the Court reiterated this point by ruling that the president might use military force within the states, whether requested or not and even against the wishes of the state government. In May 1894, due to economic conditions, the Pullman Car Company sought to impose a 20 percent wage cut on its employees. Thousands of Pullman workers went out on strike, and the American Railway Union, under the leadership of the Socialist Eugene V. Debs, resorted to a secondary boycott, refusing to move any trains with Pullman cars. Massive rioting and mob violence ensued. In order to prevent the obstruction of interstate commerce and to provide for the delivery of the mails, President Cleveland sent federal troops to Chicago (despite the protests of the Governor of Illinois, Peter Altgeld) and had the United States attorney general secure a federal court injunction against the strikers.

When the violence continued, Debs and other union leaders were found in contempt and sentenced to prison. They sought a writ of habeas corpus from the Supreme Court, but the Court denied their appeal. Though there was no explicit statutory basis for the injunction that Debs was said to have violated, the Court again ruled that the right of self-preservation was an attribute of the sovereignty the government necessarily possessed and that the president was the officer constitutionally empowered to preserve and protect that right.[11]

The Power to Discharge Federal Officials

It is obvious that, acting alone, the president could not fulfill his constitutional duty to see that the laws are faithfully executed. He must execute them through subordinates. Logically, to be an effective chief executive, the president must exercise control over his subordinates. But the degree of his control is limited by the Constitution: All officers of the United States may be appointed by the president only with the advice and consent of the Senate. Congress, however, may vest the power to fill inferior offices in the president alone.[12] While the courts have never defined what is an inferior office under the Constitution, it is clear that Congress could require senatorial confirmation for all presidential nominations to federal administrative positions.

While the Constitution provides for the appointment of federal officers, it makes no provisions for their removal, and major Court battles have been fought over this issue.[13] The political importance of the question is obvious, for the kinds of individuals occupying office determine the content of policy. The power to remove, thus, places great authority in the hands of whoever wields it. Witness the fact that over this very issue, the removal power, President Andrew Johnson was impeached.

The Decision of 1789   If senatorial confirmation is required for the appointment of all officers of the United States, does it follow that the Constitution requires the Senate to play an analogous role in the removal of those officers? No, according to the so-called decision of 1789. In establishing the Department of State, the first Congress adopted the position that the secretary of state could be removed by the president alone, without the Senate's consent.

The Tenure of Office Act   Until passage of the Tenure of Office Act in 1867, Congress tacitly indulged the idea that the president possessed an unlimited power of removal. Then, in an effort to confine President Andrew Johnson, Congress made department heads removable only with the consent of the Senate. For firing one of the members of the cabinet in violation of this statute, Johnson was impeached and very nearly convicted. After Johnson was removed from office through the electoral process, the Tenure of Office Act was amended and eventually repealed. During the same era, however, Congress had enacted a statute providing that first-class postmasters should serve four-year terms unless removed with senatorial consent. It was this statute and not the more far-reaching Tenure of Office Act that, some fifty years after its passage, gave rise to the first Supreme Court opinion on the scope of the president's removal power.

The *Myers* Case   Woodrow Wilson had appointed Frank Myers to a first-class postmastership in 1917. In 1920, however, Wilson removed Myers and appointed his successor while Congress was recessed. The Senate, thus, had not agreed to Myers's dismissal before his four-year term had expired. Myers brought suit to recover the balance of his salary for the unexpired portion of his tenure. When the case reached the Supreme Court, Chief Justice Taft found that the president's discretion in the discharge of federal officers could not constitutionally be fettered. Ironically, this was the same Taft who had once been an exponent of the executive theory of limited presidential power.

In a long and elaborate opinion excellently refuting his own earlier position, Taft relied on both the congressional "decision of 1789" and the doctrine of separation of powers. Legislative control of the executive ought to be narrowly construed, Taft argued, so as not to violate that doctrine. He found that an independent removal power had been constitutionally vested in the president as a necessary and proper means of discharging his mandate to take care that the laws be faithfully executed. Indeed, so broad was Taft's holding in *Myers v. United States*[14] that it implied Congress could not impose any limit on the president's control over executive personnel.

Humphrey's Executor   In *Humphrey's Executor v. United States*.[15] however, the 1935 Court limited *Myers*. It ruled that members of independent regulatory commissions were not removable by the president at will. These agencies, Justice Sutherland argued, were established by Congress to serve as an arm of the legislature furthering its policies and performing partly judicial and partly legislative tasks, not just executive functions. *Myers*, therefore, applied only to purely executive or ministerial offices. With respect to the independent commissions, Congress could restrict the president's removal power. The legislature might make such officers removable only for cause or only with the consent of the Senate or only by Congress itself.

Since these alternatives are impractical in a modern bureaucracy, *Humphrey's Executor* in effect strengthened the power not of Congress but of the boards and commissions at the expense of the president by further insulating their members and their policies from his control. In retrospect, however, the decision must be regarded as something of a sport. It was part and parcel of the Court's assault on the New Deal; and, after the Court's change of heart in 1937, the holding was limited.[16] Though not entirely forgotten, *Humphrey's Executor* has been invoked only once in the past forty years. In that instance it was used to prevent a relatively trivial, although flagrant, attempt at political patronage by the Eisenhower administration.[17]

The Power to Conduct Foreign Relations

As it divides the power of appointment between president and Congress, so too the Constitution divides the power over foreign relations between the president and the Senate. The president is accorded the power to make treaties, receive and negotiate with foreign ministers, and appoint ambassadors. Ambassadors, however, can be appointed only with the consent of the Senate, and two-thirds of the Senate must approve a treaty before it becomes law. Furthermore, the entire Congress has general power over appropriations. As in most other areas of policy, then, the Constitution provides for a system fraught with tension and almost invites a struggle for the privilege of making the nation's foreign policy.

In this struggle, the president is powerfully equipped by tradition, by his position as commander-in-chief of the armed forces, and by the general character of the executive office. The unitary nature of the presidency promotes secrecy and dispatch in an area where those qualities are especially important. This gives the president a major advantage over Congress in the contest to be director of international relations.

The *Curtiss-Wright* Case   Generally, the Supreme Court, realizing its lack of competence in foreign relations, has remained aloof from this struggle by invoking the "political question" doctrine. But in *United States v. Curtiss-Wright Export Corp.*[18] the Court went a long way toward officially recognizing presidential supremacy in this area as constitutionally prescribed. In 1934, Congress had passed a joint resolution that, if the President found that an embargo on the sale of arms and ammunition to certain warring nations would contribute to the cause of international peace, he should establish such an embargo by executive proclamation. Violation of such an embargo would then be a federal crime. The joint resolution did not restrict or direct the president's discretion in establishing such an embargo and, thus, clearly delegated legislative power without any standards for its exercise.

Franklin D. Roosevelt did shortly declare an embargo on the sale of arms and munitions to Bolivia and Paraguay, which were then engaged in armed hostilities. The Curtiss-Wright Corporation was subsequently indicted for conspiracy to sell arms to Bolivia. In its defense Curtiss-Wright argued that the embargo was invalid; the congressional joint resolution was an unconstitutional delegation of legislative power, the company said. In fact, the Supreme Court in several celebrated recent cases had invoked the doctrine that delegated power cannot be redelegated, in order to nullify major portions of the New Deal's economic recovery program. Curtiss-Wright's claim was, thus, well supported, and the federal district court dismissed the indictment.

The Supreme Court, however, reversed the dismissal. The rule that powers delegated to Congress by the Constitution cannot be redelegated, held Justice Sutherland, was a restriction on congressional powers in domestic matters only. It had no relevance for foreign affairs, because the power of the national government over international relations did not depend on any formal grant of power contained in the Constitution. Rather, the federal government possessed all power necessary to enable the United States to act in the international arena on an equal footing with other sovereign nations.

In essence *Curtiss-Wright* held that the federal government's power to conduct foreign relations was basically without constitutional limitation.[19] Federal power in this area goes far beyond the sum of particular functions mentioned in the Constitution. Rather, the national government automatically has power because it represents a sovereign nation in a world of sovereign nations. This power derives from the Constitution only in the sense that the Constitution established a sovereign entity. According to *Curtiss-Wright*, then, in international relations the federal government wields a sum of power in excess of the powers enumerated in the Constitution. Its residual powers cannot be precisely defined. In fact, it would be unwise even to attempt to delineate the scope of these powers rigidly, since they depend on an evolving historical context.

The next question is, in which branch of the federal government are these powers to be vested? *Curtiss-Wright* comes very close to holding that exercise of the residual powers over foreign affairs is completely consigned to the president. Justice Sutherland's opinion implies that, while the joint resolution was a nice thing for President Roosevelt to have around in case of a legal challenge, it was unnecessary to justify the embargo. Sutherland very nearly held that the president is granted such a large responsibility in international relations that Roosevelt might have established the embargo on his own initiative and authority.

On the other hand, Justice Sutherland's statement that the president is "the sole organ of the Federal Government in the field of international relations" may not resolve the problem conclusively.[20] That statement (the metaphor is traceable to John Marshall himself)[21] could be interpreted to mean only that the president is the sole executor of American foreign policy. This leaves unanswered whether the president or Congress is charged with framing that policy in the first place. Since nothing in the Constitution suggests which branch is to have ultimate responsibility for making foreign policy, it could be argued on the basis of democratic theory that, if there is conflict between the president and Congress in this twilight zone, Congress must prevail.

The Treaty Making Power   Such a resolution of the Constitutional conflict would produce substantial problems in the actual practice of American government, however. In his capacity as the sole organ of American foreign policy, the president exercises significant powers to influence the content of that policy. The president is the channel of communication to and from other nations. Negotiations, such as the Paris peace talks of recent memory, are conducted at his direction not Congress's. By virtue of his constitutionally imposed duty to send and receive ambassadors, it is the president who recognizes foreign governments; and, as the nation's changing relationship with the People's Republic of China so well illustrates, recognition or nonrecognition, even if informal, may have a substantial impact both at home and abroad. The president can use his control of the armed forces to implement *his* foreign policy. These are powers of tremendous consequence. Indeed, to a very large degree they negate the powers of Congress over foreign affairs. By his management of international relations and his use of the military, the president can, at the very least, structure the development of events so as to limit Congress's alternatives when it seeks to formulate the nation's foreign policy.

On the other hand, the necessity of securing a two-thirds vote of the Senate to ratify treaties has seldom proved a limitation on executive policy making. Originally the Framers intended the Senate to advise the president in the making of treaties as well as consent to them. But the Senate's role as an advisory body came to an abrupt end very early in the Republic. President Washington, seeking to negotiate a treaty with the southern Indians, went to the Senate for advice on several questions relating to the negotiations. The Senate was reluctant to discuss the matter in Washington's presence and sought to refer the matter to a committee. Greatly annoyed, the president stalked from the Senate chamber vowing never to return, a threat he made good. It was an unhappy experience for all, with the result that treaties are now negotiated by the executive and sent to the Senate in their final form for approval or disapproval.

The executive's attitude toward this procedure is best captured by the remark of Lincoln's biographer and McKinley's secretary of state, John Hay: "A treaty entering the Senate is like a bull going into the arena: no one can say just how or when the final blow will fall—but one thing is certain—it will never leave the arena alive."[22] Modern presidents, therefore, have increasingly bypassed the Senate by resorting to executive agreements in their conduct of foreign affairs. The use of treaties has generally been limited to fairly formal and important international agreements. Examples include military alliances, such as NATO, peace treaties, and agreements to participate in international organizations, such as the United Nations. Most United States foreign relations, however, have in recent years been conducted through executive agreements concluded between the president and the executives of other countries. These are not subject to Senate ratification. Some agreements have been specifically authorized by Congress, but many, particularly in the field of foreign trade, have been negotiated solely on the authority of the president.

The Use of Executive Agreements   The constitutionality of the executive agreement as an instrument of the president's prerogative in foreign policy has long been recognized. But, like many other aspects of presidential government, the executive agreement was used much more broadly and frequently under Franklin Roosevelt. In *United States v. Belmont* (1937) [23] and again in *United States v. Pink* (1942),[24] the Supreme Court held that such agreements should be enforced in American courts as internal law. The Constitution, of course, provides that treaties are the supreme law of the land, and there is no doubt that agreements made with congressional consent have the same effect. But *Belmont* and *Pink* held that executive agreements entered into on the authority of the president alone, without either the approval or the authorization of Congress, are legally analogous to treaties. Like treaties, they have authority above any conflicting state law.

In 1920, the Court had held that a treaty might serve as the basis for implementing legislation that Congress otherwise would not have the power to enact.[25] When *Belmont* and *Pink* were added to this ruling, the result was an unsettling sum: The power of Congress might be expanded by executive agreement in the absence of constitutional prohibitions or perhaps even in spite of them. One aspect of the Bricker Amendment, discussed more fully in chapter 5, was an effort to restrict the use of executive agreements, but for a variety of reasons that amendment failed to pass.

Today, therefore, there is little, if any, legal difference between treaties and executive agreements. The practical differences, however, are substantial. Advocates of the imperial presidency as well as apologists of simple majority rule (the two positions are not mutually exclusive) will applaud this reduction of the Senate's treaty power. After all, by voting against a treaty, one-third plus one of the members of the Senate, representing perhaps no more than 15 percent of the population, can thwart the desires of the rest of the country, their colleagues, and a popularly elected president who may be more enlightened than they. On the other hand, the thirty-four Senators from the seventeen most populous states, representing well over half of the American people, can block the actions of a president who was perhaps elected by less than 50 percent of the electorate (what with the arithmetic of the Electoral College or third-party candidates), and presidents are not always more enlightened than members of the Senate, as Vietnam and Watergate demonstrated. Thus, those concerned with limited government and adherence to constitutional form will be understandably unhappy about this development of executive power. The Supreme Court's equating of executive agreements with treaties has encouraged modern presidents to use the former in place of the latter, freeing themselves from dependence on the Senate and further diminishing the control of Congress over the conduct of foreign affairs.

The Power to Make War

This problem of control is heightened by the reality of war. One of the most important powers directly granted to the president by the Constitution and one highly visible in recent years is the power to act as commander-in-chief of the armed forces. This power has been exercised in highly personal ways, usually involving much more than signing orders for the disposition of troops. Its scope is vast and its consequences enormous. In fact, relying on the commander-in-chief provision, in times of war, the United States usually has reverted to something uncomfortably like a constitutional dictatorship.

The Role of Congress

Among the most troubling facets of the president's power as commander-in-chief has been his ability to commit troops to combat. At the Constitutional Convention, it was originally proposed that Congress have the power "to make war." But it was objected that legislatures act too slowly. Congress, therefore, could not exercise such power effectively. The proposal was then amended so that Congress was given the power "to declare war." This, it was argued, would leave the president free to repel sudden attacks. Objections were raised that this might make it too easy for the president to involve the country in war, but the amended provision carried with only a single dissenting vote.

After ratification of the Constitution, the last time Congress declared war before hostilities started was the War of 1812. Since that time presidents have taken action first and sought congressional recognition of the existence of a state of war afterwards. Congress has almost always hastened to ratify the president's course of action. A charming, though not very effective, exception occurred after the Mexican War, which Congress had declared after the fact: At the end of the war, in voting its thanks to General Taylor, Congress amended its resolution to note that he had won an unnecessary and unconstitutional war begun by President Polk.

The Prize Cases One of those voting for this resolution was Abraham Lincoln, and, ironically, it was he who later executed the most radical expansion of the war powers of the presidency. Immediately following the firing on Fort Sumter, Lincoln took a number of steps of very questionable legality, acting wholly on his own authority. These included the declaration of a naval blockade of southern ports—an act of war according to international law. The constitutionality of the blockade was resolved by the Supreme Court in the rather strange action known as *The Prize Cases*.[26] It concerned four neutral ships and their cargoes that had been seized under the presidential order before Congress formally recognized the existence of hostilities.

The Court was presented with a very ticklish political question. The federal government wanted the conflict between the states to be considered an insurrection for certain purposes. There would then be no need to recognize the Confederacy formally or to sign a peace treaty to conclude the hostilities. But, if the war were held to be an insurrection, then the laws of war would not apply, and the capture of neutral vessels on the high seas would be illegal. For other purposes, however, the federal government wished the war to be considered a war within the terms of international law. This would mean that prisoners taken would be considered prisoners of war and accorded the treatment appropriate to that status. It would also mean the blockade was legal. But, if the Court held that the conflict was a war, it would impliedly recognize the Confederacy as a legal government, which would encourage foreign governments to recognize the Confederacy as well and possibly come to its assistance with money, men, and materiel.

The Court avoided both of these positions by washing its hands of the whole matter: It declared the seizures legal and sustained the president's view of the dual status of the Confederacy. In essence the Court held that, as far as foreign nations and their citizens were concerned, the war was an insurrection, although neutral vessels might be taken as prize; for national purposes, however, the war was a war, with the exception that the confederate states were not governments in the eyes of the law.

The Court declared that it was bound to accept the president's decision that the insurgents had to be accorded belligerent status. A civil war, wrote Justice Grier, is never solemnly declared but becomes so by the number and power of those who originate it. It is still a civil war even if it is called an insurrection. "The President was bound to meet it in the shape it presented itself, without waiting for Congress to baptize it with a name; and no name given it by him or them could change the fact."[27]

The Court, thus, adopted the view urged by counsel for the government, **Richard Henry Dana** (author of *Two Years Before the Mast*), that "war is a state of things, and not an act of legislative will."[28] In short, the Court recognized that the American Civil War was a war within the meaning of that term at international law. By this holding, the Court implied that, whatever the Constitution may say about Congress's power to declare war, the president has constitutional powers to initiate hostilities, and the country is bound to accept the president's characterization of those hostilities, even if he chooses to characterize them as a war.

Undeclared Wars   Subsequent presidents have followed Lincoln's example. Congress was asked to declare World Wars I and II after hostilities had already begun and American forces had been committed. Similarly, the Tonkin Gulf Resolution was regarded by President Lyndon Johnson as sufficient congressional authorization for escalated fighting in Vietnam. In 1967, Assistant Secretary of State Nicholas Katzenbach, testifying before the Senate Foreign Relations Committee, referred to declarations of war as "outmoded." This view rather gravely distressed the committee. Katzenbach contended that the constitutional clause granting Congress the power to declare war simply meant that once a war has been commenced Congress has the power to recognize that fact. This is not a totally empty power, because declaring that a state of war exists has certain legal consequences, affecting the status of treaties, insurance policies, and relations with neutral countries, most notably. But in this day and age declarations of war are no longer relevant. Japan, for example, did not stop to declare war before bombing Pearl Harbor.

Much the same position was subsequently adopted by federal district Judge Charles E. Wyzanski, Jr., in *United States v. Sisson* (1968).[29] Noting that, in an era of thermonuclear war, diplomacy is characterized by limited military engagements, Judge Wyzanski ruled that a declaration of war is applicable only to an all-out, unlimited war. In the last third of the twentieth century, therefore, Congress's power to declare war has become obsolete.

Occasions when the president has used the armed forces to implement policy without requesting a subsequent declaration of war or other authorization outnumber even those when Congress has been asked to ratify the existence of hostilities after the fact. Woodrow Wilson, for example, dispatched a sizable American expeditionary force to Siberia in 1918. President Eisenhower sent the marines into Lebanon in 1958, and John F. Kennedy deployed the navy during the Cuban missile crisis of 1961. In all, a 1966 *Yale Law Journal* study counted 162 instances in which the president, operating as commander-in-chief, had used the armed forces on his own initiative.[30]

In this area, as *The Prize Cases* and other decisions illustrate, the Supreme Court has been extremely reluctant to restrict the president's discretionary powers.[31] Its early precedents have never been overruled and remain the leading ones today. Thus, the numerous attempts to challenge the constitutionality of the Vietnam war were futile gestures. For one thing, most of them encountered insurmountable procedural hurdles.[32] The two most promising cases were both denied certiorari by the Court, with only Justice Douglas dissenting.[33] The argument over American involvement in Vietnam, therefore, was never resolved judicially. That debate, however, was a recent manifestation of a peculiarly American trait noted by Alexis de Tocqueville nearly two centuries ago—the tendency to convert political issues into constitutional crises. Rather than debate straightforwardly the merits of a given policy, Americans debate its legality. The public confuses the question of wisdom with the question of constitutionality. With respect to foreign affairs, however, the Court has declined to indulge this passion.

The War Powers Resolution of 1973   Until quite recently, so did Congress. In the wake of Vietnam, however, Congress passed the War Powers Resolution of 1973. This provides that "the Armed Forces of the United States [may be] introduced into hostilities or into situations where imminent involvement in hostilities is clearly indicated" only under the following circumstances: (1) a declaration of war; (2) an attack on the United States or its armed forces; or (3) in pursuit of a specific statutory authorization.[34] Use of the military in these circumstances must be promptly reported to Congress, and the military engagement cannot be continued for more than sixty days unless Congress specifically authorizes continued hostilities.

Whether this legislation will significantly affect future presidential conduct is questionable. The act is not free of ambiguities. What actions, for example, constitute "hostilities," and at what point does "imminent involvement" in them become "clearly indicated"? Among modern presidents' uses of the armed forces, only Korea and Vietnam would have been unquestionably covered. Moreover, if the War Powers Resolution had been in force at the time, the Tonkin Gulf Resolution might have been construed to authorize continuation of hostilities beyond sixty days. But, whatever the effect of the War Powers Resolution, the Supreme Court has emphasized that the president is not *judicially* accountable for his emergency use of the armed forces and has denied that it, or any other court, has the power to question a presidential decision to use military power.

Domestic Aspects of the War Power

Related to the question of when, how, and by whom hostilities may be begun is the issue of the government's power to restrict the citizens' civil rights and liberties when necessary to the conduct of a war. By logical deduction, the power to engage in war must imply the power to prosecute a war successfully once begun. But is the power to wage effective warfare unlimited? Or is there a point beyond which the government may not go? Do the Constitution's prohibitions and restrictions, particularly those in the Bill of Rights, override the necessities of war? In other words, if a war cannot be successfully waged without sacrificing these rights, which—the war or the rights—must be abandoned?

The *Merryman* Case   Like many other constitutional questions of presidential power, this one first arose in acute form under President Lincoln. Determined to stifle antiwar activities (sabotage, discouragement of voluntary enlistment, and encouragement of draft resistance), Lincoln suspended use of the writ of habeas corpus by those arrested for engaging in such actions. Suspending the writ blocked these persons' access to the civil courts. In effect, this eliminated their right to indictment by a grand jury and trial by a petit jury, because those suspected of antiwar activities were subject to military arrest and trial by court martial. If convicted, often on the most meager evidence, they could be sentenced to prison or even shot, without recourse to the civilian courts.

The Constitution itself provides for suspension of the privilege of habeas corpus, if the public safety requires it. But the Constitution is silent about who is to determine that the public safety does require suspension. With Congress in recess at the time of the shelling of Fort Sumter, Lincoln simply assumed the power to suspend the writ. The president's assumption of the power was vigorously criticized from many quarters, including that of the chief justice of the United States.

John Merryman, a captain of militia in Maryland, was suspected of having southern sympathies and of having exercised those sympathies by dynamiting railway bridges between Washington, D.C., Philadelphia, and New York. Arrested at his home in the dead of night by Union soldiers, Merryman was imprisoned without trial in Fort McHenry. Chief Justice Taney, as chief judge of the federal judicial circuit for Baltimore, made a special trip to that city to receive Merryman's habeas corpus petition. Taney directed the issuance of the writ, but the commanding general at Fort McHenry respectfully declined to comply, noting that Lincoln had suspended the writ in Maryland. The chief justice then delivered a strongly worded opinion condemning the president's measure as action beyond his constitutional powers. Only Congress, Taney claimed, could suspend the writ. If the president could exercise this power, the country would be subject to military usurpation. The American people would no longer be living under a government of laws; rather, the rights to life, liberty, and property would be held at the pleasure of the military and its commander-in-chief.[35]

In his famous message to Congress on July 4, 1861, Lincoln responded to the chief justice by posing the question, "Are all the laws to go unexecuted but one?" In essence Lincoln argued that he had had to suspend habeas corpus to secure the enforcement of all other federal laws. To abide by constitutional form in the matter of habeas corpus might very well have led to Maryland's secession and the loss of the capital. While Lincoln continued to assert that his suspension of the writ was also constitutional, he called on Congress to ratify his action.

Congress complied. The Habeas Corpus Act of 1863 formally recognized the president's control of political prisoners, authorizing him to suspend the writ as needed. The act did contain some provisions attempting to restrict or modify martial law practice, but in fact these made very little difference in the arrest, confinement, and release of civilian prisoners. The military authorities continued to behave as they had before passage of the act, when they had operated on the president's orders alone.

The *Milligan* Case   During the war the Supreme Court managed to avoid all cases raising the issue of the president's power to suspend the writ. But, once the war was safely over, the Court did address the question in the elaborately argued case of Lamdin P. Milligan. Along with others, Milligan had been arrested by the Union military in Indiana and charged with conspiracy to effect the escape of several thousand rebel prisoners. Milligan and his co-conspirators planned to arm these escaped prisoners and lead them in a march through Kentucky and Missouri, wreaking havoc in the rear of the Union forces that were then confronting the Confederate army in the west. Milligan was found guilty and sentenced to be hanged, but Andrew Johnson, who had become president, commuted his sentence to life imprisonment, and Milligan petitioned the federal circuit court for a writ of habeas corpus. The circuit judges, unable to agree among themselves, certified the question to the Supreme Court.

The Court unanimously held that the writ should be issued and Milligan discharged from custody, because the procedures prescribed by the Habeas Corpus Act of 1863 had not been observed by the military and, thus, the government had no legal right to hold Milligan.[36] Five justices, however, went even further; they signed the majority opinion by Justice David Davis stating that not only did the president not have the authority but Congress also lacked the power to institute military commissions in areas remote from actual warfare. The creation of military commissions to try civilians where the civil courts were open and functioning would, according to the majority, deprive citizens of their rights to indictment by a grand jury and trial by petit jury in violation of the Fifth and Sixth Amendments. Davis did not deny that martial law might be established in times of actual invasion, but he contended that it could not be imposed merely in the face of threatened invasion.

Four justices, speaking through Chief Justice Salmon P. Chase, dissented on this last point. Chase argued that Congress did have the power, though it had not used it in the *Milligan* case, to establish military commissions for the trial of civilians anywhere in the country during time of war. This was an implied power deriving from Congress's authority to declare war and to raise and support armies, and it was not limited by the Fifth, Sixth, or any other amendment. Chief Justice Chase admitted that Congress could not apply the laws of war when a war did not exist, but when the nation was at war it was his view that Congress could authorize trial by military tribunal wherever it chose. The fact that the civil courts were open and functioning had been regarded by Congress as a sufficient reason not to excise its power, when it enacted the Habeas Corpus Act, but that fact could not deprive Congress of its power.

The *Duncan* Case   The *Milligan* case has been hailed as one of the great bulwarks of American civil liberties, an unequivocal declaration that the federal judiciary will protect the rights of Americans against military rule whether established by Congress or by the president. But, on the basis of public policy considerations, it was highly questionable at the time it was announced, and its long-range significance has been almost nil. It has been used as precedent only once since, and that was in a strangely similar case, *Duncan v. Kahanamoku* (1946).[37]

Following Pearl Harbor, the governor of Hawaii suspended the writ of habeas corpus and conferred all power, including those powers normally exercised by civilian courts, on the Hawaii military commander. Two days later, this action was ratified by President Roosevelt. Thus empowered, the United States Army erected a system of military government and martial law that continued, with some modifications and qualifications, until October 1944. In a brace of cases that reached the Court in February 1945, but that it contrived to postpone deciding until February 1946, the Supreme Court held that the establishment of military tribunals to try civilians in Hawaii had been unconstitutional.

The *Duncan* majority relied on Justice Davis's *Milligan* opinion. It is arguable, however, that the views expressed in *Milligan* and *Duncan* do not present a realistic approach to the situation that existed in either southern Indiana in 1864 or Hawaii in 1941-42. It is interesting that both decisions were announced *after* the wars were over. The most significant aspect of *Milligan* and *Duncan* is probably not the rules of law they purport to stand for but the dates when they were decided.

The Japanese-American Relocation Cases   The view that the Court generally takes a "hands off" stance in times of war is further supported by the decisions concerning forced evacuation of Japanese-Americans from the West Coast during World War II and by the result in *Ex parte Quirin* (1942). Taken together these cases strongly suggest that the Court will not interfere with governmental, particularly presidential, authority while a war is actually in progress.

Quirin involved the trial by court martial of eight Nazi saboteurs, captured in this country in 1942 shortly after they had been put ashore by German U-boats. Despite an executive order denying them access to the civil courts, the defendants' lawyers, assigned by President Roosevelt, applied to the Supreme Court for writs of habeas corpus. Counsel relied heavily on *Milligan*, claiming that the military commission before which the saboteurs had been brought lacked jurisdiction to try them while the civil courts were open and functioning. The Court unanimously rejected the contention. Noting that the Nazis were being tried for offenses against the laws of war and that Congress had provided for the trial of such offenses by military commission, the Court declined to consider the challenge of the President's power as commander-in-chief in this situation. As for the *Milligan* precedent, the Court chose to emphasize the obvious factual differences between that case and *Quirin*, rather than placing its emphasis on the equally obvious similarities.[38]

An even more striking example of judicial deference in time of war is provided by the Court's handling of the cases arising from the segregation and internment during the Second World War of more than 110,000 persons of Japanese ancestry, most of them loyal Americans. Although presented with three different opportunities, the Court never directly addressed the central issue—the legality of a military program of racial detention—and thus, in effect, lent its support to the government's actions. In *Hirabayashi v. United States* the Court sustained the militarily declared curfew imposed in the Pacific coastal area on all persons of Japanese descent, whether foreign nationals or not, but it avoided consideration of the much larger question of the constitutionality of the exclusion and confinement program.[39] In *Korematsu v. United States* the Court ruled that the threat of invasion and sabotage sanctioned the relocation program, but it carefully separated the evacuation issue from the detention question.[40] In *Ex parte Endo*, decided the same day as *Korematsu*, the Court ordered the release of a young woman whom the government conceded was a loyal American, but it did so on the ground that the legislation and executive orders establishing the detention program did not authorize the confinement of undoubtedly loyal persons.[41] Again, however, the Court refused to consider the constitutional issue of the government's power to restrict the rights of American citizens when required by military necessity.

By its refusal to address the constitutionality of the detention program, by its sustaining of the curfew and the evacuation program, and by its failure to examine rigorously the reasonableness of the military decision that these programs were necessary to the war effort, the Court in effect granted the president almost unlimited power as commander-in-chief to take measures he considers necessary to the successful prosecution of a war, particularly if he is supported by subsequent congressional action.

The Power to Seize Property in Wartime: The Steel Seizure Case As the Japanese internment cases illustrate, the president's exercise of his powers as commander-in-chief has increasing significance for domestic affairs. Actions such as economic controls, though less drastic than the relocation and detention program, are often necessitated by twentieth-century warfare. Usually acts of this nature have been authorized by congressional statute. But in some instances a president has undertaken domestic actions without specific statutory support and then sought to justify those actions by an appeal to his power as commander-in-chief or to some even broader concept of executive power in general. Usually these acts have subsequently been ratified by Congress, or the Court has managed by one means or another to avoid cases arising from them. Until the "steel seizure case," therefore, no clear test of the president's inherent power to engage in such acts had ever been presented to or decided by the Court.

The Facts *Youngstown Sheet & Tube Co. v. Sawyer* was the result of a nationwide steel strike called in the midst of the Korean War.[42] Several efforts by federal agencies to mediate the labor-management conflict had failed, and finally President Truman directed the secretary of commerce to seize and operate most of the country's steel mills. Secretary Sawyer took action as ordered. The Taft-Hartley Act would have prohibited a walkout until after an eighty-day "cooling off" period, but President Truman found it politically embarrassing to invoke that law, since his opposition to Taft-Hartley had been a key issue in his 1948 election campaign. Ignoring its relevant provisions, therefore, Truman based his action, first, on the president's power as commander-in-chief and, second, on inherent powers derived from the aggregate of powers vested in the executive by article II of the Constitution. The president twice reported his action to Congress, requesting its ratification, but none was forthcoming.

Under protest, the steel companies complied with the executive order, but they sought an injunction against Sawyer to prevent the government's seizure of their property. The federal district court issued a preliminary injunction, which was stayed the very same day by the court of appeals. The Supreme Court then granted certiorari. It heard the case and issued its opinion within two months of the seizure, indicating that the Court can occasionally move with haste if the national interest requires it. While it upheld the district court's injunction on the ground that the president had exceeded his constitutional powers, however, the Court did not categorically reject the idea of an inherent presidential power.

The Opinions   In what was labeled the opinion of the Court, Justice Black, with Justice Douglas concurring, took a hard and fast position based on a dogmatic interpretation of the concept of separation of powers. Black denied that the president could have any power not traceable to an express grant in the Constitution. He then refused to consider the argument that Truman's action might be justified by the president's status as commander-in-chief. Indeed, Justice Black disposed of the entire controversy in only thirteen paragraphs, written on such a high moral plane that he did not bother to cite a single Supreme Court precedent relevant to the substantive issue. The seven other justices, however, could not accept this separation of powers dogma.

Justice Frankfurter attached a paragraph to Black's opinion to note specifically that one did not have to define the executive power comprehensively in order to resolve the case. Rather, for Frankfurter, the problem was much simpler: to balance the equities in the case at hand. Examining the congressional acts on the use of seizure powers from 1916 through Taft-Hartley convinced Justice Frankfurter that previously the power to seize had been granted for only limited and definite periods. There was, of course, no statutory prohibition of Truman's action, but Frankfurter believed that the Taft-Hartley Act had, by implication, expressed Congress's intention to withhold the seizure power from the president in this instance. The need for legislation does not enact it, and the need for a given power does not necessarily vest it in the president.

The subtlest of all the arguments was that advanced by Justice Jackson. He began by dismissing Justice Black's notions about a strict separation of powers as fatuous. Traditional conceptions of separation of powers simply cannot be reconciled with the Constitution's other system of checks and balances, wrote Jackson. The traditional principles of separation of powers describe a system in which complementary but totally distinct powers are granted to different branches of government. But, Justice Jackson found, in the American governmental system identical powers are concurrently granted to both the president and Congress. According to Jackson, a large measure of the power to make national policy is fixed in neither the president nor

Congress but fluctuates between the two, depending on the initiatives each takes. In other words, there is a zone of constitutional power that is exclusively executive, a zone that is exclusively legislative, and between these two a twilight zone in which either branch can act in the absence of action by the other.

Jackson did not explicitly consider what would happen if both Congress and the president attempted to act in the twilight zone in conflicting ways. His opinion, however, suggests that if such a conflict occurred the legislative will would have to prevail. According to Jackson's analysis, Congress can block the president when he attempts to exercise power in the twilight zone, but the president is prohibited from blocking congressional action. He can veto legislation within the twilight zone, because that is his constitutional prerogative. But, if his veto is overridden, the legislative will must prevail. According to Jackson, then, there is a constitutional bias favoring the people's representatives as the ultimate repository of national power.

Applying this theory to the case at hand, Justice Jackson found no congressional authorization for Truman's action. Moreover, in this twilight zone, there was not an absence of congressional action; Congress had not left the executive free to act as he saw fit. Rather, for Jackson, Taft-Hartley and other statutes relating to property seizure prevented the president from acting in a manner other than that prescribed by Congress.

Justices Burton and Clark also entered separate concurrences to the effect that the president's action had not been authorized by Taft-Hartley and, in fact, violated the provisions of that act. In dissent, Chief Justice Vinson, joined by Justices Reed and Minton, defended Truman's action on the basis of sweeping assertions of presidential prerogative to meet emergency circumstances.

The Precedential Value of *Youngstown*   Today it is hard to remember that *Youngstown* was the most famous Supreme Court decision between ratification of the New Deal and *Brown v. Board of Education.* The difficulty and complexity of the case are demonstrated by the fact that, except for the dissent, no single opinion commanded the signatures of more than two justices. The Court split six to three, with seven justices writing separate opinions totaling 128 pages. Such a holding does not a strong precedent make.

For that reason alone, it is doubtful that *Youngstown* could or would be rigorously applied in future cases questioning an exercise of presidential power in an emergency. Besides, the constitutional lessons about presidential power that may be drawn from the opinions are not quite what they might at first appear to be. Justice Black's opinion explicitly denies that the president has an inherent executive prerogative, in an emergency, but only Justice Douglas subscribed to Black's view. All the other members of the Court conceded the existence of some residual powers in the presidency. Frankfurter and Burton found a consideration of inherent powers unnecessary to a decision in the case, but their opinions imply that they might uphold an executive action if no applicable statute existed to cover the situation. Justice Clark fully and explicitly accepted the doctrine of inherent executive power, and Jackson substantially did so. When these justices are added to the three dissenters, there emerges from the steel seizure case a fairly clear majority in favor of some concept of inherent executive power.

Except for Justice Black and Chief Justice Vinson, however, the *Youngstown* opinion writers never did face the question of presidential power to seize private property in the absence of congressional action. Rather, Frankfurter, Burton, Clark, and Jackson each relied to varying degrees on the fact that Congress had previously passed three different statutes giving the president limited seizure powers and the fact that, in debates on the Taft-Hartley Act, Congress had specifically rejected an amendment authorizing presidential seizure in the case of strikes. Congress, thus, had made clear that it did not approve of the sort of action subsequently taken by President Truman. All the steel seizure case means then, is that a majority of the Supreme Court thought, albeit for a variety of reasons, that the president's claim of authority to seize the steel mills was untenable because Congress had indicated an opposite intent.

Executive Privilege

A similar and more recent example of the Supreme Court saying a good deal less than it seemed to about the scope and limitations of presidential power is its decision on executive privilege. The term *executive privilege* is of recent origin, but the concept is not. It has generally been conceded that confidentiality is necessary to promote the frank and candid advice that a president requires to discharge his constitutional duties wisely. Congress, on the other hand, has the power and duty to oversee the operations of government. From time to time congressional investigatory committees have sought information about matters that the president has deemed should not be disclosed. In this situation several presidents have invoked executive privilege, whether they called it that or not, to deny the committees access to the materials sought. Usually some compromise has been worked out, forestalling serious collision between the two branches. Thus, this problem of interdepartmental relations had never come to the Court before July 1974. Even then the Court passed on the question of executive privilege in a peculiarly unique setting.

The *Nixon* Case   The case of *United States v. Richard M. Nixon* was but one of many, bizarre byproducts of the Watergate scandal.[43] Seven men, most of them intimates of the president of the United States, all of them high-ranking officials in either the White House or the president's reelection campaign organization, had been indicted by a federal grand jury on charges of conspiracy to violate a variety of criminal laws. The president himself had been named as an unindicted co-conspirator. As a result of earlier revelations about President Nixon's curious custom of taping his White House conversations, the Watergate special prosecutor, Leon Jaworski, sought to compel the release of sixty-four tape recordings as well as other papers and transcripts relevant to the pending criminal proceedings. Accordingly, the federal district court issued a pretrial subpoena, ordering the president to produce these materials for inspection in the judge's chambers to determine if they were relevant and material. The president resisted and moved to quash the subpoena, relying on a claim of executive privilege. The lower federal courts rejected the president's motion, and the case arrived on the Supreme Court's doorstep.

Unanimously, a Court including four Nixon appointees sustained the district court's issuance of the subpoena in an opinion by Chief Justice Burger that was "notable for the resolute understatement with which it marches to the ultimate doom."[44] The Court held that a presidential claim of executive privilege must yield to a demonstrated need for evidence in a criminal proceeding. But the Court also recognized, for the first time, that there is a constitutional basis for the claim of executive privilege for confidential communications with the president.

First, the Court had to negotiate some procedural and jurisdictional obstacles, any one of which might have sunk the case. The most difficult of these was the claim that the action did not satisfy the case and controversy requirement, since it concerned a dispute within the executive department alone. The president's lawyers argued that the special prosecutor, being a subordinate executive official, was not an adequately adverse party. The Court, however, rejected this contention for a variety of reasons, the most compelling being that the special prosecutor was legally authorized to contest claims of executive privilege and that he was removable not by the president but by the attorney general and then only with the consent of the congressional leadership.

The Court also rebuffed the claim that the case presented a nonjusticiable political question. But its reasoning on the political question issue is not entirely clear, for it confused the justiciability argument with its decision on the merits. However, it assumed that the political question doctrine applies only to issues that the Constitution has specifically committed to the determination of another branch, and, finding that not to be the case here, it passed without argument to the question of whether the president's executive privilege is absolute.

Counsel for the president had argued that judicial resolution of the dispute would be inconsistent with the doctrine of separation of powers. This theory would immunize presidential communications; the executive privilege would be absolute; and the case would, incidentally, present a political question. The Court, however, stood this argument on its head: It ruled that an absolute privilege, if invoked in a criminal prosecution, would itself violate the separation principle by preventing the courts from performing their constitutional duty to do justice in criminal cases. Therefore, the privilege was not absolute.

Next the Court turned to analyze the balance that should be struck between the interest in executive confidentiality and the interest in prosecuting criminals. Normally the president would be in a better position to balance these interests than would the Supreme Court, but in the singular situation presented by the Watergate prosecutions the Court was probably correct in deciding that it could strike the appropriate balance better than President Nixon. Chief Justice Burger found that the public interest in vigorous prosecution and in protecting the integrity of the criminal justice system would be seriously impaired by nondisclosure of the presidential tapes. Indeed, given the extraordinary charge of a conspiracy by the president's own advisers to obstruct justice, the need to develop all relevant facts in an adversary setting and to prevent further erosion of public confidence in that system was particularly compelling. On the other hand, the chief justice found that the executive interest in confidentiality would not be seriously undermined by judicial inspection of the tapes in closed session. Again, in view of the facts in *Nixon*, the claim that disclosure would establish a dangerous precedent likely to inhibit future advisers was very insubstantial. To argue otherwise, one would have to assume that future presidents would often require advice on how best to circumvent the nation's criminal laws. The Court, therefore, ruled that a claim of executive privilege must yield to a demonstrated need for specific evidence in a pending criminal trial.

In addition to refining the mechanics for in-chambers inspection in such cases, the *Nixon* decision established four principles: (1) in a criminal case, communications to which the president is a party do not enjoy an absolute privilege against disclosure; (2) giving due respect to a presidential claim of privilege, the trial court must weigh the president's claim against the materiality and relevance of the evidence sought and the need for its disclosure; (3) the court may order the evidence to be produced for its inspection in closed session, in order to determine whether disclosure is required; and (4) if the evidence is not forthcoming, the court may direct that the prosecution be dismissed or that the jury assume that the withheld evidence was favorable to the defendants. It was so obvious that this last alternative was inappropriate in the Watergate prosecutions that the Court did not even discuss it.

The Future of Executive Privilege   While the result in *United States v. Nixon* constituted a stunning defeat for Richard M. Nixon, it was also the first time that the Supreme Court had ruled on the existence of an executive privilege. The *Nixon* Court found that such a privilege did exist and was constitutionally based, though it was not absolute. The Court reasoned that the privilege could be implied from the separation of powers, although it was not expressed in the Constitution. The privilege derives logically from the supremacy of each branch within its own assigned area of constitutional duty. *Nixon*, thus, accorded executive privilege a constitutional status never before recognized and further found that confidential communications with the president enjoy a presumptive privilege against disclosure. That presumption may occasionally be overcome, but the balance struck in *Nixon* will not allow for easy access to presidential conversations even in a criminal trial.

United States v. Nixon did not deal with the kinds of information most commonly involved in past claims of executive privilege or with the kinds of bodies that have traditionally sought that information. The disclosure of information relating to military secrets, intelligence-gathering activities, or diplomatic negotiations was not at issue. Indeed, explicitly approving earlier decisions relevant to the subject,[45] the chief justice noted that a high degree of deference should be shown to the president's judgment in cases involving the production of such information.

The opinion was also careful to emphasize that *Nixon* dealt only with a claim of privilege in the context of a criminal case and did not discuss the scope of the privilege when invoked against Congress or one of its committees. The judicial process, unlike the president's relations with Congress, does not readily allow for compromise. In the past, the president and the courts have achieved some degree of accommodation, such as in the steel seizure case, by holding cabinet officers legally accountable for enforcing presidential directions rather than serving legal process on the president himself. But even this means of accommodation was foreclosed in *Nixon* by the president's decision to take personal custody of the tapes. These facts may have counseled the Court's resolution of the claim of privilege in this case. But, should an impasse develop between Congress and the president at some future date, could the principles enunciated in *Nixon* be extended to cover that kind of situation? Or would the Court decline to interfere with claims of executive privilege, citing the principle of separation of powers and arguing that Congress's power to impeach was the better means to force disclosure?

The dire predictions of President Nixon's counsel that a decision to force disclosure of the Watergate tapes would do profound and irreparable damage to the presidency seem unwarranted. Sudden ruin was not visited on the nation's highest office. Like many earlier Court decisions invalidating presidential actions, *Nixon* is a case in which the president lost, but not necessarily the presidency.

THE IMPACT OF THE COURT ON PRESIDENTIAL POWER

The major defeats that American presidents have suffered at the hands of the Supreme Court make a singularly short list of noticeably weak and questionable precedents. The brave words of *Milligan* were spoken after the crisis had passed. *Humphrey's Executor* was delivered at the height of the Court's attack on Franklin Roosevelt, and like most of the decisions of that period has since been ignored. The steel seizure case, decided at a time when the posture of judicial self-restraint was still very much in vogue, might have represented a notable pronouncement had there been greater agreement among the majority of the justices. As it is, the decision simply reaffirms a principle announced in the 1804 case of *Little v. Barreme*: The president may not take an action that Congress, explicitly or implicitly, has indicated shall not be taken.[46] But *Youngstown* leaves open the question of the president's constitutional powers when Congress has not expressed its intent.[47]

The Pentagon Papers case may seem to be an example of the Court restraining the presidency, but the bulk of scholarly commentary has concluded that it was not a great judicial moment.[48] The Court did reject the Nixon administration's efforts to squelch the *New York Times*, the *Washington Post*, and Daniel Ellsberg. But a decision with nine separate opinions, dealing with six different issues, none of them handled very well, and failing even to discuss at least a half a dozen more issues raised in the case, is hardly likely to be a compelling precedent.

The decision in *United States v. United States District Court* is another in the list, but this ruling was exceptionally narrow.[49] The Burger Court, again unanimous and again speaking through a Nixon appointee, Justice Powell, did rebuff a claim of presidential power, either statutory or constitutional, to authorize electronic surveillance without a judicial warrant in domestic security investigations. But the Court repeatedly emphasized that it was not concerned with the power of the president to authorize warrantless wiretapping and bugging in national security cases involving foreign affairs.

Finally, *United States v. Nixon* did force the president to turn over the tapes and thus brought his resignation. But the decision also recognized presidential claims of executive privilege to be constitutional, and its application to future invocations of presidential privilege in clashes with Congress is, at best, unclear.

These few missiles that the Court has hurled at the presidency have been judicial bricks without straw.[50] Compare them with the broad view of presidential power indulged in *Belmont, Pink, Curtiss-Wright, Quirin, Neagle,* and *The Prize Cases*.[51] If the Supreme Court is the nation's institutional political theorist, on the matter of executive power it has spoken with a voice reminiscent of Locke.

In aligning itself with the cause of the strong presidency, the Supreme Court has in part fulfilled the expectations of the Founding Fathers. But the Framers did not foresee the democratization of the presidency. In government, as in religion, the form may outlive the substance of the faith. In the modern United States, the dangers inherent in unrestrained democratic rule have proceeded not from the House of Representatives but from the plebiscitary presidency. If a constitutional republic is to survive, strong executive leadership is needed in times of severe crisis introduced by war or economic depression. But, as dangerous as economic collapse or total war are to the fabric of constitutional government, there is another threat to political liberty that contemporary Americans have come to recognize--the permanent semi-crisis. A constitutional government of limited powers is designed to function under peaceful conditions. A continuous state of emergency is a dangerous habit. Reasonable people would concede the desirability in the abstract of an energetic executive. But today, with a tremendous military machine and modern transport at his immediate disposal, the president is under little *constitutional* pressure to seek congressional authorization for his actions. Congress must insist that he do so. Traditionally, the Court has not.

SUMMARY

One of the most important themes in the history of the American Republic has been the almost uninterrupted growth in the duties and the powers of the presidency. For a number of reasons, the public has desired a strong executive. Generally the Supreme Court has functioned to legitimate this desire by rationalizing it in terms of constitutional principles. The Court has often engaged constitutional philosophy to shore up presidential actions that were otherwise legally suspect.

Instead of creating ways to restrain presidential power, the Court has labored to reinforce the presidency. This has been especially true in foreign and military affairs. But even in domestic matters the Court's handling of such issues as executive privilege and presidential seizure powers have supported the president more than they have constrained him. The Court has been a little less friendly to presidential power in recent years. But even here it has seemed to be following a public sentiment distressed by the actions of Presidents Johnson and Nixon.

Whether this distress is permanent or merely temporary remains to be seen. Over time, American opinion has favored strong presidents, and the Court has interpreted the Constitution accordingly. Increasing the scope of presidential power, however, has had consequences for the definition of congressional power.

NOTES

1 Robert Jackson, *The Struggle for Judicial Supremacy* (New York: Alfred A. Knopf, 1941), pp. ix-x.

2 Robert Scigliano, *The Supreme Court and the Presidency* (New York: Free Press, 1971), p. 146.

3 See generally ibid., pp. 1-22; Paul Eidelberg, *The Philosophy of the American Constitution* (New York: Free Press, 1968).

4 William Howard Taft, *Our Chief Magistrate and His Powers* (New York: Columbia University Press, 1916), pp. 139-40.

5 John Locke, *Concerning Civil Government, Second Essay*, chap. XIV, sec. 160.

6 *Oral Argument, Youngstown Sheet and Tube Co. v. Sawyer, Transcript*, House of Representatives, 82d Cong., 2d Sess. (1950), H. Doc. no. 534, part I, pp. 371-72.

7 Clinton Rossiter, *The American Presidency*, 2d ed. (New York: Harcourt, Brace & World, 1960).

8 U.S. Const. art. II, sec. 3.

9 135 U.S. 1 (1890).

10 Charles Warren, *The Supreme Court in United States History*, 3 vols. (Boston: Little, Brown & Co., 1922), vol. III, p. 419.

11 *In re* Debs, 158 U.S. 564 (1895).

12 U.S. Const. art. II, sec. 2.

13 Until 1976 the Court had dealt mainly with the removal power and had seldom discussed the appointment power. However, in Buckley v. Valeo, 424 U.S. 1 (1976), the Court considered the constitutionality of the post-Watergate amendments to the Federal Election Campaign Act. Among several other issues, *Buckley* dealt with the method of appointment of members of the Federal Election Commission. Because the Commission performs rule-making and rule-enforcing functions, the Court found its members to be officers of the United States within the meaning of the Constitution. Therefore, all the

justices agreed that congressional selection of some of the commission members violated the Constitution, because such a procedure did not provide for nomination by the president.

14 272 U.S. 52 (1926).

15 295 U.S. 602 (1935).

16 Morgan v. Tennessee Valley Authority, 312 U.S. 701 (1941).

17 Weiner v. United States, 357 U.S. 349 (1958).

18 299 U.S. 304 (1936).

19 In Afroyim v. Rusk, 387 U.S. 253 (1967), the Court expressed serious doubt about the inherent powers theory of *Curtiss-Wright*. But the Court did not overrule *Curtiss-Wright*, though it did overrule Perez v. Brownell, 356 U.S. 44 (1958). Moreover, Justice Black's opinion in *Afroyim*, which was acceptable to only five members of the Court, was itself qualified within only four years in Rogers v. Bellei, 401 U.S. 815 (1971). Thus *Curtiss-Wright* remains, and it is Black's sweeping language that has been limited. *Afroyim* to the contrary, it is Justice Sutherland's theory that does fullest justice to the actual holdings of the Court in the foreign policy realm.

20 299 U.S. at 320.

21 See Corwin, *The President*, pp. 177-78.

22 William R. Thayer, *The Life and Letters of John Hay* 2 vols. (Boston: Houghton Mifflin Co., 1915), vol. II, p. 393.

23 301 U.S. 324 (1937).

24 315 U.S. 203 (1942).

25 Missouri v. Holland, 252 U.S. 416 (1920).

26 67 U.S. (2 Black) 635 (1863).

27 67 U.S. (2 Black) at 671.

28 67 U.S. (2 Black) at 659.

29 294 F. Supp. 511 (D. Mass. 1968). But see Holtzman v. Schlesinger, 361 F. Supp. 553 (E.D. N.Y. 1973). It should be noted that the decision in *Holtzman* occurred in a much different context from that in *Sisson*: American troops had been withdrawn from southeast Asia; there was a peace agreement; and, although bombing continued, Congress and the president had agreed to a bombing cutoff date. The legal significance of this agreement could be interpreted in a number of ways; and, indeed, the lower federal courts disagreed on what it meant. Compare the district court's reasoning in *Holtzman* with Drinan v. Nixon, 364 F. Supp. 854 (D. Mass. 1973).

On appeal, the circuit court in *Holtzman* concluded that the nature of presidential tactics used to conclude a war presented a nonjusticiable political question. But the court then about-faced and suggested that the bombing cutoff date might provide a judicially manageable standard. Holtzman v. Schlesinger, 484 F.2d 1307 (2d Cir. 1973).

With the bombing cutoff date rapidly approaching, the Supreme Court declined to intervene. See Holtzman v. Schlesinger, 414 U.S. 1304 (1973); Holtzman v. Schlesinger, 414 U.S. 1316 (1973); Schlesinger v. Holtzman, 414 U.S. 1321 (1973).

The whole, convoluted story is traced in Clinton Rossiter, *The Supreme Court and the Commander in Chief*, expanded ed. with an introductory note and additional text by Richard P. Longaker (Ithaca, N.Y.: Cornell University Press, 1976), pp. 148-50.

30 "Legality of United States Participation in the Viet Nam Conflict: A Symposium," *Yale Law Journal,* 75 (June 1966), 1085-160.

31 See Martin v. Mott, 25 U.S. (12 Wheat.) 19 (1827); Luther v. Borden, 48 U.S. (7 How.) 1 (1849).

32 See generally Anthony A. D'Amato and Robert M. O'Neil, *The Judiciary and Vietnam* (New York: St. Martin's Press, 1972).

33 Mitchell v. United States, 369 F.2d 323 (2d Cir. 1966), *cert. denied,* 386 U.S. 972 (1967); Mora v. McNamara, 387 F.2d 862 (D.C. Cir.), *cert. denied,* 389 U.S. 934 (1967).

34 87 Stat. 555.

35 *Ex parte* Merryman, 17 F. Cas. 144 (No. 9487) (1861).

36 *Ex parte* Milligan, 71 U.S. (4 Wall.) 2 (1866).

37 327 U.S. 304 (1946).

38 *Ex parte* Quirin, 317 U.S. 1 (1942).

39 320 U.S. 81 (1943).

40 323 U.S. 214 (1944).

41 323 U.S. 283 (1944).

42 343 U.S. 579 (1952).

43 418 U.S. 683 (1974). The tawdry events of Watergate have been rehearsed in publications almost too numerous to count. Perhaps the most complete and objective is *The End of a Presidency* (New York: Bantam Books, 1974).

44 Paul A. Freund, "The Supreme Court, 1973 Term—Foreword: On Presidential Privilege," *Harvard Law Review,* 88 (November 1974), 13.

45 See Chicago & S. Air Lines, Inc. v. Waterman S.S. Corp., 333 U.S. 103 (1948); United States v. Reynolds, 345 U.S. 1 (1953).

46 6 U.S. (2 Cranch) 170 (1804).

47 Compare United States v. Midwest Oil Co., 236 U.S. 459 (1915). When oil was discovered on publicly owned land, President Taft took steps to prohibit private access to a large tract of the land, even though such a policy lacked congressional authorization. Taft asked Congress to ratify his action, but it failed to do so. In upholding the president's closing of public land to the public, the Supreme Court reasoned that the legislative failure to challenge the president constituted an implicit approval.

48 New York Times Co. v. United States, 403 U.S. 713 (1971). See, e.g., Harry Kalven, Jr., "The Supreme Court, 1970 Term—Foreword: Even When a Nation Is at War—," *Harvard Law Review,* 85 (November 1971), 3, 25-36.

49 407 U.S. 297 (1972).

50 See Edward S. Corwin, "The Steel Seizure Case: A Judicial Brick without Straw," *Columbia Law Review,* 53 (January 1953), 53-66.

51 See also Buckely v. Valeo, 424 U.S. 1 (1976), discussed in note 13 above which also favored presidential over congressional power.

SUGGESTED ADDITIONAL READING

Abraham, Henry J. *Justices & Presidents: A Political History of Appointments to the Supreme Court.* New York: Oxford University Press, 1974.

Berger, Raoul. *Executive Privilege: A Constitutional Myth.* Cambridge, Mass.: Harvard University Press, 1974.

———. *Impeachment: The Constitutional Problems.* Cambridge, Mass.: Harvard University Press, 1973.

Corwin, Edward S. *The President: Office and Powers.* 4th rev. ed. New York: New York University Press, 1957.

Henkin, Louis. *Foreign Affairs and the Constitution,* Mineola, N.Y.: Foundation Press, 1972.

Longaker, Richard P. *The Presidency and Individual Liberties.* Ithaca, N.Y.: Cornell University Press, 1961.

Miller, Arthur S. *Presidential Power in a Nutshell.* St. Paul: West Publishing Co., 1977.

Rossiter, Clinton. *The Supreme Court and the Commander in Chief.* Expanded ed. with an introductory note and additional text by Richard P. Longaker, Ithaca, N.Y.: Cornell University Press, 1976.

Schubert, Glendon A., Jr. *The Presidency in the Courts.* Minneapolis: University of Minnesota Press, 1957.

Scigliano, Robert. *The Supreme Court and the Presidency.* New York: Free Press, 1971.

THE COURT AND CONGRESS

CHAPTER 4

CONGRESSIONAL DELEGATION OF POWER

As a practical matter, the growth of presidential power owes less to judicial validation—or judicial avoidance—than to congressional delegation. The most numerous and important powers wielded by a modern president are not those vested in the presidency by the Constitution as interpreted by the Supreme Court but those delegated to the president or his subordinates by Congress. The Court's most significant statement affecting the presidency, therefore, has probably been its sweeping approval of this delegation of legislative power. Ironically, the expansion of presidential power has been accomplished, in part, by expanding Congress's power—its power to give away its power.

Contrary to popular teaching and belief, the United States does not have a government of separated powers. Rather, American government is characterized by a separation of institutions sharing power. The doctrine of separation of powers was never intended by the Framers to be strictly enforced. The Constitution, in fact, was criticized by the Anti-Federalists for its fusion of the executive, legislative, and judicial powers. But James Madison argued that this sharing of powers through a scheme of checks and balances constituted a valuable additional restraint on government by providing each department with weapons to defend itself against potential encroachments by one of the other branches. The president, for example, exercises a legislative function through the veto power. Similarly, he has some influence over the judiciary by virtue of the power of appointment. And, today, in the conduct of foreign relations, the functions of advising and consenting to treaties and of declaring war, originally entrusted to Congress, have come largely under executive control. Congress, on the other hand, may significantly interfere with the process of administration through its investigative powers, its control of the budget, and the Senate's authority to confirm or reject presidential nominations.

This mixture of supposedly separate powers has been aggravated by the need to delegate law-making authority. No statute is precise enough to detail every possible regulation or procedure by which its policy is to be executed. Statutes may succeed in establishing comprehensive goals, but legislatures lack the time and expertise to specify the means for realizing such general policies. These legislative limitations have become increasingly apparent with the expansion of government, particularly in its management of the economy. The effective operation of government often requires the exercise of legislative authority by the executive and, thus, the delegation of law-making powers to it. The chief beneficiary of such congressional generosity has been the president who, in turn, sub-delegates much of his authority to subordinate administrative agencies. But even the Supreme Court has received a delegation of legislative power: Congress has empowered it to prescribe the rules of procedure for the federal judiciary.

The Court's View of Delegation

Delegation of congressional powers raises a serious constitutional question, for it is an ancient constitutional maxim that delegated power may not be redelegated (*Delegata potestas non potest delegari*). Since Congress's powers are delegated to it by the sovereign—the people of the United States—its redelegation of those powers jeopardizes the principle of separated powers. Nonetheless, the delegation of legislative power seems to be a necessity, not just of modern government, but of government generally. Thus, Congress has delegated its power to executive agencies almost from the beginning of the Republic.

In view of this necessity and in spite of the orthodox constitutional theory of the separation of powers, the Supreme Court has been extremely permissive in recognizing Congress's power to delegate its power. But the doctrine of nondelegation of legislative power has placed the Court in a dilemma; it has been able to resolve the problem only by adopting an outright fiction. Congress may engage in extensive delegation of power, according to the Court's theory, as long as it provides clear and explicit standards to guide and control the actions of those to whom it delegates its power. Congress, then, is not delegating law-making power after all; it really is legislating, and the delegee merely executes the legislation by filling in the details of a general plan.

Marshall Court Origins The leading cases enunciating this theory have been *Field v. Clark (1892)*[1] and *United States v. Grimaud (1911)*,[2] but the rationale may be traced back to the Marshall Court. In 1813 the Marshall Court sustained the constitutionality of the Embargo Act of 1809, which granted the president power to suspend the Non-Intercourse Act if he should determine that certain conditions existed.[3] *Field v. Clark* simply upheld similar contingent legislation empowering the president to enact tariffs specified on commodities if he found that foreign countries were not treating the United States with reasonable reciprocity.

Similarly, in 1825, the Great Chief Justice himself ruled that, while important subjects must be entirely controlled by Congress, minor matters of detail might be left to administrative regulation.[4] *Grimaud* then sustained a delegation to the secretary of agriculture of power that was legislative in all but name: the power to make rules and regulations for grazing on national forests. The fact that the statute provided for criminal penalties for violations of the secretary's rules did not bother the Court in the least.

An administrative officer, thus, may be authorized to determine if the facts of a particular case bring it within the operation of a given statute or to enact appropriate regulations to fill in the gaps left in a statute. Such delegations do not violate the constitutional separation of powers if Congress has clearly stated a standard to guide the administrative officer's exercise of discretion. But the Court has normally been willing to accept rather broad and general, if not vague and opaque, standards as meeting this constitutional requirement. The Interstate Commerce Commission, for example, is empowered to set rates that are "just and reasonable," and this been found an adequately specific guideline.[5]

The New Deal Cases Indeed, before 1935, no statute had ever been held invalid as an unconstitutional delegation of legislative power. Then the Court twice used this particular rationale to invalidate some of the early New Deal legislation. In *Panama Refining Co. v. Ryan*[6] the Court struck down section 9(c) of the National Industrial Recovery Act, which authorized the president to prohibit the shipment in interstate commerce of so-called "hot oil"—oil produced or stored in violation of state regulations. All of the justices except Cardozo found section 9(c) objectionable because it did not require any finding by the president as a condition for his action but merely permitted him to act.

An even sharper blow was delivered in *Schechter Bros. Poultry Corp. v. United States*,[7] invalidating the NIRA codes of fair competition. It is of some significance, however, that the Court in *Schechter* was unanimous; even Justices Cardozo and Brandeis could not stomach the virtually unfettered delegation and minute regulation of the act. In reality, the law delegated congressional power not to the president but to the private individuals and business groups that promulgated the codes. It was, as Cardozo put it in a concurring opinion, "delegation run riot."

Actually, Franklin Roosevelt was probably relieved by the *Schechter* decision. The National Recovery Administration was collapsing of its own weight and had become a political albatross about the president's neck. But, consummate political tactician that he was, Roosevelt got good mileage out of the decision in his battle with the Supreme Court. By 1938 both Congress and the Court had learned a lesson. Congressional enactments of the so-called Second New Deal contained slightly more explicit standards than had the legislation of the famous "Hundred Days." For the Court's part, in *Opp Cotton Mills v. Administrator*,[8] it upheld the Fair Labor Standards Act against charges that the standards established to guide the administrator of the Wage and Hour Division were so vague that they invested him with uncontrolled power of legislation. The Court ruled that the statute's lengthy list of factors to guide the administrator's discretion presented a sufficiently clear standard to overcome the constitutional limitation. On the other hand, after the Court-packing battle of 1937, perhaps the Court would not have struck down any of this later legislation even had it not contained more explicit standards. The factors listed in the FLSA are, after all, indefinite to the point of meaninglessness; or, as Justice Stone euphemistically observed, the statute leaves room for administrative "judgment."[9]

Modern Permissiveness   Recent decisions suggest that the Court has returned to a permissive attitude toward delegation.[10] Congress has been accorded broad powers of delegation under the vaguest of standards, especially if the delegation is to the president. Since 1839 the Court has held that the president then may redelegate the powers bestowed upon him to subordinates, whether or not the statute empowers him to do so.[11] The Court has been particularly reluctant to challenge Congress's power to delegate its authority in foreign affairs and in times of emergency.[12] *Mora v.*

McNamara[13] is instructive. In *Mora* the Court denied certiorari to a suit brought by three soldiers who contended that the war in Vietnam was illegal. Only Justice Stewart, dissenting from the denial of certiorari, raised the possibility that the Gulf of Tonkin Resolution, which President Johnson had relied on heavily to support his actions in Southeast Asia, might have constituted an unconstitutional delegation of congressional power to declare war. As a consequence of the Court's permissive approach, an enormous quantity of congressional power has passed to the independent regulatory commissions and administrative agencies charged with filling in the procedural and substantive details of exceedingly general statutes.

Delegation to Administrative Agencies

This delegation had its effect on the judicial process. Today, adjudication involving administrative agencies is a major portion of the Supreme Court's docket, perhaps as much as one-third of the cases decided each term. These decisions claim a significant share of the Court's time and attention and have a noteworthy impact on public policy, but only rarely do they involve constitutional questions. Much more commonly a citizen's dispute with an administrative agency raises questions of statutory interpretation. Each party interprets the applicable statute to favor its position, and the Court, as an independent third party, must determine which interpretation shall prevail. But the Court's thinking in nonconstitutional cases is often colored by its orientation toward constitutional issues.

The Court's power over administrative agencies is seldom derived from its capacity to declare their actions unconstitutional; rather, it has the power to find them illegal. In other words, their actions are not beyond the powers that government may legitimately exercise but simply beyond the authorization of the statute specifying how the administrative agency is to conduct itself. Because of the modern Court's tendency to approve very broad and extremely ill-defined congressional delegations of power, the constitutional question of how much power Congress *could* give an agency almost never arises. In cases involving administrative agencies the crucial question for the Court is usually how much decisional power *did* Congress give the agency. In these cases, therefore, the Court very often must decide precisely the same question the administrative agency itself decided. When an administrative agency takes some action, it is expressing its own opinion of the scope of its power under the applicable congressional statute. When the Supreme Court reviews that action, it must make the same kind of factual determinations and policy choices as the agency did, even if it arrives at a contrary conclusion.

Judicializing the Administrative Process   In the period immediately after the New Deal, the Court not only was willing to accord Congress great latitude in delegating power to administrative agencies but also was exceptionally deferential to the agencies' interpretations of their own powers. The contemporary Court, however, has indicated that that judicial mood has passed. A favorite new mode of attack has been to acquiesce in an agency's power to make a substantive decision but to reverse that decision on the ground that the agency arrived at it through procedures that violate due process of law. This approach fastens on administrative agencies' trial-like adversary hearings—in effect judicializing the administrative process.[14]

As in an earlier era, this decision-making trend has been influenced not by hostility to administrative agencies in themselves but by the Court's attitude toward the subject matter the agency oversees. At the turn of the century an economically conservative Court was mistrustful of the Interstate Commerce Commission and like regulatory agencies. The modern Court has been wont to examine closely the actions of welfare agencies, correctional institutions, and the Selective Service System.

The Perspective of a Generalist   If the Court and the agency make essentially the same decision, why is judicial review of administrative decisions necessary? This process of double decision results in delays, costs to the taxpayers, and yet more stress and strain on an overworked federal court system. The answer is that courts are generalists, and agencies are specialists, and it has frequently been found desirable to introduce an element of generalism into the making of public policy in order to offset a too narrow perspective. There is always the danger that bureaucrats, spending a good deal of their lives in close contact with a single subject, may develop a peculiar view of the world. The intrusion of the Supreme Court into the administrative process represents the intrusion of a generalist into a process dominated by highly specialized experts who claim justification for their projects on the basis of technical competence. If a judge is an expert at anything, it is at law itself—which is to say, at nothing. There is, to be sure, a legal ideology absorbed in the law schools, but the study of law does not make one an expert at any substantive social or economic problem. Therefore, judges, who are almost exclusively drawn from the legal ranks, are not likely to make the mistake of thinking that agriculture, or education, or selective service alone will save the world. A judge may believe that the rule of law will save the world. But that belief, history has shown, is a relatively harmless romanticism.

Thus, regardless of the constitutional theory that Congress is the lawmaker in American society, a very great deal of law is made by both the administrative agencies and the courts. Statutory interpretation involves filling in the details of statutes that provide only general statements of legislative intent. It is exercised by both administrative agencies and the Court, but the Court's word is final. When the Court examines a challenged agency action, it must decide whether the details filled in by the agency agree with the intent of Congress or whether the agency's action is illegal in the sense of being out of harmony with the statute. The necessary generality of statutes and the Court's permissive approach to congressional delegations of power have resulted in delegations not only to the executive branch but also to the Supreme Court.

CONGRESSIONAL INVESTIGATORY POWER

The job of overseeing administrative action is shared by the Court with Congress. True, Congress has not played the role of generalist overseer of administrative action to the degree that it can or should. But, should the sleeping giant choose to bestir itself, it has substantial powers in this area, among them an investigatory power whose broad range has been recognized by the Supreme Court fairly consistently.

Legislative investigations and the legal and political debates surrounding them are not of recent vintage. Although commonly associated in the modern mind with the Red-hunting days of the House Un-American Activities Committee and Senator Joe McCarthy, congressional investigations enjoy a long history. Indeed, before World War II, liberals and reformers were the principal supporters of a sweeping congressional investigatory power, while such practices were most often attacked by conservatives. But the charges against congressional investigations whether from the Right or from the Left, have tended to be the same. Many have been condemned as "fishing" expeditions, conducted without any obvious legislative purpose, to expose for the sake of exposure. Congressional inquiries into personal beliefs and political affiliations allegedly invade privacy, constitute thought control, and violate the First and Fifth Amendments. Congressional committees, it has been argued, often deliberately seek out hostile witnesses, subpoena them, and when they refuse to testify imprison them for contempt, thereby systematically suppressing dissent.

The Requirement of Legislative Purpose

The Supreme Court's first brush with these issues came in *Kilbourn v. Thompson*.[15] In 1876, after the failure of Jay Cooke's banking firm, which had been a depository for federal funds, the House of Representatives authorized one of its committees to investigate the financial dealings between Cooke and a real estate pool of which Kilbourn was the manager. The House resolution authorizing the committee stated that Jay Cooke and Company were debtors of the United States, were creditors of the real estate pool, and had dealt with the latter to the financial loss of the former. For refusing to answer various questions about the pool's dealings, Kilbourn was, by an order of the House, imprisoned in the District of Columbia jail for forty-five days. He brought suit for false imprisonment against the sergeant-at-arms of the House who had executed the order.

Justice Miller's opinion for the Court in *Kilbourn* proceeds in veritably Caesarean fashion. All Washington is divided into three parts: a legislative part that makes laws, an executive part that administers them, and a judicial part that decides individual cases under them. These three parts being mutually exclusive, a function exercised by one may not be exercised by another. Inquiry into the propriety of private business transactions was, according to Miller, a judicial function, because it was designed to establish individual wrongdoing. Since it was judicial, it could not be a proper legislative function. Therefore, it exceeded the power of the House of Representatives. Congress might conduct investigations, conceded Miller, but to be valid those investigations had to be related to some legislative purpose.

The critical question about *Kilbourn* is: What is meant by "legislative purpose"? It may mean simply pertaining to the legislature. Any purpose Congress may have, whether in making laws or otherwise, may be a legislative purpose, since Congress is a legislature. On the other hand, it may mean pertaining to law making. A legislative purpose, in this view, means directed toward the passage of a statute. It was this latter understanding that Justice Miller adopted in *Kilbourn*. An investigation not aimed at the making of a law is not legislative and, hence, is beyond the power of Congress.

The Presumption of Legislative Purpose

This limitation on the investigative acts of Congress was severely qualified as a result of the Teapot Dome scandal. The Senate had sought to investigate the misconduct in office of President Harding's attorney general, the infamous Harry Daugherty. Daugherty's brother refused to testify and challenged the

Senate's power to compel his testimony. Though his position was upheld in the lower courts, he lost in the Supreme Court. The Court began by recognizing that the power of inquiry and its enforcement are essential to the legislative function, because accurate information is needed for wise legislation. But, according to *Kilbourn*, that power could be exercised validly only in aid of the legislative function. Daugherty alleged that the Senate was not seeking information relevant to law making; rather it was, in effect, trying the attorney general. His allegation was strengthened by the fact that the Senate's resolution authorizing the investigation contained no mention of any possible legislative purpose as defined by *Kilbourn*. Strict adherence to that precedent would obviously have required the Court to find the investigation invalid. But, much to Daugherty's chagrin, the Court ruled that Congress must be presumed to have a proper intent.[16]

A much simpler course would have been to recognize that Congress had often investigated for purposes other than law making—to expose governmental chicanery, for example. However, the Court could not adopt this approach and rely on *Kilbourn* as well. It chose to follow *Kilbourn* and thus was forced to create a doctrine of presumption of legislative purpose in order to sustain an investigation that seemed legitimate to Congress, to the public, and to the Court. In essence, *McGrain v. Daugherty* held that, even though no lawmaking purpose is evident, the fact Congress has the power to make laws concerning whatever subject is being investigated creates a presumption that Congress intends to pass such laws as a result of the challenged investigation. The burden rests on the person challenging the investigation to prove that the inquiry is not directed toward law making. *Kilbourn's* limitations on congressional investigations sank beneath the ooze of the Wyoming oil fields.

The Scope Requirement

McGrain did suggest two possible limitations on Congress's investigatory power. A witness might legitimately refuse to answer (1) if the investigating committee exceeded the scope of its authority, or (2) if the questions asked were not pertinent to the subject under investigation. For the next quarter of a century the significance of these limits was lost, as the Court consistently deferred to Congress whenever one of its investigations was challenged. Then, in *United States v. Rumley*,[17] the Court gave some indication that it might be abandoning this uncritical approach.

Rumley, secretary of the Committee for Constitutional Government, had been convicted of contempt of Congress for his refusal to produce the books and records of his organization for inspection by the House Committee on Lobbying Activities. He challenged the investigation as going beyond its authorized scope. By narrowly construing the committee's authorization, a majority of the Supreme Court found that Rumley's refusal to answer was justified. Noting that the resolution authorizing the committee's investigation referred to "lobbying activities," the Court defined "lobbying" to mean direct appeals to members of Congress. Since the Committee for Constitutional Government had not been engaged in such activites, investigation of its papers was not warranted. No investigatory committee could extend the bounds of its power by its own interpretation of the congressional resolution creating it. Justice Frankfurter, the majority's spokesman, emphasized that any other interpretation of the resolution in this case would raise serious First Amendment questions. A broader definition of lobbying might make the resolution an infringement on the freedom of speech.

The Fifth Amendment Privilege

During the 1940s some witnesses before the House Un-American Activities Committee did attempt to avoid answering the committee's questions on the ground that its investigation violated their First Amendment rights to free speech and association. These claims uniformly failed. Apart from the limits implied in *McGrain*, the only constitutional restriction on congressional investigations that the judiciary would recognize was the Fifth Amendment's privilege against self-incrimination. The Supreme Court in 1955 affirmed that the privilege was as applicable in a legislative investigation as in a court of law and further ruled that it might be claimed in layman's language, as long as the assertion was reasonably clear.[18] The result was that, as legislative investigations of allegedly subversive activities increased in number and scope during the early 1950s, many witnesses who would no doubt have preferred to "take" the First Amendment wound up invoking the Fifth. This created a widespread, unfavorable attitude toward "Fifth Amendment Communists," an attitude at variance with the purposes of the self-incrimination privilege and an attitude that the Court itself bitterly criticized but could do very little to change.

It might, of course, have confronted the First Amendment problems presented by HUAC's and Senator McCarthy's investigations. But in 1957 *Watkins v. United States*[19] rather clearly signaled that it was not going to do that.

The Pertinence Requirement

Watkins, a union official, had appeared as a witness before HUAC. He testified with complete candor about his own earlier political associations and activities but refused to answer questions about his former Communist Party colleagues. He was cited for and convicted of contempt of Congress, and his appeal came before the Supreme Court. Speaking for the Court in a long, rambling, and diffuse opinion, Chief Justice Warren held Watkins's conviction invalid because the House resolution creating HUAC was too vague. With such a broad and indefinite authorization for the inquiry, a witness had no way of knowing the relevance of the questions asked to any legislative purpose. The chief justice stated a rule like that used in cases of delegation of legislative power to administrative agencies: In creating committees and vesting them with investigatory power, each house of Congress must provide a clear and definite statement of the committees' jurisdiction. Citing Watkins for contempt under the overbroad standard contained in the HUAC authorizing resolution was a denial of due process in violation of the Fifth Amendment. Watkins, however, had rested his appeal on the First Amendment and a supposed right to privacy under it. The Court, thus, did not decide for Watkins on his own grounds; it merely reiterated the *McGrain* limits. Due process requires that the questions put to a witness by an investigating committee be pertinent to the matter under inquiry, and the inquiry must inform Congress relevant to some contemplated legislation. In short, the *Walkins* Court retained the old standard, although obviously dissatisfied with it.

Watkins and a companion case decided the same day,[20] applying similar limits to state legislative investigations, were widely hailed by liberal critics of HUAC, who read these opinions broadly. (Supreme Court "winners" always do.) Consequently, the decision two years later in *Barenblatt v. United States*[21] came as a bit of a shock, for the Court not only declined to strike HUAC dead but also appeared to retreat from its *Watkins* decision in the face of congressional hostility.

The facts in *Barenblatt* differed hardly at all from those in *Watkins*. Barenblatt, a college professor, had invoked the First Amendment in refusing to cooperate with a HUAC investigation into Communism in higher education. He had then relied very heavily on *Watkins* in appealing his contempt citation. But the Court majority denied that *Watkins* was an applicable precedent. In spite of Chief Justice Warren's broad, condemning language in *Watkins*, the majority opinion in *Barenblatt* found that the earlier case had been decided on the basis of the pertinence test, *not* the vagueness of the HUAC authorizing resolution! That resolution, reasoned the *Barenblatt* majority, could not be read in isolation; the gloss of history had made HUAC's charge quite clear. That history, furthermore, demonstrated that education was within HUAC's jurisdiction.

In contrast with Watkins, Barenblatt had raised no objection at the time of his interrogation to the pertinence of the questions put to him. Indeed, his prepared memorandum of constitutional objections was clear evidence that he knew and understood HUAC's authority and purpose.

Having set aside the pertinence and vagueness claims, the Court turned to the issue that *Watkins* had studiously avoided, the First Amendment objections to HUAC's investigations. It resolved this issue adversely to Barenblatt. When the nation's right to self-preservation is involved, argued the majority, the balance between the governmental interest in disclosure and an individual's interest in privacy of association must be struck in favor of the former. Finally, the Court had come to grips with the First Amendment problem, but its resolution was hardly that anticipated by the opponents of the Un-American Activities Committee. In essence, *Barenblatt* overturned *Watkins* by distinguishing it to death, and a companion case did the same for state legislative investigation.[22]

In the subsequent cases of two journalists who were being harassed by subpoenas from HUAC, the Court made it abundantly clear that *Barenblatt*, not *Watkins*, was to be the controlling precedent for the law of legislative investigations.[23] During the 1960s the Court acknowledged a virtually unlimited congressional power of investigation. In those rare instances when the Court did reverse contempt convictions, it scrupulously avoided giving the impression that it was making a general judicial limitation on congressional investigations. Almost the only cases in which the scope of legislative inquiry was challenged were a few decisions designed to frustrate state investigations of civil rights organizations.[24] Despite some brave language about judicial scrutiny of legislative investigations, however, these were not very broad precedents. Their essential holding was that groups with a demonstrated connection with or engagement in subversive activities may be investigated. This is the very question such investigations are designed to decide—whether an organization *is* subversive. Since the Court is unlikely to determine this question in advance and in opposition to legislatures, especially Congress, this holding is not likely to prove a very great limitation. About all the Court really did was to offer a special exemption for civil rights organizations, such as the NAACP, from harassment by southern legislatures.

Shortcomings of the Legislative Purpose Doctrine

This state of the law is likely to continue unless the Court abandons the legislative purpose doctrine. It is politically unrealistic to limit Congress's investigatory power by insisting that legitimate investigations can be directed only toward the making of laws. Rather, congressional investigations may serve many purposes other than legislating—supervision of the administrative process for one. "Congress's principal source of influence over the bureaucrats is not in legislative correction of administrative wrongdoing subsequent to its exposure but in the exposure itself or more frequently in the threat of exposure."[25] In fact, despite Chief Justice Warren's comment in *Watkins* condemning exposure for exposure's sake, this tactic may serve a public purpose, as it did in Watergate and in Senator Estes Kefauver's earlier investigation of organized crime.

Yet another purpose served by investigations is to keep the balance of powers in balance by allowing Congress to compete effectively with the president for media coverage. Finally, investigations may inform the public, and no less an authority than Woodrow Wilson concluded long ago that "the informing functions of Congress should be preferred even to its legislative function."[26]

By its refusal to recognize that these are legitimate congressional purposes and by its insistence that the only possible justification for investigations is to aid Congress in legislating, the Court has cut itself off from any effective supervision of investigations. By insisting on a whole loaf, the Court has wound up with no loaf at all: In order to sustain legitimate investigations that frankly were not directed toward law making, the Court was forced to adopt the *McGrain* doctrine of presumption of legislative purpose; having adopted the presumption doctrine, the Court cannot really supervise congressional investigation at all.

It might be desirable for the Court to redefine legislative purpose to mean for the purposes of the legislature, not for the purposes of legislation, and then to abandon the presumption doctrine. "[B]y looking the judicial purposes of certain investigations straight in the face, the Court could claim the right to impose strict supervision over those matters in which judges are admitted to have special competence."[27] In particular, the Court could attempt to establish fair investigatory procedures by carefully examining congressional investigations in light of the Fifth Amendment's guarantee of due process of law.

CONGRESSIONAL IMMUNITY

Rather than take such a forthright approach, the Court has recently adopted the curious device of weakening the speech or debate clause. The Constitution provides that senators and representatives "shall not be questioned in any other Place" "for any Speech or Debate in either House."[28] Ironically, the Court's dilution of this legislative immunity has been accomplished in cases that extended the privilege's protection to individuals other than members of Congress.

In *Gravel v. United States*[29] the Court found this provision to prohibit grand jury interrogation of a congressman's alter ego, the congressional aide. In *Doe v. McMillan*[30] the Court ruled that this immunity applied to government printing officials, and in *Eastland v. United States Servicemen's Fund*[31] the clause was held to bar a suit against the chief counsel of a Senate subcommittee to enjoin enforcement of a subpoena issued by that subcommittee. Yet two of these decisions, *Gravel* and *McMillan*, enunciate doctrines that, by implication, limit Congress's investigatory and informing functions.

Obtaining Information

Senator Mike Gravel, having obtained copies of the Pentagon Papers, placed the entire study in the public record at a meeting of the Subcommittee on Buildings and Grounds of the Senate Public Works Committee. He then undertook to have it privately published. A federal grand jury, investigating possible criminal violations committed in the acquisition and release of the papers, subpoenaed one of Gravel's staff members to testify before it. Gravel sought to quash the subpoena on the ground that such testimony would violate his own constitutional privilege as a member of Congress. The Court agreed, reasoning that congressional assistants must enjoy an immunity to the same extent as their superiors, since a contrary holding would require legislators to perform all their legislative tasks personally in order to retain the protection of the speech or debate clause. This is obviously impossible under contemporary conditions.

The Court then went on to consider which of Gravel's and his aide's acts were immune from grand jury inquiry, however. It found that only their behavior *at the hearing*, the motives for that behavior, and the communications between them related to the hearing were constitutionally privileged. Matters relating to Gravel's preparation for the hearing, including questions about how he obtained the Pentagon Papers in the first place, as well as matters relating to his conduct after the hearing, including his plans to publish the papers, were judged nonessential to the deliberative and communicative processes of the Senate and, thus, not protected by the speech or debate clause from grand jury questioning.

Effects on the Use of Informants   Although consistent with another Court ruling on the same day (that journalists had no First Amendment privilege against the disclosure of their sources), the *Gravel* decision has potentially very harmful consequences. It could impair Congress's ability to wield its investigatory ower effectively in order to oversee the bureaucracy, for Congressmen as well as newsmen rely on informants to uncover problems and deficiencies. Administrators are seldom eager to volunteer information about their agencies' corruption, malfeasance, misfeasance, or simple inefficiency, and the number of times the executive branch has attempted to frustrate a congressional investigation or to conceal the need for one almost defy counting. Numerous, too, are the instances in which the congressional camel's nose has slipped inside the bureaucratic tent with the aid of an individual employee turned informer. The leak of the Pentagon Papers is itself an example. Another was the action of a B. F. Goodrich engineer who informed Congress of deficiencies in certain products supplied to the government by his company and brought about a congressional investigation. Yet another was the role palyed by a Pentagon employee in bringing to Congress's attention more than $2 billion in cost overruns for the C-5A cargo plane. And the list goes on.

Gravel, particularly coupled with the Courts recognition in *Nixon* of a constitutional basis for executive privilege claims (see chapter 3), would make it extremely difficult, if not impossible, for Congress to obtain such information. After *Gravel*, no member of Congress can guarantee confidentiality for a possible informant, because the release of such information may constitute a crime that is subject to investigation by a grand jury. Indeed, under *Gravel*, individual legislators may be subject to criminal prosecution for even receiving, let alone releasing, classified information or stolen government documents.

Publishing and Distributing Information

McMillan arose from an action for damages brought by the parents of junior high school students. Their children had been named as students who presented academic and disciplinary problems in a report by a House subcommittee investigating the District of Columbia school system. Alleging an invasion of privacy, the parents, on behalf of their children, filed suit against the subcommittee and its staff, officers of the Government Printing Office, which had printed and distributed the report, and various other defendants. The federal district court dismissed the suit against all of the defendants. But the Supreme Court, while affirming the immunity of the members of the subcommittee and their aides, allowed the suit against the public printer and the superintendent of documents for preparation and publication of the report. These printing officials had relied heavily on the earlier decision in *Gravel*, arguing that they were as much deputies of the legislature as were congressional staff members. The Court accepted this argument but found that legislators themselves would not necessarily have been protected by the speech or debate clause, had they personally printed and distributed the report.

Unable to agree on any single theory of congressional immunity, though unanimously concurring in the result, the Court produced five separate opinions. Under all the approaches, however, the result was to narrow the scope of the privilege accorded to members of Congress. The five-man majority took the position that the members of the subcommittee would not have been personally protected by the speech or debate clause unless they could show that publication and distribution of the report was necessary to "legislative acts."[32] This is reminiscent of *Kilbourn's* talk of "legislative purpose" and probably as unrealistic. Nevertheless, the majority opinion was emphatic that the judiciary is to decide what are and what are not the legitimate legislative needs of Congress.

Indeed, the *McMillan* majority endorsed the view that informing the public is not necessarily a legislative act, even if authorized by one or both houses of Congress. Thus, while clothing government printers with the same immunity as the congressional representatives whose orders they execute, *McMillan* raises the possibility that the Court, perhaps in league with the president, might prohibit the public broadcast of information obtained by Congress in the exercise of its investigatory powers. Such judicial interference with the legislative process seems clearly improper.

MEMBERSHIP OF THE HOUSE

The modern Supreme Court's interference with the internal affairs of Congress has been even more spectacular in its decisions affecting the composition and membership of the House of Representatives. Article I establishes certain qualifications of age, citizenship, and residence for senators and representatives. Each house is also to be "the Judge of the Elections, Returns and Qualifications of its own Members."[33]

Congressionally Imposed Qualifications

In *The Federalist* No. 60 Alexander Hamilton contended that the qualifications of members of Congress were fixed by the Constitution and unalterable by the legislature. But the Constitution changes through legislative as well as through judicial action, and on several subsequent occasions both houses of Congress in effect enforced additional qualifications by refusing to seat duly elected members who met the constitutional qualifications. The Test Oath Act of 1862, for example, required all members of Congress, as well as all other federal officers, to take an oath that they had never participated in rebellion against the United States. In 1900 the House of Representatives refused to seat a Utah polygamist, and nineteen years later Victor L. Berger, a

Wisconsin Socialist, was denied his seat because he had been convicted under the Espionage Act for opposing American intervention in the First World War. His constituents reelected him, and the House again refused to seat him. Before his third election, his conviction was reversed, and the House then admitted him. In the 1920s the Senate refused to seat two senators-elect because of scandals involving their campaign funds.

The *Powell* Case

The most colorful episode occurred in 1967 when Adam Clayton Powell, the representative-elect from Harlem, was denied his seat in the House. The previous year Powell had been convicted of criminal contempt of court for failure to pay a defamation of character judgment against him. His manner of conducting the House Education and Labor Committee, of which he was chairman, his deception of the House in the matter of expenditures of foreign currency during his highly publicized trips abroad at public expense, and his cashing of salary checks issued to his estranged wife, who was a member of his committee's staff but apparently performed no services for the committee, all served as bases for the House exclusion of Representative Powell. Others attributed the House action to hysteria generated by Powell's race and the swagger and defiance of his personality.

Claiming that the House had no constitutional power to deny him his seat, Powell and some of his constituents sued to regain it. The federal district court dismissed the case on the ground that it presented a political question, and the court of appeals likewise ruled against Powell. But the Supreme Court, in the last major opinion written by Chief Justice Earl Warren, reversed.[34] The chief justice reasoned that no political question was presented by the *Powell* case, because the Constitution made no textually demonstrable commitment to Congress of a power to exclude members on whatever grounds it pleased. Rather, the House could exclude only those whose age, residence, or citizenship failed to meet the standards set forth in Article I. Since Adam Clayton Powell met all these criteria, his exclusion had been illegal.

The Intent of the Framers   To reach this holding, *Powell v. McCormack* relied very heavily on the fact that the Constitutional Convention had defeated a measure that would have allowed Congress to impose additional membership qualifications. This piece of historical evidence, however, does not support the Court's conclusion about the intent of the Framers. When the convention debated the question of what qualifications should be required of congressmen, three points of view were expressed. First, there were those who favored a property qualification. A second group opposed listing any qualifications, because they might be interpreted as exclusive, and favored instead a clause giving Congress the power to set the qualifications for its members. A third faction favored a statement of only minimal and exclusive qualifications.

After a good deal of maneuvering and debate, a clause was proposed that would set minimal and exclusive qualifications, with the exception that Congress would be empowered to set a property qualification. Those who had opposed listing any qualifications moved to amend the exception clause by striking the words "with respect to property," thus leaving Congress free to alter qualifications as it saw fit. This amendment was defeated, and the *Powell* Court saw great significance in this. But this amendment was defeated through a coalition of those who opposed a property qualification and those who wanted a property qualification specifically written into the Constitution. After more debate over whether the legislature should be able to impose additional qualifications, the convention elected to resolve the issue, as it resolved a number of others, by simply leaving the Constitution silent and allowing subsequent events to settle the matter. Thus, the constitutional silence cannot be taken to indicate that the Framers meant the article I qualifications to be exclusive.

The Interests of Powell's Constituents   In assessing the merits of the *Powell* decision, it is best to separate Adam Clayton Powell's interests from those of his constituents. The most appealing argument advanced in *Powell* involved not the personal interests of Congressman Powell but his constituents' interest in representation. Because neither history nor precedent shed much light on the question of Congress's power to judge the qualifications of its own members, the *Powell* Court was presented with a difficult task of weighing competing interests to determine the scope of that power.

On the one hand, a societal interest would be served by allowing either house to exclude members on the basis of its own qualifications—the elimination of corrupt legislators from positions of public trust. On the other hand, the presence of dissenting voices in Congress is also beneficial to society; it encourages debate, ensures that divergent views have an opportunity for expression, and checks repressive legislation. Allowing Congress to exclude on its own standards could be detrimental to this interest. Of course, the First Amendment would prevent the exclusion of members solely on the basis of their publicly expressed political views. But, given the realities of the political process, most members excluded for corruption or similarly undesirable behavior would probably also happen to belong to dissenting minorities. Therefore, though the interest of society in honest government would be furthered by allowing Congress to exclude the corrupt, the societal interest in having dissenting voices in Congress would be harmed.

When there is no clear guide from history, precedent, or policy, the Court must attempt to interpret a given provision of the Constitution in harmony with existing constitutional law. An important branch of constitutional law concerns voting rights. According to a number of Court decisions, the Constitution establishes an electoral process that protects the right to cast a ballot in a regular or primary election and to have that vote counted. Chief Justice Warren, therefore, was probably correct in reasoning that to allow the House to exclude Powell on the basis of qualifications of its own choosing would impinge on the interest of his constituents in effective participation in the electoral process.

But, conceding that the *Powell* decision was the correct one for Powell's constituents, it was also unnecessary. *Powell* was announced after Adam Clayton Powell had been reelected *and seated* in the Ninety-first Congress. In terms of the constituents' interests, what purpose was served by informing the House of Representatives that it had not had the power to exclude Powell from the Ninetieth Congress? Those two years would never be recaptured. The eighteenth New York congressional district was and always shall remain unrepresented during that time. As far as Powell's constituents were concerned, a declaratory judgment that they had been unconstitutionally deprived of representation served no end other than some small psychological or moral vindication. But the Supreme Court is not in the business of providing moral vindication in the abstract, and from the point of view of the House of Representatives, a body constitutionally equal to and coordinate with the Court, the decision in *Powell* was more than offensive—it was a gratuitous insult.

Powell's Own Interests   As for Adam Clayton Powell, his reelection and admission to the Ninety-first Congress had already served to vindicate him in a much more concrete manner than could any declaration after the fact by the Supreme Court. But Powell's seating in the Ninety-first Congress had been conditioned by two factors. He had been stripped of his seniority and fined $25,000. Powell, therefore, had several personal interests distinct from those of his constituents: restoration of his salary from the Ninetieth Congress, restoration of his seniority, and remission of the fine. Could the Court provide relief for any of these interests?

The Court addressed this aspect of the controversy by dismissing Powell's suit against five named members of the House of Representatives, but not against named employees of the House—the sergeant-at-arms and the doorkeeper. This was consistent with the Court's understanding of the speech or debate clause, but it did not avoid the practical difficulties. Exactly what would happen if the House fired these employees and entrusted their functions to elected members posed one interesting question.

Even short of that, granting relief to Powell presented other very difficult problems. These were, however, glossed over in the chief justice's opinion. The Court limited itself to a declaratory judgment that Powell was entitled to his seat. Then, observing that the propriety of remedies was a question more appropriately considered in the lower courts, it remanded the case to the district court. But, as that court was shortly to discover, there was very little it could do for Congressman Powell.

The sergeant-at-arms of the House could not be served with a writ of mandate, since he was not covered by the statute authorizing the federal courts to issue such writs against federal officials. Since the House, unlike the Senate, is not a continuing body, the sergeant-at arms of the Ninetieth Congress was no longer a legal entity at the time of the decision in *Powell.* Since that sergeant-at-arms could pay only those members who took an oath of office for the Ninetieth Congress, and since Powell did not, the sergeant had no legal authority to reimburse Powell. Besides, because any congressional surplus reverts to the Treasury at the end of the session, the sergeant-at-arms had no funds with which to pay Powell.

For all of these reasons, Powell had no chance at law of securing the recovery of his back salary or the remission of his fine. A more appropriate recourse would have been a suit not in the regular federal courts but in the United States Court of Claims, which, as Justice Stewart noted in his *Powell* dissent, has the authority to compel payments from the Treasury if it determines that a wrong has been committed. As Stewart also observed, this would have avoided a Supreme Court declaration on the constitutional issue.

As for the seniority question, there was no conceivable way in which a court could restore Powell's seniority. The seniority system is an informal, extralegal arrangement controlled by the members of Congress, who were beyond the reach of judicial power, by virtue of the speech or debate clause. The question of Powell's seniority rested with his colleagues, not the courts. With regard to the interests that Powell had distinct from those of his constituents, he had no recognized legal remedy. Therefore, in spite of Chief Justice Warren's opinion, *Powell v. McCormack* seems to have presented a nonjusticiable, political question.

Apportionment

Powell is not the only case in which the modern Court has ignored the wisdom of the political question doctrine, including its own formulation of that doctrine, to render decisions altering the composition and membership of the House of Representatives. Following *Baker v. Carr* (1962),[35] the first case to find that legislative apportionment was a justiciable issue, the federal judiciary embarked on a campaign to reapportion virtually every legislative chamber in the United States on the basis of population alone. Only the United States Senate, which was constitutionally immune, was excepted from this onslaught. While the campaign was of greater significance for the political institutions of the states, the Court also imposed its "one man, one vote" standard on congressional districting in *Wesberry v. Sanders*.[36]

Wesberry is a classic example of the inadequacies of historical jurisprudence, especially when the Court chooses to distort the historical facts. Justice Black's majority opinion in *Wesberry* was subjected to immediate, vehement, and almost unanimous criticism and condemnation from professional historians.[37] Black argued that it was the intent of the Framers to ensure equal representation for equal numbers of citizens when, in the so-called Great Compromise, they agreed to apportion the Senate with equal representation for states as states and to apportion the House on a population basis. But, as Justice Harlan pointed out in a biting dissent, Black confused the apportionment of representatives among the states with the apportionment of seats within the states. For the *Wesberry* majority, the basic principle of justice in a republican regime is equality of election. But it is demonstrable that the Constitution's Framers were not concerned with mere equality; rather they wanted to create the institutional elements necessary for good government. Representation, undoubtedly, is a part of good government. But it is only a part. For the Founding Fathers representation, and a mixed system of representation at that, was viewed as a means conducive to the end of good government, not as an end itself.

Moreover, as again Harlan noted in dissent, *Wesberry* contravened *Baker v. Carr*. In *Baker*, Justice Brennan had attempted to reduce the political question doctrine to a substantive rule, rather than leaving it a matter of discretion or merely prudence. (Since the political question doctrine refuses to be domesticated in this fashion, it was not surprising that *Baker* proved inadequate from almost its first application.) Brennan had argued that political question cases concerned only the relationship between the Supreme Court and the coordinate branches of the federal government. It did not affect the federal judiciary's relationship with the states. Since *Baker* involved the apportionment of seats in the legislature of Tennessee, it did not present a political question and was justiciable.

But *Baker* also stated that the nonjusticiability of a political question arose from the separation of powers. *Wesberry* touched the very separation of powers questions that *Baker* had said would always be political and, thus, nonjusticiable. The logical consequence of the decision in *Wesberry* was to declare that most of the House of Representatives had been unconstitutionally elected.

The Court has, nevertheless, continued to press resolutely ahead in its self-proclaimed role as the protector of the majority against the minority. Having established that legislative districts must be of substantially equal population, the Court was required to define how substantial was substantial. Recognizing the difficulty of drawing district lines with mathematical precision, the Court has tolerated some deviation from exact numerical equality in state apportionment plans. But at the congressional level no population disparity, no matter how small and how justified, has ever been approved.[38] Apparently nothing short of strict egalitarianism will suffice.

CONGRESS'S REGULATORY POWERS

While it has been increasingly restrictive in its interpretations affecting Congress's internal operations, the Court, particularly during the past two generations, has generally construed Congress's external powers very broadly. Among the most important of these are the power of Congress to regulate interstate commerce, the power to tax, and the implied power derived from the necessary and proper clause.

The Implied Power

The first judicial exposition of the doctrine of implied powers was penned by the Great Chief Justice, John Marshall, in the case of *McCulloch v. Maryland*,[39] generally regarded as the most important decision in American constitutional law. At issue was the constitutionality of the Bank of the United States, a financial institution unpopular in the southern and western states. Maryland had sought to drive the bank from its borders by levying a discriminatory tax on the Baltimore branch. The case presented two questions: Did Congress have the power to incorporate a bank? If so, could a state constitutionally impose a tax on it?

Marshall began by readily admitting that the power to charter a bank was not to be found in the article I enumeration of congressional powers. But, Marshall continued, the federal government possesses implied as well as enumerated powers. The constitutional source of these implied powers is the necessary and proper clause, a provision normally referred to since *McCulloch* as the elastic clause. Necessary, said Marshall, did not mean absolutely necessary but merely convenient, and proper simply meant appropriate. "Let the end be legitimate, let it be within the scope of the constitution, and all means which are appropriate, which are plainly adapted to that end, which are not prohibited, but consist with the letter and spirit of the constitution, are constitutional."[40]

To the argument that implied powers were in fact prohibited by the Tenth Amendment, Marshall answered that that amendment, reserving to the states the powers not granted to the federal government, did not contain the word "expressly." This omission was critical, for had the Tenth Amendment reserved to the states all powers not expressly granted to the federal government by the Constitution, no implied congressional power could exist. But, since that was not the case, the doctrine of implied powers could be logically reconciled with the Tenth Amendment, although the practical effect of *McCulloch* was to reduce that amendment to a tautology.

Marshall entered a strong and compelling plea for constitutional flexibility. Indeed, perhaps one of the reasons that Marshall's earlier handiwork in *Marbury v. Madison* survived was that his view of the scope of legislative and executive power possessed a certain grandeur. True, Marshall saw it as the function of the Court to expound the Constitution with finality, but it was also Marshall who, in *McCulloch*, enjoined posterity never to forget "that it is *a constitution* we are expounding." And for Marshall *a constitution* must not "partake of the prolixity of a legal code ... [but be] adapted to the various crises of human affairs."[41]

The Power to Tax

Turning to the issue of Maryland's power to tax the bank, Marshall had recourse to the principle of national supremacy. Pointing to the supremacy clause, he observed that, when a state law conflicts with a national law, the latter must prevail. The act of Congress creating the bank as a lawful instrument of federal authority must prevail against any state attempt to limit, control, or exclude it, because "the power to tax involves the power to destroy."[42]

On the other hand, the Great Chief Justice made it quite clear that, though a state might not tax a constitutional entity of the federal government, the federal government was not conversely prohibited from taxing a state government's institutions. During the latter part of the nineteenth century, however, justices less nationalist in sentiment than Marshall stood this doctrine on its head; more accurately, they reasoned that, in taxation, what was good for the goose was good for the gander. This reasoning gave rise to a number of cases elaborating the tangled and technical doctrine of intergovernmental tax immunities.

Intergovernmental Immunities   Although *McCulloch* had involved a discriminatory tax that was indeed designed to destroy the Bank of the United States, Marshall himself subsequently expanded the doctrine of federal immunity from state taxation to invalidate a nondiscriminatory, nondestructive state personal property tax levied on privately owned United States government bonds.[43] This was viewed by the Court as a tax on the borrowing power of the United States. In 1842 *Dobbins v. Commissioners of Erie County*[44] held that the salaries of federal officials were immune from state taxation; since these officials were the instrumentalities of the federal government, to tax them constituted state interference with effective use of the power of the United States. In 1871 *Collector v. Day*[45] inverted the theory of *Dobbins* to hold state officers immune from federal taxation.

Following *Collector v. Day*, the Court steadily inflated the doctrine of intergovernmental tax immunity, until by 1930 the two governmental systems were almost totally immune from taxation by the other. Making little effort to analyze or justify the immunity doctrine, the Court invalidated a federal income tax levied on state bonds, a state sales tax applied to sales made by a private contractor to the federal government, and a federal excise tax levied on motorcycles sold by a private enterprise to a state police agency. The most extreme case found that the states could not tax income derived from patents, since patents were granted by the federal government.

The doctrine had clearly grown out of all proportion to its usefulness, especially in light of the governmental need for revenue during the depression. After 1937, therefore, the immunity of individuals from taxation because of government employment or business relationships with government rapidly declined, and eventually *Collector v. Day* was expressly overruled.[46] Congress can statutorily exempt federal employees from state taxation, as it has done for military personnel, and it can exempt from federal income taxation interest payments derived from state and municipal bonds, as it has also done. But today the employees, officers or instrumentalities of one jurisdiction have no constitutional immunity from taxation by the other.

The Court, however, has continued to wrestle with the problem of the direct taxation by one jurisdiction of the activities of the other. The general rule, at least since 1946, has been that activities traditionally within state governmental functions, such as education, may not be subjected to federal taxation but that activities not within the scope of tradition, such as New York's sale of mineral water from Saratoga Springs, are taxable. On the other hand, the Court has uniformly held federal functions immune from state taxes unless Congress consents to the taxation.

The Commerce Power

The tax immunity cases provide an apt example of how the Supreme Court, acting as the umpire of the Federal system, officiates with a prejudice in favor of one side, the federal government. The principle is equally well illustrated by the Court's interpretation of the scope of Congress's commerce power. Here, as in the tax cases, the Court has construed congressional power very generously.

The Exclusive View of the Commerce Power The initial problem presented by the Constitution's grant of power "To regulate Commerce . . . among the several States" was to determine if this were an exclusive grant. In the absence of congressional legislation, did the states retain any power to regulate interstate commerce?

The extreme nationalists of the formative era contended that they did not. The Constitution, they argued, gave the power to regulate interstate commerce to Congress alone. If Congress did not legislate over a certain subject, the commerce clause possessed a dormant potency of its own that would prevent the states from legislating with respect to that subject.

Others, however, contended that the states enjoyed a totally concurrent power over interstate commerce. If Congress did not legislate, the states were completely free to regulate as they saw fit. In *Gibbons v. Ogden*,[47] the earliest commerce clause decision, John Marshall intimated that he favored the dormant commerce power theory. But, since the state legislation in *Gibbons* was voided on the ground that it conflicted with a federal statute, Marshall's veiled expression of opinion was dictum, not a holding.

The Cooley Rule Complicated by the slavery question, the commerce controversy seethed for decades, with the Court so fragmented that no ruling principle could be discerned from its decisions. Then, in *Cooley v. Board of Wardens*,[48] the newly appointed Justice Benjamin Robbins Curtis hit upon an ingenious solution. In sustaining a pilotage regulation by the Philadelphia Port Authority, Curtis enunciated the doctrine of selective exclusiveness. According to *Cooley*, the constitutional grant to Congress of the power to regulate interstate commerce did not necessarily prohibit state regulation in the absence of congressional action. But neither did the states possess a totally concurrent power. Rather, the nature of the subject regulated must be considered. Those aspects of commerce that required a uniform national rule were exclusively reserved to Congress to regulate. If Congress did not exercise its regulatory power, these matters could not be subjected to state regulation. On the other hand, in the absence of congressional legislation, the states might regulate those aspects of interstate commerce that were amenable to diverse local regulations.

Historically, application of the *Cooley* rule has produced two schools of judicial thought. In one school are those justices who, fearing the balkanization of American commerce, have consistently preferred uniform national rules. They have been unwilling to countenance much, if any, state regulation of commercial matters. In the other school are the justices who have feared that a broad application of *Cooley* would create a regulatory void in which Congress would not legislate and the states could not. They, consequently, have been willing to tolerate much greater exercise of state concurrent regulatory power.

The Narrow View of the Commerce Power   From approximately 1886 to 1937, an economically conservative Court used the commerce clause to protect business enterprise from almost all governmental regulation, either federal or state. This was accomplished, in part, by adopting an extremely narrow view of interstate commerce matters in which local conditions might permit state regulation. This virtually reintroduced the dormant commerce theory.

At the same time, the Court embraced some very questionable doctrines limiting Congress's own commerce power. The power to regulate commerce, for example, was found not to include the power to prohibit it. Congress might only encourage commercial enterprise; it could not discourage it. Nor could Congress use the commerce power to fulfill other aims, such as the elimination of child labor. As a corollary to this, the Court on a number of occasions made it perfectly clear that it would go behind statutes and examine congressional motivations to determine if challenged legislation was, in fact, commercial regulation or social experimentation masquerading as an exercise of the commerce power.

The Court also resurrected the Tenth Amendment as a substantive bar to congressional regulatory action. In particular it ruled that manufacturing, as distinguished from commerce, was a matter reserved to the states to regulate. Most American industry, thus, fell beyond the reach of such federal statutes as the Sherman Antitrust Act. The result was to create a twilight zone in which the states were incompetent to act and congressional regulation was barred. This judicial construction reached its peak in 1935-36 when the Court laid waste the New Deal's economic recovery program.

The Broad View of the Power   In a change of heart, allegedly in response to Franklin Roosevelt's Court-packing scheme, the Court abandoned all the formulas that had guided its decisions in this field of constitutional law for over half a century. The task of adjusting the balance between Congress's power over commercial matters and the states' interests in regulating matters of local concern was abdicated to the state legislatures and Congress, with the final remedy in Congress's hands by virtue of the supremacy clause.

In the modern era, essentially anything goes, if Congress says so and in saying so invokes its commerce power. The modern Court has, for example, used the commerce clause to sustain various provisions of federal civil rights legislation. *Heart of Atlanta Motel v. United States* and its companion case, *Katzenbach v. McClung*, provide prime illustrations.[49] Both involved challenges to the constitutionality of the Civil Rights Act of 1964. The act allows persons injured by racial discrimination in public accommodations such as hotels, motels, gas stations, and restaurants to obtain federal injunctions to prevent such injury in the future. The Court reasoned that discrimination against blacks impaired interstate commerce by discouraging a substantial portion of the black community from traveling. This artificially restricted the market, since blacks were lost as customers, and businesses such as motels and restaurants had fewer customers. These businesses as a result sold less than they would if there were no discrimination and consequently bought less. Thus, racial discrimination tended to depress interstate commerce, and Congress had the power to correct this condition.

Nor was Congress's commerce power restricted by the fact that it was legislating against a moral evil. Rather, the Court ruled that the only fit questions for judicial inquiry were whether Congress had a rational basis for finding that racial discrimination affected interstate commerce and whether the means it selected to eliminate the evil were reasonable and appropriate.

A second issue presented by *Heart of Atlanta* and *McClung* was whether the 1964 Civil Rights Act, if constitutional, actually applied to the businesses in question. The Court found that the Heart of Atlanta Motel was subject to Congress's commerce power for three reasons: It was readily accessible to interstate highways; it solicited patronage through advertising in various media, including magazines with interstate circulation; and approximately 75 percent of its customers were engaged in interstate travel.

But it was not so easy to show that Ollie's Barbecue, the Birmingham restaurant involved in *McClung*, was subject to the commerce power. Ollie's was not located on or near any interstate highways, bus stations, railroad depots, or the like. It did not solicit business from interstate travelers, and there was no claim that a substantial portion of its clientele were interstate travelers. Ollie's transactions were entirely local, and it drew less than one-half of its foodstuffs from suppliers who bought the produce outside Alabama. Nevertheless, the Court held that Ollie's was subject to congressional commercial regulatory legislation. Even though it drew an insignificant amount of its foodstuffs from interstate commerce, its contribution to that commerce, when taken together with that of all other similar buinesses, was far from trivial.

Actually, the decisions in *Heart of Atlanta* and *McClung* did little more than reiterate four settled principles of constitutional law that had been established in the 1940s. First, Congress may regulate any activity, however local, that affects interstate commerce. Secondly, the Court will not review a congressional determination that a local activity does affect interstate commerce, if there is any evidence giving rational support to that determination. Thirdly, questions of degree are exclusively within the province of the legislature; the Court will not invalidate an act of Congress merely because the activity regulated is local and its effect on interstate commerce remote. And, fourthly, the predominant purpose of a congressional statute is not subject to judicial scrutiny; thus, it was constitutionally irrelevant, even though it was true, that the essential purpose of the Civil Rights Act of 1964 was to eliminate racial segregation from one aspect of American life and not to regulate or encourage interstate commerce.

The Power to Enforce the Reconstruction Amendments

Congress had based the 1964 Civil Rights Act on the equal protection clause of the Fourteenth Amendment as well as on its power to regulate interstate commerce. Section 5 of that amendment empowers Congress to enforce the amendment through appropriate legislation. Only Justices Douglas and Goldberg, concurring, reached the equal protection issue in *Heart of Atlanta* and *McClung*. The majority's commerce clause reasoning made such an analysis unnecessary.

The Civil War amendments, however, have been an increasingly important source of power for Congress. Through expansive interpretations both of Congress's constitutional power to enforce these amendments and of the statutes enacted under that power, the modern Court has recognized a far-reaching congressional ability to remedy racial discrimination not only in public accommodations but also in the sale and rental of housing, in electoral procedures, and in employment practices.

Discrimination in Employment   A provision of the 1964 Civil Rights Act companion to the provision sustained in *Heart of Atlanta* outlawed discrimination in hiring, job placement, and promotion. In *Griggs v. Duke Power Co.*[50] the Supreme Court read this provision to prohibit an employer from requiring a high school education or a passing grade on a standardized aptitude test as a condition for employment, if such requirements operated to eliminate a disproportionately large number of minority applicants, unless the employer could demonstrate that the requirements were significantly related to successful job performance.

In a subsequent case in which the employer had introduced evidence to verify the job-relatedness of its entry-level aptitude tests, the Court found the verification inadequate for a variety of reasons, even though statistically significant correlations were shown between employees' scores on the tests and their on-the-job performance.[51] Moreover, the Court went on to hold that the 1964 Civil Rights Act was designed not only to ensure equality of employment opportunity but also to compensate the victims of past discrimination. Therefore, in this case, the employer's good faith efforts to comply with the act were not sufficient to protect it from liability to its black workers for many years' back pay, given the racially discriminatory effects of the company's seniority system.

Discrimination in Voting Rights   The Voting Rights Act of 1965 has enjoyed similar permissive treatment at the hands of the Court. One section of this act invalidated state literacy tests for any otherwise qualified citizen who had completed a minimum of six grades in an American-flag school where the language of instruction was not English. The purpose of this provision was clearly and simply to enfranchise New York City's Spanish-speaking Puerto Rican minority. It was upheld in *Katzenbach v. Morgan*,[52] but the language of the opinion was so sweeping it suggested there were almost no limits to Congress's power to identify and correct what it perceived to be denials of equal protection. Speaking for the Court, Justice Brennan argued that, in light of the special importance of voting, congressional scrutiny of any state-imposed limitation on suffrage might be very strict. On the other hand, judicial scrutiny of the justification for legislation directed at such limitations would be minimal indeed. Congress need only have some basis for concluding that an unfair differentiation was made between an enfranchised group and an unenfranchised group. Once that determination was made, Congress might enact *any* enforcement measures it thought appropriate.

Another section of the Voting Rights Act requires that, before certain states or their political subdivisions may initiate any change in voting qualifications or practices, they must first obtain a decision from the United States attorney general or from the federal district court for the District of Columbia that the alteration does not intend to and will not deny or abridge the right to vote on the basis of race. According to the terms of the act, this provision applies to states and political subdivisions that used literacy or character tests to screen voters on November 1, 1964, and in which less than 50 percent of the voting age population either were registered to vote or voted in the 1964 presidential election.

By interpreting this portion of the act very broadly, the Supreme Court has further strengthened federal control of local elections. *Allen v. State Board of Elections*,[53] for example, applied the requirement of prior federal approval of changes in voting procedures not only to acts that might prevent blacks or other minorities from voting but also to acts that might dilute their voting strength. Even though the ability to cast a ballot would not be impaired, the *Allen* Court found that at-large elections could not be substituted for single-member district systems in states affected by the Voting Rights Act. Such a ruling implied that the act had almost no limits. It might now reach alterations of previous election practices, such as changing the location of polling places, that would only very indirectly affect the electoral process yet that would have the potential for diluting the votes of identifiable ethnic minority groups.

This implication was carried further in *Perkins v. Matthews*,[54] ruling that municipal annexations were changes in voting practices within the meaning of the Voting Rights Act. Such annexations presented the potential for racial gerrymandering, reasoned the Court, because the addition of new, white voters to a given jurisdiction could dilute black voting power. After *Perkins*, however, the Court ruled that an annexation changing a city's racial composition might still be permissible under the Voting Rights Act, if it furthered legitimate governmental goals and established a ward election system.[55]

The Court also held that the ward election system had to reflect only the black community's postannexation voting strength not its preannexation electoral power, and this seems difficult to reconcile with the holding in *Allen* that racial minorities have a statutory right to preserve their relative voting strength against the diluting effects of electoral change. Yet, if minority voting blocs are overrepresented in postannexation elections in order not to dilute their strength, this arrangement might violate the Fifteenth Amendment and contravene the Court's "one man, one vote" rule. Moreover, municipal annexation of white suburbs is a particularly important tool for integrating urban schools. Ironically, therefore, if the Court held that racially imbalanced annexations were on their face violations of the Voting Rights Act this would undercut its efforts to desegregate education.

Discrimination in Contractual Matters   Unquestionably, the most significant recent development in congressional power to protect civil rights has been the rediscovery of the Thirteenth Amendment. Before *Jones v. Alfred H. Mayer Co.*,[56] the Thirteenth Amendment, which prohibits slavery or involuntary servitude anywhere in the Unites States, was regarded as little more than a prohibition of chattel slavery. Thus, congressional power under this amendment has been viewed as relatively narrow. In *Jones*, however, the Court considered the case of a black man whose efforts to purchase a home in an exclusive suburb of St. Louis had been frustrated purely on account of his race. Joseph Lee Jones had then sought redress under the Civil Rights Act of 1866. This federal statute, which had lain dormant for over a century, provides that all citizens of the United States shall enjoy an equal right to inherit, purchase, lease, sell, hold, or convey real and personal property.

The lower federal courts dismissed Jones's claim on the ground that the 1866 act had been passed under Congress's power to enforce the Fourteenth Amendment, and that amendment requires some state action before the discrimination rises to a constitutional level. Since the Fourteenth Amendment prohibits racial discrimination only when a state is involved, congressional action enforcing that amendment could apply only to such instances; since there had been no state action in the denial of Jones's offer to buy a house, the Civil Rights Act of 1866 could not apply. So reasoned the lower courts.

The Supreme Court, however, took the position that the act had been an exercise of Congress's power to enforce the Thirteenth Amendment, which prohibits private as well as state actions. The *Jones* majority, speaking through Justice Stewart, emphasized that the Thirteenth Amendment, unlike the Fourteenth Amendment, affects private conduct, whether sanctioned by state law or not. Stewart went on to reason that the denial of a right to purchase or lease real property might be viewed as a badge of slavery. The Thirteenth Amendment was construed to forbid the infliction of such badges of slavery as well as imposition of the actual condition of slavery. It followed that under the Thirteenth Amendment Congress could enact legislation to prohibit discrimination not only by states but also by private individuals.

This view was further elaborated in *Sullivan v. Little Hunting Park, Inc.*,[57] holding that the 1866 Civil Rights Act prohibited discrimination in access to community facilities normally open to all owners or lessees of a property. In this case the owner of a home in a residential community in Fairfax County, Virginia, had leased his property to a black family, assigning to the family as part of the lease his membership share in a nonstock corporation organized to operate a park and swimming pool for residents of the community. The board of directors of the corporation, however, refused to approve the assignment because of the family's race. Taking a liberal view of congressional power under the Thirteenth Amendment, the Court found that the board's action violated the 1866 act.

Such an interpretation potentially transformed the Civil Rights Act of

1866 from a weapon for combatting racially restrictive housing covenants into a vehicle for attacking discrimination in most forms of commercial dealings. Following *Sullivan*, for instance, a black family seeking to buy a house could sue a bank for refusing to issue it a mortgage on the ground that the lender's refusal had been racially motivated and that the family's inability to obtain a mortgage interfered with its right to purchase real property. Similarly, since the 1866 Civil Rights Act applies to personal as well as to real property, people who felt that they had been denied credit by a store or finance company because of their race could also sue, alleging a violation of their rights under the act.[58]

That such prophecies were correct was acknowledged by *Runyon v. McCrary*.[59] In *Runyon*, the Court held that a private, nonsectarian school could not refuse to admit a black applicant, because such a refusal impaired the statutory right of the applicant's parents to enter into commercial contracts. The Court was quick to emphasize that, since its holding was based on the 1866 Civil Rights Act, it did not touch sex-segregated schools, and it avoided the question of how the 1866 act might affect parochial schools that practiced racial exclusion on religious grounds. But it did uphold congressional power to compel racial equality against Runyon's challenges based on constitutional rights to privacy, parental choice, and freedom of association.

RESTRICTIONS ON CONGRESSIONAL POWER

While the modern Court has been willing to indulge Congress's power to do good, as perceived by the Court, it has strictly scrutinized legislative efforts touching on other of the justices' subjective values. A corollary of the Court's broad recognition of congressional power to protect civil rights has been an increasingly severe restriction of Congress's power to categorize or to regulate various aspects of individual conduct.

Two milestones in the Court's history typify the change in judicial temperament: Despite numerous prior challenges, no act of Congress was ever struck down as violating the First Amendment until 1965;[60] and the first important case since 1936 to invalidate federal legislation for exceeding Congress's delegated power under the Constitution was decided in 1970.[61] During the past decade the Court has invoked its power of judicial review on more than thirty occasions. Among other things, it has limited the jurisdiction conferred on military tribunals, nullified efforts to aid sectarian higher education, and frustrated congressional reform of election campaign practices.[62]

Fifth Amendment "Equal Protection"

The most important tool for the contemporary Court's constraint of Congress has been its creation of a law of equal protection where none existed previously. As recently as 1937, the Court could dismiss a challenge to the constitutionality of the Social Security Act with the observation that the statute's exemptions did not violate the Fifth Amendment because that amendment, unlike the Fourteenth, had no equal protection clause;[63] and the equal protection claim was of little avail in combatting the exclusion and internment of a racial minority during the Second World War.[64] In 1954, however, the Supreme Court was practically forced to find some kind of equal protection restraint on Congress in order to avoid the creation of an anomalous situation. Having declared that racially segregated education violated the Fourteenth Amendment, the Court was faced with the fact that public schools within the District of Columbia were also segregated by act of Congress. Yet Congress is not restrained by the Fourteenth Amendment, which applies only to state action. The Court found it "unthinkable" that the Constitution should impose a lesser duty on the national government than on the states. Turning to the Fifth Amendment, the Court laid to rest racially separate education throughout the country with the cavalier observation that segregation "constitutes an arbitrary deprivation of . . . liberty in violation of the Due Process Clause," thus giving birth to a new constitutional right.[65]

Nonracial Classifications   The 1954 decision is understandable as an act of political necessity, though not of legal logic. But from little acorns such as this do mighty oak trees grow. Since its inception, the Fifth Amendment's unwritten equal protection provision has proved exceptionally vigorous. In *Frontiero v. Richardson*,[66] for example, the Court overturned congressional statutes discriminating on the basis of sex in the payment of fringe benefits to armed forces personnel. Under these statutes, a married servicewoman could obtain various dependent's allowances for her husband only if she could prove that she provided more than one-half of his living expenses, whereas married male members of the armed forces were granted these benefits automatically. The Court found this differential treatment to be unconstitutional, although no majority could agree on the exact contours of the Fifth Amendment protection against unequal treatment by the federal government.

While the result in *Frontiero* may be explained by the contemporary Court's growing sensitivity to gender-based classifications,[67] this does not explain *United States Dep't of Agriculture v. Moreno*,[68] another recent example of judicial invalidation of a congressional classification scheme. Eligibility for federal food stamps is determined on a household rather than an individual basis. To be eligible under the program, a household must have a collective monthly income of less than a specified amount. As originally drafted, the Federal Food Stamp Act of 1964 defined a "household" as a "group of related or non-related individuals ... living as one economic unit sharing cooking facilities and for whom food is customarily purchased in common."[69] In 1971, however, the act was amended to exclude from the definition of "household" groups of nonrelated individuals under the age of sixty.

Moreno held this exclusion an unconstitutional violation of the equal protection component of the Fifth Amendment due process clause, because it was not rationally related to some legitimate governmental interest. Inquiring into the governmental interest underlying the 1971 amendment, the *Moreno* majority concluded that what little legislative history there was indicated a desire on the part of Congress to prevent "hippie communes" or the "voluntary poor" from receiving food stamps. But this, the Court observed, could not be a legitimate governmental interest, for the doctrine of equal protection was specifically designed to inhibit legislative efforts to harm politically unpopular groups. The stated goals of the Food Stamp Act, however, were and are legitimate governmental interests: the alleviation of malnutrition and the stimulation of the nation's agricultural economy. Given these goals, the exclusion of households containing unrelated members was irrational; the familial relationships within a household have nothing to do with nutritional need or economic stimulation.

The difficulty with this line of reasoning, which is otherwise unexceptionable, is that it ignored the government's central argument in *Moreno*. The Department of Agriculture, which is charged with administering the food stamp program, had contended that exclusion was a rational means to prevent abuse of the program. Unrelated households were especially likely to contain abusers, and such abusers were difficult to detect. Congress could reasonably believe that unrelated households of persons under sixty were likely to be composed of low-income students and the voluntary poor, who actually have alternative sources of food money. Recognizing the importance of keeping welfare funds out of administration and in the hands of the truly poor, Congress might rationally conclude that it was better to eliminate an entire class of potential recipients than to allow the abuses to continue or to devote funds to the expensive process of weeding out the abusers. This was certainly a reasonable argument, if not a powerful one, but the Court simply dismissed it, noting that the government's position was unsubstantiated; yet precedent indicated that substantiation was not required. As in *Katzenbach v. McClung*, the law demanded only that Congress have some rational basis for finding a chosen regulatory scheme necessary.

Unenumerated Substantive Rights

Congressional efforts to introduce some measure of efficiency and economy into administration of the welfare program have been scuttled by the judicial creation of new, unenumerated, substantive rights as well as by the use of equal protection arguments. Thus, in *Washington v. Legrant* and its companion state cases, one-year residence requirements for the receipt of welfare payments were overturned by the Court.[70] These requirements discourage mass migrations of the poor into states providing significantly higher welfare benefits. State imposition of residence requirements was disposed of on equal protection grounds; the federal requirement was prohibited, according to the *Legrant* majority, because it would impede the constitutional right to travel interstate.

In dissent, Chief Justice Warren, joined by Justice Black, railed against the creation of a fundamental, unenumerated right to travel. Viewing the welfare program as a major experiment in cooperative federalism, the chief justice argued that, while the states could not constitutionally impose residence requirements, Congress could under its interstate commerce power. As Warren viewed the situation, Congress had authorized the states to enact such requirements. Almost unique in modern memory, however, *Legrant* represents a case in which congressional invocation of the commerce clause did not prevail.

THE COURT'S CURRENT STANCE

This judicial activism may not be simply a function of the Warren Court, a phenomenon of the past now that four Nixon appointees and a Ford appointee sit on the Supreme Court. As of 1976, only eight cases in the Court's history had declared congressional statutes unconstitutional on equal protection grounds, and six of them were decided by the Burger Court.[71] Moreover, the Burger Court has voided more national laws on First Amendment grounds than all of its predecessors combined. Thus, it can hardly be characterized accurately as self-restrained.

A striking example of this difference in judicial attitudes toward the executive and the legislative branches is afforded by the immunity from private suit that has been recognized for each. Under the niggardly interpretation accorded the speech or debate clause by *Doe v. McMillan*, a member of Congress who maliciously ordered the publication and distribution of a libelous statement would be subject to a defamation suit unless the legislator could prove that the release was necessary to "legislative acts." But an executive officer who did the same thing would not be liable, for in *Barr v. Mateo*,[72] adopting an expansive view of official immunity, the Court held that the acting director of a federal executive agency was absolutely privileged, without regard to malice, in issuing a libelous press statement designed to allocate blame for corruption that had been publicly exposed in his agency. Thus, while the cases dealing with legislative investigations have often taken the position that Congress has no authority to expose for the sake of exposure, *Barr* implicitly recognized that the executive branch does and may perform such an informing function.

"Even ... while tendering power under the enabling clauses of the Thirteenth, Fourteenth, and Fifteenth Amendments," the Court has behaved as if this power "were the Court's to grant."[73] *Oregon v. Mitchell*, for example, declared unconstitutional the Voting Rights Act Amendment of 1970, which attempted to lower the voting age to eighteen. Previously, the Court itself had used the equal protection clause to strike down state laws disenfranchising armed forces personnel, non-property-holders, and residents of federal enclaves. Since Congress's power to enforce the Fourteenth Amendment is theoretically as broad as that of the Court, these holdings lead necessarily to the conclusion that Congress had the power to prohibit state franchise discriminations that were nonracial as well as those that were racially based. But the Court held otherwise. While the *Mitchell* decision has been mooted by ratification of the Twenty-sixth Amendment, the fact remains that the Court has never upheld congressional invalidation of state action on nonracial grounds.

The Court has been willing to share with Congress the burden of solving the problem of racial discrimination. But, if the exercise of legislative power has moved too slowly or too cautiously for the Court's taste, it has shown a remarkable ingenuity in adapting old legislation to its purposes. *Jones v. Alfred H. Mayer Co.* not only revived the Civil Rights Act of 1866 to strike at discrimination in housing but also rendered the Civil Rights Act of 1968 inconsequential.

In the 1968 act, passed just before the decision in *Jones*, Congress had endeavored to promote open housing, but on a limited basis. The act was to take effect in three stages, and in none of them would it fully outlaw discrimination in the sale, rental, or lease of residential dwellings. The first stage, to become operative immediately on passage of the act, prohibited discrimination in federally assisted housing projects. The second stage, which began in 1969, extended coverage to include sales of homes by developers and sales of units in cooperative developments. It also affected the private sale or rental of residential property containing five or more dwelling units and one-family houses sold or rented by owners of more than three such houses. The third stage went into effect on January 1, 1970, when the act was extended to cover all one-family houses sold or rented with the aid of a real estate broker. However, single-family homes sold exclusively by the owner and apartments rented by owners of four or fewer units were not to be affected. By finding that the 1866 Civil Rights Act was based on the Thirteenth Amendment, which makes no such distinctions of degree, the *Jones* Court in effect precipitously extended federal fair housing legislation far beyond the coverage that the contemporary Congress in its wisdom had chosen to provide.

Congressional Response

As a consequence of this judicial behavior, it is not surprising that historically most retaliatory measures directed toward curbing the Court have been initiated by Congress, not the president. The Eleventh Amendment, designed to overturn *Chisholm v. Georgia*, the Fourteenth Amendment, securing the reversal of *Dred Scott*, and the Sixteenth Amendment, responding to *Pollock v. Farmers' Loan & Trust Co.* were all products of congressional action.[74] More recently, Senator Everett Dirksen's efforts in the 1960s to amend the Constitution to allow for public school prayer and to permit the states to apportion one house of their legislatures on some basis other than population, and Senator John Bricker's earlier proposal to limit the president's power to enter into treaties and executive agreements have enjoyed some support on Capitol Hill but not at the White House.

Similarly, attempts to reverse Supreme Court decisions by statute, some of them successful, have usually originated with Congress.[75] To speak only of the modern era, provisions of the Labor-Management Relations Act of 1947 were directed against certain of the Court's decisions. *Watkins* was followed by the introduction of a number of bills, none successful, to limit the Court's jurisdiction, and the Crime Control Act of 1968 may certainly be viewed as an expression of congressional opinion on the work of the Warren Court.

That so many of these congressional efforts to curtail the Court have failed may be attributed largely to the fact that the president, remaining benevolently neutral, has not lent them support. Indeed, the United States has not witnessed a major disturbance in the relations between the president and the Court since FDR's Court-packing plan of 1937. Even Richard Nixon, no fan of the Warren Court, limited himself to campaign invective and an aborted program for diminishing the quality of the justices by nominating acknowledged mediocrities—which was his constitutional prerogative, if not a wise policy. What might happen to the Court if some future President lent even tacit support to a congressional retribution effort is easy to predict, if not pleasant to contemplate. But thus far, by allying itself with the presidency, the Supreme Court has, more often than not, won its bet.

SUMMARY

Over time, the Supreme Court has been less indulgent of congressional power and policy making than of presidential authority. In contrast to its relatively infrequent and generally insignificant nullifications of presidential actions, the Court has on more than one hundred occasions invoked its power of judicial review to invalidate acts of Congress, and the incidence of the exercise of this power has increased, not decreased, in recent years.

In particular, the modern Court has been very restrictive in its decisions affecting Congress's internal operations. The Court has taken an unrealistic approach toward the scope of the investigatory function, impaired the informing function through its dilution of congressional immunity, and presumed to dictate to the House of Representatives concerning its own membership.

The Court has been more charitable in the matter of delegation of legislative power. But it might be argued that this is a part of the Court's favorable attitude toward the presidency, since most congressional delegations serve to strengthen the president's power.

When exercising its "external" powers, Congress has been given wider latitude by the Court. In the modern era, Congress's powers to tax, to regulate commerce, and to enforce the Reconstruction amendments have been broadly interpreted.

At the same time, however, the modern Court has recognized or created new personal rights that restrain Congress's sphere of action. Unlike the old, conservative Court that, from the late nineteenth century until 1937, took a very modest view of Congress's power, the contemporary Court has acknowledged expansive congressional regulatory power but has reserved to itself the authority to define the manner in which that power may or may not be used.

These twists in judicial ideology have influenced and been influenced by twists in popular ideology. The late nineteenth century was chary of government power generally. Modern Americans have been more positive about the exercise of public authority. But they have also exhibited less confidence in the quality of the legislative process than in presidential leadership and bureaucratic expertise.

In the wake of Watergate, there are signs that these attitudes may be changing. Indeed, the War Powers Resolution, the increasing use of congressional vetoes of administrative rules, and the cautious revitalization of the impeachment mechanism are all signs of increasing congressional energy in dealing with the presidency. If these represent enduring trends, they will find their way into Supreme Court decision making. But still Woodrow Wilson's 1885 observation that "Congress is establishing itself as the one sovereign authority in [the federal] government"[76] sounds odd, if not false, to the modern ear.

One can, however, readily concur with the first part of Wilson's sentence: "The central government is constantly becoming stronger and more active...."[77] Centralization of power in the federal government has been another major theme in American politics. While Congress has generally not fared as well at the hands of the Court as has the president, it has done considerably better than the states.

NOTES

1 143 U.S. 649 (1892).

2 220 U.S. 506 (1911).

3 The Brig Aurora, 11 U.S. (7 Cranch) 382 (1813).

4 Wayman v. Southard, 24 U.S. (10 Wheat.) 1 (1825).

5 Interstate Commerce Comm'n v. Illinois Cent. R.R., 215 U.S. 452 (1910).

6 293 U.S. 388 (1935).

7 295 U.S. 495 (1935).

8 312 U.S. 126 (1941).

9 312 U.S. at 144.

10 See, e.g., Zemel v. Rusk, 381 U.S. 1 (1965).

11 Wilcox v. Jackson, 38 U.S. (13 Pet.) 498 (1839).

12 See United States v. Curtiss-Wright Export Corp., 299 U.S. 304 (1936).

13 389 U.S. 934 (1967).

14 See Richard Funston, "The Judicialization of the Administrative Process," *American Politics Quarterly*, 2 (January 1974), 38-60.

15 103 U.S. 168 (1881).

16 McGrain v. Daugherty, 273 U.S. 135 (1927).

17 345 U.S. 41 (1953).

18 Quinn v. United States, 349 U.S. 155 (1955); Emspak v. United States, 349 U.S. 190 (1955).

19 354 U.S. 178 (1957).

20 Sweezy v. New Hampshire, 354 U.S. 234 (1957).

21 360 U.S. 109 (1959).

22 Uphaus v. Wyman, 360 U.S. 72 (1959).

23 Wilkinson v. United States, 365 U.S. 399 (1961); Braden v. United States, 365 U.S. 431 (1961).

24 E.g., Gibson v. Florida Legislative Investigation Comm., 372 U.S. 539 (1963).

25 Martin Shapiro, *Law and Politics in the Supreme Court* (New York: Free Press, 1964), p. 59.

26 Woodrow Wilson, *Congressional Government* (Boston: Houghton Mifflin Co., 1885), p. 303.

27 Shapiro, *Law and Politics*, p. 69.

28 U.S. Const. art. I, sec. 6.

29 408 U.S. 606 (1972).

30 412 U.S. 306 (1973).

31 421 U.S. 491 (1975).

32 412 U.S. at 312.

33 U.S. Const. art. I, sec. 5.

34 Powell v. McCormack, 395 U.S. 486 (1969).

35 369 U.S. 186 (1962).

36 376 U.S. 1 (1964).

37 See generally Charles A. Miller, *The Supreme Court and the Uses of History* (Cambridge: Harvard University Press, 1969), chap. VII.

38 See Kirkpatrick v. Preisler, 394 U.S. 526 (1969); White v. Weiser, 412 U.S. 783 (1973).

39 17 U.S. (4 Wheat.) 316 (1819).

40 17 U.S. (4 Wheat.) at 421.

41 17 U.S. (4 Wheat.) at 407.

42 17 U.S. (4 Wheat.) at 431.

43 Weston v. Charleston, 27 U.S. (2 Pet.) 449 (1829).

44 41 U.S. (16 Pet.) 435 (1842).

45 78 U.S. (11 Wall.) 113 (1871).

46 Graves v. New York *ex rel.* O'Keefe, 306 U.S. 466 (1939).

47 22 U.S. (9 Wheat.) 1 (1824).

48 53 U.S. (12 How.) 299 (1852).

49 Heart of Atlanta Motel, Inc. v. United States, 379 U.S. 241 (1964); Katzenbach v. McClung, 379 U.S. 294 (1964).

50 401 U.S. 424 (1971).

136   A VITAL NATIONAL SEMINAR

51 Albemarle Paper Co. v. Moody, 422 U.S. 405 (1975). See also McDonald v. Santa Fe Trail Co., 427 U.S. 273 (1976), in which the Court held that the legislative history of the ban on racial discrimination in private employment protected whites as well as non-whites. The white appellants, therefore, were successful in challenging their firing for misappropriating cargo when a black employee, charged with the same offense, had not been discharged.

52 381 U.S. 641 (1966).

53 393 U.S. 544 (1969).

54 400 U.S. 379 (1971).

55 City of Richmond v. United States, 422 U.S. 358 (1975).

56 392 U.S. 409 (1968).

57 396 U.S. 339 (1969).

58 A second and very significant aspect of the *Sullivan* decision involved the question of what judicial remedies were appropriate for the victim of private racial discrimination. The *Sullivan* Court found that the injured party could obtain monetary damages as well as injunctive relief.

In an important sequel to *Sullivan*, Griffin v. Breckenridge, 403 U.S. 88 (1971), the Court further expanded the range of federal civil remedies available to those discriminated against on the basis of their race. But see Paul v. Davis, 424 U.S. 693 (1976), which seems to modify *Griffin* substantially. It may be important to note, however, that *Paul* was decided under 42 U.S.C. sec. 1983 (1964), while *Griffin* involved an entirely different statute, 42 U.S.C. sec. 1985(3) (1964).

59 427 U.S. 160 (1976).

60 Lamont v. Postmaster-General, 381 U.S. 301 (1965).

61 Oregon v. Mitchell, 400 U.S. 112 (1970).

62 See O'Callahan v. Parker, 395 U.S. 258 (1969); Tilton v. Richardson, 403 U.S. 672 (1971); Buckley v. Valeo, 424 U.S. 1 (1976).

63 Steward Machine Co. v. Davis, 301 U.S. 548 (1937).

64 Hirabayashi v. United States, 320 U.S. 81 (1943); Korematsu v. United States, 323 U.S. 214 (1944).

65 Bolling v. Sharpe, 347 U.S. 497, 500 (1954).

66 411 U.S. 677 (1973).

67 The constitutional status of sex-based discrimination is discussed in chapter VI. See, e.g., Weinberger v. Wiesenfeld, 420 U.S. 636 (1975) (Social Security Act's granting of survivor's benefits to widows with dependent children but not to similarly situated widowers held unconstitutional).

68 413 U.S. 528 (1973).

69 7 U.S.C. sec. 2012(e) (1970). See generally 7 U.S.C. secs. 2011-25 (1970).

70 394 U.S. 618 (1964); Shapiro v. Thompson, Reynolds v. Smith, 394 U.S. 618 (1969).

71 The trend continued unabated in 1977. See Califano v. Goldfarb, ___U.S.___, 97 S. Ct. 1021 (1977), and Califano v. Webster, ___ U.S. ___, 97 S. Ct. 1192 (1977), both invalidating sections of the Social Security Act on equal protection grounds. Interestingly, both involved questions of sex-based discrimination; see note 67 above.

72 360 U.S. 564 (1959).

73 Philip B. Kurland, *Politics, the Constitution, and the Warren Court* (Chicago: University of Chicago Press, 1970), p. 87.

74 Chisholm v. Georgia, 2 U.S. (2 Dall.) 419 (1793); Dred Scott v. Sandford, 60 U.S. (19 How.) 393 (1857); Pollock v. Farmers' Loan & Trust Co., 157 U.S. 429 (1895); Pollock v. Farmers' Loan & Trust Co., 158 U.S. 601 (1895).

75 See generally Note, "Congressional Reversal of the Supreme Court, 1945-1957," *Harvard Law Review*, 71 (May 1958), 1324-37.

76 Wilson, *Congressional Government*, p. 316.

77 Ibid.

SUGGESTED ADDITIONAL READING

Barber, Sotirios A. *The Constitution and the Delegation of Congressional Power.* Chicago: University of Chicago Press, 1975.

Beck, Carl. *Contempt of Congress.* New Orleans: Hauser Press, 1959.

Dunne, Gerald T. *Monetary Decisions of the Supreme Court.* New Brunswick, N.J.: Rutgers University Press, 1960.

Frankfurter, Felix. *The Commerce Clause under Marshall, Taney and Waite.* Chapel Hill: University of North Carolina Press, 1937.

Murphy, Walter F. *Congress and the Court.* Chicago: University of Chicago Press, 1962.

Pritchett, C. Herman. *Congress versus the Supreme Court, 1957-1960.* Minneapolis: University of Minnesota Press, 1961.

Schmidhauser, John R., and Larry Berg. *The Supreme Court and Congress: Conflict and Interaction, 1945-1968.* New York: Free Press, 1972.

Shapiro, Martin. *The Supreme Court and Administrative Agencies.* New York: Free Press, 1968.

Truman, David B., ed. *The Congress and America's Future.* Englewood Cliffs, N.J.: Prentice-Hall, 1965.

THE COURT AND THE STATES

CHAPTER 5

"It is one of the happy incidents of a federal system," Justice Brandeis once wrote, "that a single courageous state may, if its citizens choose, serve as a laboratory and try novel social or economic experiments."[1] While that may be the case, it is also true that the Supreme Court has shown little solicitude for experimentation. Rather, the history of American federalism has generally been a story of the diminution of state power, with the Court serving as one of the principal agents of nationalization.

THE FEDERAL SYSTEM

In the American constitutional system power is divided spatially as well as functionally. In addition to separating powers at the national level, the Constitution also establishes a federal system. There are two reasons for the creation of this dual sovereignty. Historically, the original colonies regarded themselves as entities independent from one another. Following their declaration of independence from Britain, the new states each assumed the sovereignty previously exercised by the Crown. This arrangement was confirmed by the character of the Articles of Confederation government. By the time the Constitutional Convention convened, therefore, the states were too well established to be abolished. But the Framers saw this as fortuitous, for they did not consider federalism less desirable philosophically because it was inevitable historically. To cure the mischief of faction, the Founders advocated a geographically extensive republic. But then to prevent the accumulation of too much power in the central government, to keep government close to the people, and to enhance local decision-making control they advocated decentralization of political power. They saw the federal principle, therefore, as necessary to the promotion of a good regime.

The Federal-State Division of Power

The relationships among the various states and between the states and the central government is, in part, constitutionally prescribed. But it was impossible for the Framers to draw neat and precise lines between the powers of the states, on the one hand, and those of the national government, on the other. Categoric statements about the actual powers possessed by either jurisdiction are, therefore, impossible. Constitutional law and American politics would be greatly simplified if it were possible to say that certain functions (such as control over educational matters) are always performed by the states, while other powers (control of banking and commerce, for example) are exclusively accorded to the federal government. But such statements cannot be made; or, if they are made, they fail to describe the actual conduct of American government.

The powers of the states are nowhere enumerated in the Constitution. Instead, the Tenth Amendment reserves unspecified residual powers to them. If pressed to define these reserved powers, the constitutional scholar will usually beg the question by relying on that vaguest of all constitutional concepts, "the police power"—the power to legislate for the health, welfare, safety, or morals of the citizenry. It can be inferred that the states are to prescribe voter qualifications, but the federal government is empowered by the Fourteenth, Fifteenth, Seventeenth, Nineteenth, and Twenty-sixth Amendments to take certain actions in the same field. It can be inferred that the states have the power to establish their own militias, but the National Guard can be called into national service and sometimes, as in Arkansas in 1957, has even been used to quash the acts of its own state officials.

Nor is the authority of the national government necessarily exclusive, for the states may share a concurrent power, for example in the construction of roads. This bifurcation of governmental authority has led to the development of numerous joint, cooperative federal-state programs that, like several other aspects of the constitutional system, no political philosopher has been able to fit into a coherent theory. But that should not be surprising, because the American Constitution does what is theoretically impossible: It divides sovereignty.

Like other constitutional relationships, the division of power under federalism is constantly evolving. Even if the Framers had been able to draw a clear line of demarcation between the spheres of federal and state authority, that line would have needed revision from time to time to meet new and changed conditions. Far from precluding conflict between federal and state authorities, therefore, the distribution of powers agreed on at the Constitutional Convention actually invited it and made it inevitable. The struggle was continued in politics, it flowed over into the courts, and eventually the contestants carried it to the battlefield in the Civil War. However, the North's victory merely established the supremacy of the Union over the individual states. The problem of determining the extent of national and state power and of resolving conflicts between the two centers of authority within the federal system was left to the Supreme Court.

THE COURT'S AUTHORITY OVER STATE COURTS

Today we accept almost without question that the Supreme Court should be the agency to referee the federal-state division of power. But the Court's position was achieved after a history of far more struggle than is generally remembered. In the formative era the sentiment that the Supreme Court should have final and authoritative say in matters of federal-state relations was a good deal less universal and well entrenched than it is now. The Court's role in relation to the states was intertwined with the question of the nature of the Union, the principal legal and political issue of the first seventy years of the nation's existence. Indeed, while John Marshall's assertion of the power of judicial review went almost unchallenged, he had much greater trouble in establishing the Court's ultimate authority over the states. It was not until seven years after *Marbury* that he first exercised the Court's power to declare a state statute unconstitutional, in what was an extremely unpopular decision. It took even longer for the Court to gain acceptance of its power to review decisions of state courts on appeal and, if necessary, to reverse them.

The *Martin* Case

The controversy over appellate jurisdiction first presented itself in the case of *Martin v. Hunter's Lessee.*[2] During the Revolution, Virginia had confiscated the lands of the loyalist Lord Fairfax. Following the war, Fairfax's heirs sought to recover the land. Such recoveries were provided for by the Treaty of Paris, which the United States and Great Britain had negotiated to terminate the hostilities. The Virginia courts, however, upheld that state's anti-alien-inheritance statutes and denied the heirs' claim, despite their rights under the federal treaty.

Section 25 of the Judiciary Act of 1789 had provided that state courts should exercise a concurrent jurisdiction with the federal judiciary in some cases, with an appeal going to the Supreme Court, if specified conditions were met. The measure had clearly been framed with economy in mind: The idea had been to use the existing judicial machinery of the states to try federal cases, thereby relieving Congress of the expense of creating a large federal court system with numerous judges. Since their case fell within the terms of the Judiciary Act, the Fairfax heirs appealed.

Chief Justice Marshall, who had previously been involved in the case, absented himself from the bench. Even without him, the Supreme Court ruled in favor of the heirs and reversed the Virginia courts, but the Virginia Supreme Court, speaking through its highly regarded chief justice, Spencer Roane, declared section 25 of the Judiciary Act unconstitutional and refused to carry out the Supreme Court's decision. A second *Martin* appeal was then taken to the Supreme Court.

With Marshall again absent, Justice Joseph Story delivered the opinion of the Court. Under article III, he noted, Congress has the right to assign the federal judicial power. It might have vested all such power in a federal judiciary, but it had seen fit to vest part of this power in the state courts. This grant of concurrent power did not divest the Supreme Court of jurisdiction, however, for the Court's jurisdiction depends on the nature of the case and not on the nature of the court in which the action was first filed. Since the Court's jurisdiction in such cases is not original, it must be appellate. This appellate jurisdiction is necessary, Story continued, first, to prevent injustices that might be committed by state judges moved by local prejudices and, secondly, to ensure uniformity of federal law throughout the United States. In essence, then, state courts had, for certain purposes, been incorporated into the federal judicial system.

The *Cohens* Case

The decision in *Martin* was bitterly attacked throughout the South and particularly in Virginia, where the leading critic was Chief Justice Roane. Writing in a series of pseudonymous pamphlets, Roane contended that the Constitution had not intended to establish a consolidated union. It was true that state judges were bound by the supremacy clause, but in Roane's view that were bound as *state* judges. They had not been and could not be incorporated into the federal judiciary. As the courts of last resort within their respective jurisdictions, state supreme courts were precisely that, courts of *last* resort, and their decisions were final in cases originally filed within their jurisdictions. Such a system, Roane readily admitted, would probably produce a lack of uniformity in the interpretation of federal law, including the Constitution, but this problem should be resolved by interstate diplomacy, not by central judicial power. To allow the national government—that is, the Supreme Court—to be the judge of the limits of its own power would be dangerous to popular liberty.

Marshall's answer to Roane came in the case of *Cohens v. Virginia*.[3] The Cohens brothers had been convicted of selling lottery tickets in Virginia, contrary to state law. They claimed protection, however, under a congressional franchise authorizing them to sell such tickets for a District of Columbia lottery. When they appealed the state court verdict, counsel for Virginia denied the constitutionality of section 25 of the Judiciary Act and denied that Virginia could be sued by the Cohenses' appeal, given the eleventh Amendment.

Dispensing with the first contention, Marshall began by observing that the Constitution implies that the federal courts exercise a double jurisdiction. The first is determined by the nature of the case—that is, it includes cases arising under the Constitution, laws, and treaties of the United States. The second is determined by the nature of the parties—for example, it includes cases in which the United States may be a party or those between two or more states. By ratifying the Constitution, Marshall argued, the states had surrendered part of their sovereignty to the federal union. While the federal government is limited in its powers, it must be supreme within its sphere of action, and within that sphere all state laws must conform to the Constitution and laws of the United States.

> That the United States form, for many, and for most important purposes, a single nation, has not yet been denied. In war, we are one people. In making peace, we are one people. In all commercial regulations, we are one and the same people. In many other respects, the American people are one; and the government which is alone capable of controlling and managing their interests, in all these respects, is the government of the Union. It is their government, and in that character they have no other. America has chosen to be, in many respects, and to many purposes, a nation; and for all these purposes her government is complete; to all these objects, it is competent. The people have declared, that in the exercise of all powers given for these objects, it is supreme. It can, then, in effecting these objects, legitimately control all

individuals or governments within the American territory. The
constitution and laws of a State, so far as they are repugnant to
the constitution and laws of the United States, are absolutely
void. These States are constituent parts of the United States.
They are members of one great empire—for some purposes sovereign,
for some purpose subordinate.[4]

In order to maintain national supremacy within its appropriate sphere, the Supreme Court had to exercise an appellate jurisdiction over state judiciaries.

Nor did the Eleventh Amendment protect Virginia, in Marshall's view. Strictly construing that provision, which denies jurisdiction to the federal courts in any suit "commenced or prosecuted against any of the United States by Citizens of another State," Marshall ruled that the *Cohens* case did not fall within its prohibition, because the Cohenses had not commenced the action. This was merely an appeal from a legal action begun by the state. Marshall then awarded Virginia a nominal victory by finding that the congressional lottery ordinance under which the Cohens brothers had been operating had been limited to the District of Columbia and, thus, when the brothers had crossed the Potomac to sell their tickets in Virginia they had exceeded the limits of their commission.

Like *Martin*, the decision in *Cohens* was vigorously criticized in the South. But it stood—first, because President Monroe passively approved of it and, secondly, because Marshall had used the same tactic he had applied in *Marbury*—by deciding the surface issue in their favor, he gave his opponents no way to avoid his ruling. Virginia was not about to set the Cohenses free in protest of the Great Chief Justice's opinion. Marshall's victory was then consummated three years later in *Gibbons v. Ogden*,[5] Marshall's last major opinion, voiding a state-granted monopoly over steamboat traffic between New York and New Jersey because it conflicted with the Federal Coasting Act. As an antimonopoly expression, *Gibbons* enjoyed great popularity; its nationalistic implications were generally overlooked.

THE COURT'S DIVISION OF POWER

Establishing the Court as the agency empowered to determine the relations between the federal and state governments was only the first step. The second was to chart the actual division of power. In other words, once it had been agreed, however reluctantly, that the Supreme Court was to declare which functions belonged to the states and which to the federal government at any given time, the next question was which powers did in fact belong to which jurisdiction.

The Tenth Amendment

In theory, the powers of the federal government are limited to those delegated to it by the Constitution. *McCulloch v. Maryland*,[6] of course, advanced the proposition that these powers might be delegated implicitly as well as expressly. In order to give effect to any specifically granted power, the federal government may, through the necessary and proper clause, employ any and all means not explicitly prohibited by the Constitution. But the necessary and proper clause does not, at least in theory, grant any new or additional powers to the federal government. Moreover, the Tenth Amendment does provide that the "powers not delegated to the United States by the Constitution, nor prohibited by it to the States, are reserved to the States respectively, or to the people."

Over the years, however, judicial interpretation has nearly reduced the Tenth Amendment to a truism. To be sure, all powers not granted to the federal government are reserved to the states; but in modern times what powers are not granted to the federal government?

National power is three-dimensional. There is, first, the sum of the constitutional grants of power. Next there is the discretionary choice of means of executing the enumerated powers. Finally, there is the supremacy clause directive that, if legitimate exercises of federal and state powers conflict, the former shall prevail. Under this three-dimensional scheme of national authority, no subject matter whatever is withdrawn from federal control or regulation simply because it also lies within the traditional domain of state power. According to this view, any power exercised by the states is also enjoyed concurrently by Congress, even though the only example of a power expressly delegated as concurrent is the now-defunct Eighteenth Amendment. Powers delegated to the federal government, on the other hand, are exclusive under the following conditions:

(1) if the right to exercise the power is made exclusive by the Constitution's express delegation (for example, Congress is given exclusive jurisdiction to legislate for the District of Columbia);

(2) if one section of the Constitution grants a power to Congress and another section prohibits the states from exercising a similar power (for example, Congress is given the power to coin money, and the states are expressly prohibited from doing so); or

(3) if a power granted to the federal government, though not stated in exclusive terms, is such that the exercise of a similar power by the states would be incompatible.

The Marshall Court's View

This state of constitutional affairs is the product of many decades of Supreme Court decision making. But its broad, recognizable outlines were traced by the Marshall Court. Marshall extended federal judicial authority over state courts and state legislatures, while liberally construing the powers granted to the national government. Marshall's doctrine of national supremacy was built on the proposition that the Constitution had been implemented by the people of the United States; he did not see it as a compact among the several states. The central government and the states, therefore, confronted each other in the relation of superior and subordinate. If the exercise of Congress's express or implied powers was legitimate, the fact that this exercise encroached on the states' powers was of no significance. For Marshall the principal danger to the federal system lay in erosive state action, not in unrestrained national power.

Developments under the Taney Court

Marshall's doctrines did not go unchallenged. The concept of federalism held by his most extreme critics saw the Constitution as a compact of sovereign states not an ordinance of the people. Although Marshall's successor, Roger Brooke Taney, did not share this view, the Court under his leadership did try to redefine federalism in terms more favorable to the states. In *Briscoe v. Bank of Kentucky*,[7] for example, the Taney Court held that bank notes issued by a state-owned and state-controlled bank were not bills of credit within the meaning of the Constitution and might, therefore, validly circulate. *Briscoe* severely limited an earlier decision of Marshall's, if it did not actually overrule it, and, coupled with the simultaneous decline of the Bank of the United States, severely undermined the Constitution's limitations on state issuance of currency.

Similarly, in *Bank of Augusta v. Earle*,[8] Chief Justice Taney granted the general right of a corporation to do business within other states under interstate comity, but then recognized the right of a state to take positive action to exclude corporations not chartered by itself. The dissenters argued that such a course would be disastrous to national business enterprise. Again, in *Charles River Bridge v. Warren Bridge*,[9] Taney held that any ambiguity in a public contract must be construed in the state's favor. While *Charles River Bridge* did enhance state power, it did not do so at the expense of national power, however; nor did it overturn the fundamental principle of Marshall's holding in *Dartmouth College v. Woodward*,[10] that a charter of incorporation is a contract within the meaning of the contract clause and, thus, constitutionally protected from state impairment.

Indeed, the Taney Court did not move far from Marshall's conception of federal judicial power in relation to the states. Marshall's limited view of federal admiralty jurisdiction was even reversed by Taney, who extended the scope of federal judicial power to encompass the Great Lakes and all of the country's navigable streams. *Swift v. Tyson*[11] asserted that, in matters of general law, when the federal courts exercised jurisdiction in a case because the parties were citizens of different states and there was no controlling statute, federal judges were free to form judgments independent of the prior rulings of the state courts. And in *Ableman v. Booth*[12] Taney reversed an attempt by the Wisconsin Supreme Court to interfere with the federal fugitive slave law, issuing a ringing statement of national supremacy that out-Marshalls Marshall. Taney, in short, did not break sharply with the Marshall tradition. At most, he was a moderate dual federalist. And the final arbiter of the scope of state power remained, for him, the United States Supreme Court.

For Marshall's concept of national supremacy the Taney Court substituted a theory of federal equilibrium. Perhaps its most famous statement on the issue, *Cooley v Board of Wardens*,[13] is essentially a compromise between the apologists of states' rights and the extreme advocates of national power. But it is a compromise that does not elevate the states to a position of parity with the federal government. As Roscoe Pound facetiously observed, commenting on the doctrine of selective exclusiveness:

> Now congress has a wonderful power that only judges and lawyers know about. Congress has a power to keep silent. Congress can regulate interstate commerce just by not doing anything about it. Of course when congress keeps silent, it takes an expert to know what it means. But the judges are experts. They say that congress by keeping silent sometimes means that it is keeping silent and sometimes means that it is speaking. If congress keeps silent about the interstate commerce that is not national in character and that may just as well be regulated by the states, then congress is silently silent, and the states may regulate. But if congress keeps silent about the kind of commerce that is national in character and ought to be regulated only by congress, then congress is silently vocal and says that the commerce must be free from state regulation.[14]

Not only is a silently vocal legislature a fiction, but it is also a concept difficult to reconcile with the constitutionally prescribed legislative process. The *Cooley* Court's recognition of a congressional power to legislate by silence, after all, leaves no role for the president to play.

The Post-Civil War Policy

Once recovered from the debacle of *Dred Scott*, an essentially business-oriented Court did revive the Tenth Amendment and again invoke the doctrine of dual federalism. Certain areas of economic life were held to be within the exclusive purview of state legislation, and in such areas Congress could not legislate because that would contravene the principles of federalism. But this position was hardly motivated by judicial solicitude for state power. The Taney Court had upheld state power in order to deal with certain economic or social problems, because the states were at that time the only governmental entities capable of dealing with them; the post-Civil War, laissez-faire Court, on the contrary, upheld state power because it knew that the states were in fact powerless to deal with such business problems as the trusts.

State Regulation as Violation of Due Process   In those areas where the states might meaningfully regulate corporate activity, the Supreme Court after 1890 erected the due process clause of the Fourteenth Amendment as a substantive bar to state legislation. Rather than treating the concept of due process as a merely procedural guarantee, the Court found in it an independent, identifiable content that coincidentally was closely tied to the doctrines of laissez-faire economics. It was not enough to satisfy the due process requirement that government decisions were arrived at through a fundamentally fair process. Instead, some decisions always denied due process, no matter how fair the procedures used to arrive at them. Invariably, these decisions involved the regulation of business enterprise. For example, state efforts to prevent cutthroat competition or usurious railroad practices were held unconstitutional. According to this conception, most state regulatory legislation by its very nature as regulation violated the due process clause and was absolutely prohibited.

The Court did countenance state regulation of businesses affected with a public interest, but it also held that it was the judiciary and ultimately the Supreme Court itself that had the constitutional authority to determine which businesses were affected with a public interest and, hence, subject to regulation. Increasingly the Court took a narrow view of the categories of business affected with a public interest, eventually including only public utilities, monopolies, and a handful of others (such as hotels) that had for centuries been regarded by the common law as affected with a public interest. Moreover, even these businesses could be regulated only in a reasonable manner, and the Court went on to establish that the judiciary would make an independent determination of a statute's reasonableness. According to the Court's view, a reasonable legislative regulation was one that permitted a fair return on the value invested, and the Court's definition of a fair return can only be described as most congenial to the captains of industry.

Liberty of Contract   A second line of cases decided under the due process clause of the Fourteenth Amendment held further that there were substantive limits on the states' power to restrict liberty, in particular the liberty to enter into contractual agreements. This doctrine of liberty of contract was introduced into constitutional law directly from laissez-faire economics. It asserted that, whenever two parties came together to enter into a contract that was not inherently contrary to the public welfare and did not violate a criminal statute, the legislature had no power to interfere with either the terms of the agreement or the conditions under which it was to be performed.

In application, this meant that maximum hours and minimum wage legislation was unconstitutional. The Court might permit the regulation of hours in admittedly hazardous occupations, such as mining, or for women, given the "general knowledge" of woman's frailty.[15] But liberty of contract was the rule, not the exception, and the burden of proof rested on the states to demonstrate that their regulation of that liberty was reasonable. Not surprisingly, few could shoulder that burden. Wage and hour legislation was, at best, constitutionally suspect. In essence, the doctrine of liberty of contract was, as Justice Holmes charged, a medium by which economically conservative justices read their own social preferences and prejudices into the Constitution of the United States.

The New Deal Court and After

This practice was curtailed in the economic realm once the Court and Franklin Roosevelt came to a meeting of the minds. But their agreement hardly constituted a victory for state regulatory power. Once the New Deal's adherents gained a majority on the Court, it virtually bowed out of the business of economics; Congress then bowed in, and, under the doctrine of preemption, when Congress occupies a field, the states are forbidden to legislate in that area. Thus, the states were little better off after 1937 than they had been before.

Generally the modern Court has deferred to Congress and limited state regulatory power through application of the doctrine of selective exclusiveness. Given the nature of modern business enterprise, the aspects of interstate commerce that might still be regulated by the states—those in which a uniform national rule is unnecessary—have become fewer and fewer. After a little more than a century and a half, then, the Court has come almost full circle, arriving where it set out in this field of adjudication, *Gibbons v. Ogden.*

Expansion of Federal Habeas Corpus   The post-New Deal Court also returned to another of Marshall's principal concerns in the area of federalism, federal court control of state judicial proceedings. This was accomplished through the Court's nationalization of the Bill of Rights, to be discussed shortly, and the redefinition of federal habeas corpus policy.

Traditionally, the Great Writ—the writ of habeas corpus—was available only to a prisoner who challenged the jurisdiction of the court under whose authority he was being held or who argued that he was being restrained by the executive branch of government in excess of its lawful power. The Federal Habeas Corpus Act of 1867, however, provided that the federal courts should hear the habeas petition of any person, including a state prisoner, claiming to be "in custody in violation of the Constitution of the United States."[16] In 1953, in *Brown v. Allen*,[17] the Supreme Court concluded that this language meant that *any* constitutional challenge to state imprisonment was reviewable in a federal court in a habeas corpus proceeding.

The significance of this holding was not immediately apparent. But, when coupled with tremendous expansion of the scope and application of constitutional rights through Supreme Court interpretations during the 1960s, the result was to convert *Brown* into a means for federal control of state criminal courts. The Great Writ's original concerns about excessive executive actions or improper court jurisdiction faded into obscurity. Then, in a brace of cases decided in 1963, the Court went further and ruled that state prisoners' constitutional claims were subjected to federal habeas review even if those claims had been fully and fairly adjudicated in the state courts.[18] As a consequence, every constitutional issue raised in a state trial could be litigated twice: once by the state courts at trial and on appeal and once by the federal judiciary in a habeas corpus proceeding. Predictably, the number of constitutional issues raised in state trials multiplied rapidly.

Indeed, a state prisoner might even raise issues he had failed to raise at trial. Before 1963 the accepted view had been that only the decision of the trial court was subject to review on habeas corpus. If a defendant did not raise a particular constitutional claim at trial, obviously the trial court would not rule on it, and thus the issue would be foreclosed from habeas review. Now, however, the Supreme Court adopted the position that federal courts had habeas corpus jurisdiction whenever a person in custody challenged his detention on constitutional grounds, whether or not the grounds were within the scope of the state court's ruling. Relief should be denied only if the applicant had failed to raise the issue at trial in an effort to "deliberately bypass" state court procedure. Unfortunately, the Court did not elaborate on what would constitute a deliberate bypass.

Similarly, the accepted rule had been that a state prisoner must exhaust all state remedies before petitioning the federal courts for relief. Now the Supreme Court found that this did not really mean *all* state remedies. Federal courts would have jurisdiction once the applicant's claim had been considered by the state courts on direct appeal; prisoners need not apply for state habeas corpus before turning to the federal courts. Nor did the applicant have to be actually in prison. The federal habeas corpus statute provides that the writ shall not extend to a prisoner unless he is in custody, but the Court concluded that being on parole was sufficient custody to give the federal courts jurisdiction over the matter. The result of this expansion of federal habeas corpus beyond review of a court's jurisdiction over a prisoner was to inundate the lower federal courts with habeas petitions, while leaving the states in great uncertainty about the finality of their criminal convictions.

Federal Injunctions Against State Prosecutions   Even more severe inroads into state court proceedings were countenanced by *Dombrowski v. Pfister*.[19] Direct federal intervention in ongoing state prosecutions was mandated by the Supreme Court there. Decided at the height of the civil rights movement when there was great concern over the harassment of civil rights workers by state officials in the South, *Dombrowski* permitted the federal courts to enjoin the enforcement of state criminal statutes.

The *Dombrowski* Court reasoned that the threat of prosecution under overbroad statutes that affected freedom of expression would have a "chilling effect" on the exercise of First Amendment rights. The opinion was not clear, however, about whether the mere existence of such statutes was sufficient to trigger federal relief or whether bad faith enforcement was a prerequisite. In any case, *Dombrowski* drastically increased the applications for federal injunctions against state law enforcement and, like the habeas corpus decisions, further exacerbated frictions between state and federal courts.

The Burger Court and the New Federalism

During the 1970s the Court has made efforts to reverse the trend toward federal intervention in state proceedings and more generally to correct disruptions of the balance of federalism. Under Chief Justice Burger, the Supreme Court has curtailed the availability of federal habeas corpus review, confined the scope of *Dombrowski*, given at least passing recognition to the Tenth Amendment, and even struck down a congressional effort to prescribe state voter qualifications. But each of these decisions is likely to be of limited significance.

Limits on Federal Habeas   *Stone v. Powell*[20] limited federal court review on habeas corpus of state court applications of the "exclusionary rule"—a rule that prohibits the admission at trial of evidence seized in violation of the Fourth Amendment. Emphasizing the nature of the government illegality and the fairness of the state process of review, a six-man majority concluded that the benefits of further federal habeas review did not outweigh its costs. The Court noted that state courts have equal responsibility with the federal judiciary for interpreting and enforcing the Constitution and that it would be inadmissible to presume that state judges would not discharge this duty with care and fidelity. The Court also emphasized that federal consideration of claims that had already been rejected by two or more levels of state courts tended to be an inefficient use of the nation's limited judicial resources. *Stone*, therefore, prohibited federal judges from entertaining habeas corpus allegations that evidence had been admitted in violation of the exclusionary rule if the state had provided the opportunity for a full and fair adjudication of the Fourth Amendment claim.

Stone, however, may be read as suggesting that the Fourth Amendment's exclusionary rule is merely a judicially created rule of evidence designed to deter illegal police conduct, not a constitutional right. If that is so, *Stone* can be reconciled with the ruling in *Brown v. Allen* that all constitutional claims are proper subjects for federal habeas corpus petitions. All constitutional claims remain reviewable on habeas; the exclusionary rule is simply not such a claim. The *Stone* majority did not state that this was its view, however; it merely indicated in a puzzling footnote its belief that the holding was limited to the Fourth Amendment context.

Limits on Federal Injunctions   The Burger Court decision in *Younger v. Harris* blunted the impact of *Dombrowski* by requiring that, before federal injunctive relief can be granted against a state criminal action in progress, the complaining party must show that state officials have no reasonable expectation of ultimately prevailing on the merits and are enforcing the law in bad faith against an individual or group merely for harassment.[21] This rule was subsequently extended to state-initiated civil cases.[22] But the Court has also ruled that *Younger's* doctrine of federal abstention does not apply if the challenged proceedings are "extrajudicial" in nature or if a state prosecution is merely threatened but has not yet been commenced.[23] *Younger*, then, represents some judicial fine tuning rather than an outright rule against federal court intervention in state judicial processes.

Tenth Amendment Interpretation   In 1976 the Court did acknowledge the possibility that the Tenth Amendment might, under some circumstances, prevent federal regulation of the states and their institutions. *National League of Cities v. Usery*[24] found that the amendment prevented congressional control of the wages and hours of almost all state and municipal employees. The justices, however, were bitterly divided, and the decision's closest student has concluded, "One cannot read the several opinions of the case and be confident about its future.... [S]overeignty over state employees may be the only thing left [for the states] to claim at this late date in the advance of national power."[25] The Tenth Amendment is not likely to be resurrected, nor did *National League of Cities* attempt to do that. In fact, the majority expressly distinguished and approved the Court's decision of only the previous year upholding the application of a federally imposed wage freeze to state and local employees.[26]

Federal Imposition of Voter Qualifications   The tortured constitutional construction in *National League of Cities* is reminiscent of the reasoning in *Oregon v. Mitchell*,[27] mentioned in chapter 4. There the Court, by a studied rejection of its own precedents, denied Congress the power to lower the voting age to eighteen in state elections. But this was not the only surprising reading of constitutional law to be found in *Mitchell*.

Although article I, section 4, which permits Congress to alter state regulation of the "Times, Places and Manner" of holding elections to the Senate and House of Representatives had previously been interpreted as merely a means for Congress to prohibit electoral irregularities such as vote fraud, the Court in *Mitchell* converted this into a grant of power to Congress to regulate voter qualifications in federal elections. Therefore, in spite of the fact that the Constitution explicitly grants to the states the power to specify voter qualifications for congressional elections and implicitly seems to give the states control over the process for choosing presidential electors, the *Mitchell* Court upheld Congress's lowering of the voting age in congressional and presidential elections. It also sustained the congressional prohibition of literacy and other tests as prerequisites for voting and federal establishment of a state residence requirement for voting in presidential elections. Finally, as noted in chapter 4, the section of *Oregon v. Mitchell* that overturned the lowering of the voting age in state elections was itself reversed by ratification of the Twenty-sixth Amendment within six months of the decision.

EXPANSIONS OF FEDERAL POWER

The Court's attitude toward the proper distribution of power in the federal system, thus, has made only a partial shift. Despite these recent developments, the general trend of Supreme Court decision making in the area of federalism has historically been toward expansion of *McCulloch* and denigration of the Tenth Amendment. The Court, to be sure, has not been the sole or even the chief cause of the nationalization of American political problems and processes. At most, it has contributed to that transformation, and in many ways its decisions have merely ratified choices made elsewhere. The evolution of the business corporation has undoubtedly had more to do with the nationalization of political issues, the centralization of government power, and the decline of federalism than the Supreme Court has. But, in adjusting the federal-state balance of power, the Court, as a branch of the national government, has a vested interest in seeing that the balance is struck in favor of federal power.

"I do not think the United States would come to an end if we, the Supreme Court, lost our power to declare an act of Congress void," Justice Oliver Wendell Holmes once declared. "I do think the Union would be imperiled if we could not make that declaration as to the laws of the several states. One in my place sees how often a local policy prevails with those not trained to national views."[28] While Holmes's observation may very well be correct, it is also symptomatic of the effect that service on the nation's highest Court can have on a judge's perspective. It is sometimes argued forcefully, even lyrically, that the Court functions as a balance wheel in the federal system, countering not only the provincialism of state legislation but also the centralizing tendencies of congressional and presidential policy. The Court, in a metaphor favored by some, is the umpire of the federal system. Be that as it may, "the Court has no more achieved neutrality between the interests of state power and national power than would any umpire paid by one of the two contestants."[29]

The Treaty Power

In perhaps no single decision has this bias on the part of the Court been more manifest than in *Missouri v. Holland*.[30] The case arose out of the efforts of the federal government to impose restrictions on the hunting of migratory birds. In 1913 Congress had passed the Migratory Bird Act, but this statute was held unconstitutional by two different federal district courts on the ground that the subject matter was not within Congress's constitutional powers; it was in fact a matter reserved to the states, said the courts.

The United States and Great Britain then entered into a treaty that noted the danger of extinction to certain species in their annual migrations between Canada, then a British Dominion, and the United States and that provided for closed hunting seasons and other forms of protection. Both nations agreed that they would propose statutes to their legislatures to implement the treaty effectively. In pursuance of this treaty, Congress then enacted the Migratory Bird Act of 1918.

This legislation was shortly attacked in court by Missouri. The state argued that the act exceeded the enumerated powers of Congress, violated the Tenth Amendment by invading regulatory areas reserved to the states, and was, thus, unconsitutional. Basing its claim on the earlier district court decisions, Missouri in effect asked: How can a treaty vest the federal government with powers it did not possess in the absence of the treaty?

The *Holland* Decision   Avoiding Congress's commerce power, a doctrinal path that might not have commanded a majority of the Court in 1920, Justice Holmes upheld the implementing legislation as a constitutional exercise of the treaty power. While Holmes's opinion for the Court is certainly no model of clarity, he appears to have erected an irrebuttable presumption of constitutionality for statutes enforcing treaty provisions. If the treaty is valid, there can be no question about the validity of the statute. Then focusing his analysis on the validity of the treaty, Holmes turned to the wording of the supremacy clause: "This Constitution, and the Laws of the United States, which shall be made in Pursuance thereof; and all Treaties made, or which shall be made, under the Authority of the United States, shall be the supreme Law of the Land."[31] From this wording, Holmes drew the lesson that, in order to be the supreme law of the land, treaties need not be made in pursuance of the Constitution; they need only have been made under the authority of the United States, as was the treaty with Great Britain. Since the treaty was valid, the Migratory Bird Act implementing it was constitutional. The Tenth Amendment was simply irrelevant to the case at hand.

Now, there is something a little startling about a situation whereby ratification of a treaty gives Congress powers it did not have and could not have had before the treaty. "If an enactment which is otherwise unconstitutional becomes constitutional when passed pursuant to a treaty, then for all practical purposes the Constitution can be amended without resort to the formal amendment process."[32] Can there then be any limits to the power of the federal government?

In *Holland* Holmes endeavored to suggest that there were limitations on the treaty power. To be constitutionally valid, a treaty must deal with a matter of national concern. He then justified the migratory bird treaty on the ground that here was a national interest of nearly the first magnitude. "But for the treaty and the statute," wrote Holmes, "there soon might be no birds for any powers to deal with."[33]

There are, however, objections to a "national interest" test as a limit on the treaty power. It is arguable that the decision that a particular matter is or is not a proper subject for international negotiation should not be made by the judiciary. Should the Supreme Court, with its limited resources and limited diplomatic expertise, second-guess the Senate and the Department of State about whether a particular issue is of sufficient national concern to be dealt with by international agreement? Yet that is exactly what it must do to apply the "national interest" test as a limit on the treaty power. If it does not do this, it must accept that a matter of national interest is anything Congress and the president declare to be a matter of national interest. The mere fact that they are interested in the subject becomes evidence sufficient to meet Holmes's test, and Holmes himself in *Holland* recognized at length that the national interest was an elastic concept.

The Bricker Amendment   The *Holland* case has raised fears that the treaty power really is unlimited, and these fears have gained some support from the fact that the Supreme Court has never declared a treaty unconstitutional. In the early 1950s fears that the treaty power might be used to amend the Constitution and to curtail constitutional rights flared up and were given material expression in a constitutional amendment sponsored by Senator John W. Bricker. Support for the Bricker Amendment was also generated by postwar isolationism and resentment against a decade of strong executive leadership, which had involved the United States more deeply in foreign affairs than it had ever been previously. In particular, supporters of the amendment were opposed to American participation in the United Nations. They were or purported to be concerned that, since the United Nations Covenant on Human Rights was less stringent in its protection of civil liberties than is the Bill of Rights, American involvement with the U.N. might endanger the rights of American citizens. According to *Holland*, Congress, acting pursuant to a treaty, might exercise powers it did not previously have; since American participation in the United Nations was based on a treaty, the Bricker advocates argued that Congress could, in implementing the U.N. treaty, pass statutes that would otherwise have been precluded by the Bill of Rights.

The Bricker Amendment sought to accomplish two purposes. First, it would have reversed the decision in *Holland*. In its most celebrated form, the so-called "which" clause, the amendment provided that "a treaty shall become effective as internal law in the United States, only through legislation which would be valid in the absence of the treaty."[34] If this language had been added to the Constitution, no treaty could have been self-executing within the United States. Before a treaty might become internal law, after ratification it would have to be repassed as domestic legislation to be enforceable in American courts. The Bricker Amendment would also have required that the legislation reenacting the treaty be within the existing power of Congress. Congress, thus, would have been prevented from dealing on the basis of treaty with any domestic matter over which it otherwise lacked constitutional authority. The amendment very probably would have rendered foreign governments reluctant to enter into treaties with the United States and might have impaired the federal government's ability to protect the rights and interests of Americans abroad through treaties granting reciprocal protections to aliens within the United States.

Secondly, the Bricker Amendment sought to limit the president's power to enter into executive agreements. It provided that "executive agreements shall not be used in lieu of treaties."[35] If this hopelessly vague language meant anything at all, it must have meant that executive agreements would be completely banned. Although the Bricker Amendment was clumsily worded and overbroad, however, its objective of restricting the president's power to enter into executive agreements was probably well taken. As noted in chapter 3, subordinating executive agreements to treaties as a matter of law would be a desirable revision in light of late-twentieth-century circumstances. The Framers restricted the president's discretion to make appointments by requiring Senate participation because they considered the power of appointment a potential menace to constitutional government. Does not the power to make international agreements belong in the same category? Ironically, however, it was this part of the Bricker Amendment, and not its effort to circumscribe the treaty power, that certified its doom. The portion dealing with executive agreements incurred the opposition of President Eisenhower, and the amendment failed of passage in the Senate by one vote less than the necessary two-thirds.

Some of the fears that gave rise to the Bricker Amendment have since been allayed by the decision in *Reid v. Covert*.[36] In *Reid*, the Court held that an executive agreement could not deprive American citizens—civilians accompanying armed forces personnel abroad—of their constitutional right to trial by jury. Since executive agreements are constitutionally the functional equivalent of treaties, the same would presumably hold true for treaties. The limitations on the treaty power recognized by *Reid* and later cases following that holding, however, do not touch on the questions of federalism raised by *Holland*. While the treaty power may not be used to encroach on the liberties guaranteed to individuals by the Constitution, *Holland's* holding that it may serve as a foundation for federal invasion of areas previously reserved to the states remains undisturbed. True, *Holland* has been deprived of much of its significance by the Court's post-1937 approval of a sweeping congressional commerce power. But that is of cold comfort to the states.

Federal Reapportionment Mandates

In the past generation the Supreme Court has gone beyond any previously contemplated intervention in the affairs of the states, rendering decisions fundamentally affecting not merely state governmental power but the very structure of state government as well. The reapportionment decisions have imposed a uniform rule of political organization on all state legislatures and have raised serious questions about the continued vitality of the principle of bicameralism.

The *Baker* Case   Until the 1960s the issue of legislative apportionment was treated by the Court as presenting a nonjusticiable "political question." Because there was no neutral way to apportion legislative districts, the Court took the position that in this subject area there were no objective, judicial standards to apply in making a judgment. Then, in 1962, *Baker v. Carr*[37] reversed this line of precedent and found that the political question doctrine should not prevent the federal judiciary from taking a hand in these matters. According to Justice Brennan, the majority's spokesman in *Baker*, there was no absence of standards to be applied to suits challenging state legislative apportionments, since such cases arose under the equal protection clause of the Fourteenth Amendment, the meaning of which had been fully elaborated by previous judicial interpretation. Indeed, the standard appropriate to use in such suits was so well understood by Justice Brennan that he failed even to discuss what it might be.

Justice Clark argued that the appropriate standard was rationality; population disparities among districts might be constitutionally permissible if the apportionment plan promoted some reasonable purpose. Clark, however, could find no such purpose in *Baker* and, therefore, concurred in the judgment. The dissenters noted with emphasis that inequality in and of itself was not prohibited by the Fourteenth Amendment. Rather, the states were precluded from enacting or enforcing inequalities based on impermissible standards, such as race. The mere fact that legislative districts within a state contained differing populations, whether rationally contrived or not, was constitutionally irrelevant. The *Baker* majority, however, held only that legislative malapportionment was a fit subject for judicial resolution and sent the case back to the federal district court for a ruling, declining to offer any analysis of the standard to be employed in resolving the case.

The *Reynolds* Case   In the immediately subsequent litigation, states whose electoral structures were being challenged relied on the so-called federal analogy. They argued that their legislatures were modeled on the United

States Congress, with one house apportioned on a population basis and the other apportioned on a geographical basis without respect to population. State efforts to invoke this analogy in justification of their governmental structures were thunderingly rejected by *Reynolds v. Sims*.[38] Employing a slogan coined the previous year by Justice Douglas, Chief Justice Warren ruled that the Constitution required "one man, one vote." Both houses of bicameral state legislatures must be apportioned on the basis of population and *population only*. "Ours is a representative form of government," the Chief Justice expostulated.[39] Therefore, the constitutional standard the states must meet in allocating legislative seats is equality of population across districts. To note that Chief Justice Warren's noble sentiments rather seriously begged the question presented in *Reynolds* would be to emphasize the obvious. Of course, the Constitution is committed to representative government. But there are several different, possible forms of representative government. That Warren ignored this fact only serves to demonstrate that the chief justice's major premise was his conclusion.

When Is Equal Representation Inequitable? Arriving at an adequate understanding of the concept of representation, exactly what it is that the representative represents about his or her constituents and how, has proved one of the knottiest problems in all political theory. Among the difficulties inherent in the idea of representation and, thus, in the construction of representative institutions is that the very characteristics that are the foundation of politically relevant interests—race, religion, sex, wealth—are not evenly distributed throughout the population. Not all citizens are equally affected by every governmental policy, nor are all issues equally salient to every citizen. It can, then, reasonably be argued that those most affected by a given decision or those who feel most intensely about it should have a proportionately greater say in the making of that decision. To represent people on the basis of a simple arithmetic equality only is to reduce them to faceless ciphers, devoid of political interests. The result may very well be that only those interests shared by a numerical majority will receive effective representation.

One of the principal problems in the construction of representative institutions, therefore, is to prevent the creation of permanent minorities. If all the citizens of a political community voted unanimously for a governmental policy that would benefit them all equally, one would have ideal democratic equality: equality of participation, equality of decision-making power, and equality of benefit. But, of course, this never happens in the real political world. Rather, some portion of the electorate, 55 percent, say, votes for a policy that will benefit it while the other portion of the electorate votes for an opposite policy that will benefit it (or votes against a policy that will do it harm). Usually this situation is resolved by resort to majority rule. But consistently following simple majority rule does not result in ideal democratic equality. The majority makes the decision; the minority does not. The majority receives the benefits of the policy it chooses; at best, the minority gets nothing. The Supreme Court's facile equation of equality of participation with democratic equality obscures the fact that for the minority the reapportionment decisions merely protected the right to vote and lose. A person who consistently casts one equal vote on the minority side of issues will probably not feel the equal of someone who consistently casts a vote with the majority and always gets what he or she wants.

One way to attempt to avoid the creation of permanent minorities is to use complex rather than simple systems of government, whereby different institutions represent differing constituencies. The American governmental scheme is one of the most complex of all, being organized on the principles of both federalism and separation of powers. An essential element of this blueprint for the construction of good government has been the bicameral legislature with one house apportioned on the basis of population and the other apportioned on some other basis in an attempt to provide some representation for at least the more significant minority interests. Generally this was achieved by apportioning the upper house on the basis of geography. In most states this was done in emulation of the United States Senate. At the state level, moreover, residence-based apportionment achieved more effective interest representation than it did in the Senate. States are far too heterogeneous for residence within a state as a whole to be a significant indicator of interests that will be reflected by Senate representation. But at the state level, given American housing patterns, geography serves as an imprecise but not inaccurate indication of politically relevant interests. Two residence patterns—the single-family dwelling and Americans' tendency to segregate themselves by age, race, and income into ethnically and economically homogeneous neighborhoods—make residence a rough but reasonable guide to the interests of different constituencies.

The *Lucas* Case   *Reynolds*, however, erected a constitutional barrier to the use of geography as a basis for legislative apportionment and, thus, prevented states from granting an extra margin of representation to certain minorities, which would contribute to their real participation in the formulation of public policy. As a result, *Reynolds* "deprived us of one means of overcoming the dilemmas that arise when we realize that rule by the majority is not the same as rule by the people."[40] The absurdity of this position was well illustrated in a case handed down on the same day as *Reynolds*. *Lucas v. Forty-fourth General Assembly of Colorado*[41] overturned an apportionment plan approved by a vast majority of Colorado's voters. In a 1962 referendum the Colorado electorate had by a landslide rejected a plan that would have apportioned the state legislature on a population basis only. By an equally overwhelming vote it had adopted a scheme apportioning the lower house by population and the upper house by a complex formula that considered a number of factors in addition to population. The Supreme Court, however, found that this apportionment plan failed to comply with the mandate of "one man, one vote." Thus, a rule of law designed to ensure majority rule was used to thwart the will of the majority.

Chief Justice Warren arrived at this holding by relying on the unexceptionable premise that a majority may never override a constitutional right. Since *Reynolds* had established an individual right to cast a vote equally weighted with all others, the outcome in *Lucas* was easily reached. Too easily for Justice Stewart. In dissent Stewart argued that the Court should, instead, have recognized the more subtle and complex right to fair and effective representation. For Stewart, the proper judicial concern was not with the individual as an individual but with the overall fairness and reasonableness of any challenged legislative apportionment. In Colorado at the time of *Lucas* the people had recourse to the initiative process. The governor was popularly elected. The lower house was apportioned on a population basis, and more than half of the state's total population lived in the Denver metropolitan area. Taking judicial notice of these facts, Stewart concluded that it was neither unfair nor unreasonable to apportion one-half of one-third of the state government on some basis other than straight population in order to promote the effective representation of inhabitants of western Colorado.

An Assessment of the Reapportionment Decisions   Undoubtedly the result in *Baker* was correct. Despite the failure of Justice Brennan's effort to define the political question doctrine, he was justified in concluding that the federal courts could hear malapportionment claims. It was a hollow mockery to tell urban voters to rely on the state political processes in malapportioned states to vindicate their grievances. Undoubtedly the gross population disparities between legislative districts that had developed in many states had to be corrected, and clearly correction had to come from the judiciary.

But *Reynolds* was not the logically necessary extension of *Baker*. The Court could have embraced the federal analogy and permitted the apportionment of one legislative chamber on some basis other than population without undermining its concern for overall political fairness. No apportionment that does not ensure ultimate effective majority rule can be considered reasonable or fair. But, in addition, it is desirable that governmental structures promote the adequate articulation of minority interests. *Reynolds* confused arithmetic with representation and in so doing substituted a slogan for a rationale.

Early in this century, Justice Holmes chided his colleagues that the Constitution did not enact any particular economic philosophy.[42] The modern Court might have done well to take his lesson to heart in its reapportionment decision. Like *Lochner v. New York* which elevated a single economic theory, laissez-faire capitalism, to the status of constitutional doctrine, *Reynolds* accorded constitutional status to a particular political philosophy, majoritarian democracy.

The Court under Earl Warren's successor, Warren Burger, has shown some appreciation of this fact. It has upheld state statutes requiring extraordinary majority votes for the passage of bond issues, although these obviously contradict the reasoning in *Reynolds*; and it has permitted greater population disparities among districts than the Warren Court might have countenanced.[43] But in its continued insistence that there is only one principle on which state legislatures may be constitutionally apportioned, although it is to be applied flexibly, the Burger Court, no less than the Warren Court, has undermined bicameralism and the diversity of governmental arrangements that the principle of federalism envisioned.

Nationalization of the Bill of Rights

The modern Court's preference for legal uniformity among the states has also been manifest in its nationalization of the Bill of Rights. Originally the Bill of Rights was intended as a curb on the power of the national government only. Many of the proponents of these first amendments were, in fact, more concerned with the preservation of state perquisites than with the protection of civil liberties as such, and in 1833 Chief Justice Marshall himself confirmed this view.[44] Having been a member of the Virginia ratifying convention, Marshall was personally familiar with the motives behind the proposal and adoption of the Bill of Rights, and relying on his knowledge of that history he denied a claim that the Fifth Amendment required a state to provide just compensation for property taken for a public purpose.

The question of the applicability of the Bill of Rights to the states was, however, reopened by ratification of the Fourteenth Amendment. That amendment provides, "No state shall ... abridge the privileges or immunities of citizens of the United States," and it might be argued that among the privileges and immunities enjoyed by virtue of federal citizenship are the rights and liberties guaranteed in the Bill of Rights. But this argument was rejected in the Court's very first interpretation of the Fourteenth Amendment, the *Slaughter-House Cases*.[45]

Following *Slaughter-House*, focus shifted to the due process clause of the Fourteenth Amendment, which prohibits the state from depriving people of "life, liberty, or property without due process of law." Several cases shortly arose urging the notion that the guarantees contained in the Bill of Rights were inherent in the notion of due process of law. Most of these early cases involved the jury—grand or petit, criminal or civil—because at the time some legal writers equated due process with jury trial. These claims, however, were uniformly unsuccessful.

Total Incorporation   The Supreme Court has never adopted the theory that the Fourteenth Amendment applies the entire Bill of Rights to the states, despite the consistent, often eloquent appeals of Justice Hugo Black, the greatest advocate of this "total incorporation" theory. Black was convinced, on the basis of both history and policy considerations, that the due process clause of the Fourteenth Amendment should be equated with the Bill of Rights and only the Bill of Rights. His historical claim that it was the intention of the framers of the Fourteenth Amendment to enforce all of the checks of the Bill of Rights against the states has been the subject of considerable criticism. At best, there appears to be insufficient evidence to give a clear, definitive answer about what the framers' intentions may have been. Some respected constitutional scholars have argued that Black's view is correct; equally respected scholars, after researching the same materials, have found a strong probability that there was no intention to incorporate the whole Bill of Rights into the Fourteenth Amendment.

Justice Black, however, also argued that, whatever may have been the original intent of the amendment's framers, it would be sound policy to make the due process clause mean the Bill of Rights and nothing more, for he saw this as a way to curtail judicial discretion. In Justice Black's view the deficiencies of the old, laissez-faire Court's interpretations of the due process clause arose because the clause was not tied to specific provisions in the Constitution; thus, the justices had been allowed to decide questions of constitutionality on the basis of their personal standards of justice and fairness. Such unlimited judicial discretion was inappropriate, Justice Black contended, and total incorporation of the Bill of Rights into the Fourteenth Amendment was the way to avoid the old Court's error. For Justice Black this meant total incorporation of only the express guarantees of the first eight amendments, however. No "cognate" or "penumbral" rights were to be found in the due process clause; nor was the Ninth Amendment, with its implications of natural law, to be used by the courts to invalidate state legislation.

Selective Incorporation   The Court consistently rejected the Black theory. In part it was influenced by the view espoused first by Justice Cardozo and later by Justice Frankfurter—that due process is an evolving concept whose content changes as the mores and capabilities of society change. But, through a process of selective incorporation, the modern Court has achieved almost the same result that would have been produced by total incorporation.

In the beginning this process was random and haphazard, almost accidental. The Fifth Amendment eminent domain provision was applied to the states in 1897,[46] and after thirty years so was the First Amendment protection of freedom of speech.[47] Within the next decade various other provisions of the First Amendment followed.[48] But during the same period the Court was rejecting claims that the states were bound by the Eighth Amendment ban on cruel and unusual punishments, the Fifth Amendment self-incrimination privilege, the Sixth Amendment guarantee of a jury trial in serious criminal cases, and other portions of the Bill of Rights.[49] A mere look at the precedents suggests that the selection was arbitrary.

Then, in 1937, Justice Cardozo enunciated a coherent principle to explain the division between rights that had and had not been absorbed into the Fourteenth Amendment. According to *Palko v. Connecticut* the rights that the states had been constitutionally required to honor were "implicit in the concept of ordered liberty."[50] Neither liberty nor justice would exist if these freedoms were sacrificed. On the other hand, those rights that had been denied incorporation into the Fourteenth Amendment, such as jury trial, while important, were not essential to the realization of a fair and enlightened system of justice. Although *Palko* concluded that the Fifth Amendment prohibition against double jeopardy was not applicable to the states, it provided the doctrine under which most of the guarantees of the Bill of Rights were eventually to be incorporated into the due process clause of the Fourteenth Amendment. After *Palko* all that was necessary to apply a given protection to the states was for the Court to find it essential to the concept of ordered liberty, and that proved an expandable concept indeed.

For some time the process of selective incorporation continued to move slowly. But in 1961 it suddenly accelerated and soon reached breathtaking speed. In that year *Mapp v. Ohio*[51] reversed an earlier decision that the Fourth Amendment exclusionary rule was not required in state criminal proceedings. The exclusionary rule was first established in federal courts in 1914. It holds that evidence secured by an unreasonable search and seizure may not be used by the prosecution at trial. The purpose of the rule is to deter unconstitutional police conduct, although little evidence exists to suggest that the rule actually does so. A dozen years before *Mapp* the Supreme Court had announced, in a very confused opinion by Justice Frankfurter, that the values of privacy at the core of the Fourth Amendment were applicable against the states because of the due process clause of the Fourteenth Amendment but that the "fruits of" (evidence obtained by) unreasonable searches need not be excluded from state trials.[52] This holding did not clarify whether the exclusionary rule was required by the Constitution but simply was not at the core of the Fourth Amendment or whether it was a judicially created rule of evidence applicable in federal trials only. *Mapp* answered that question, fastened the exclusionary rule on the states, and provoked a storm of criticism from police officials across the country.

Nevertheless, within two years the Court returned to the fray by finding that the Sixth Amendment right to counsel was incorporated in the due process clause of the Fourteenth Amendment and that states would have to meet the same standards required of the federal government in complying with the amendment.[53] For nearly three decades the Court had been saying that the Sixth Amendment did not merely protect a defendant's right to employ counsel but also required the appointment of counsel at government expense, if the defendant were too poor to employ a private attorney. The Court, however, had shied away from holding that the states had a constitutional duty to appoint counsel for all indigent defendants in serious criminal cases. Instead, it had evolved an exceptional circumstances rule requiring the appointment of counsel in *state* trials according to a number of factors in addition to proverty (for example, the age and intelligence of the defendant and the degree of his familiarity with the criminal process).[54] The exceptional circumstances rule had grown so complex and unwieldy it was almost unworkable, however. Therefore, when Clarence Earl Gideon petitioned the Court to require the appointment of counsel for any indigent on trial for a felony, twenty-three states filed a brief amicus curiae (as friends of the court rather than adversary parties) on his behalf, and the Court unanimously injected the Sixth Amendment right into the body of the Fourteenth.

The following year the Fifth Amendment self-incrimination privilege, long denied application to the states, was incorporated,[55] and more Bill of Rights provisions followed in quick succession.[56] Finally, *Palko* itself was overruled through use of the very rationale enunciated by Justice Cardozo. In *Benton v. Maryland*[57] the Court concluded that Cardozo had stated the correct rule for determining whether a given Bill of Rights guarantee should apply to that states but that he had erred in his resolution of the question presented—whether the Fifth Amendment double jeopardy prohibition was necessary to the concept of ordered liberty.

Burger Court Developments   By 1969, when Chief Justice Warren retired, only a handful of Bill of Rights provisions, among them the rarely litigated Second and Third Amendments, remained unincorporated. Moreover, while the contemporary Court, composed largely of Nixon appointees, has differed somewhat from its predecessor in interpreting the substantive meaning of the Bill of Rights guarantees, particularly as they affect law enforcement, it has shown no enthusiasm for reversing the application of the Bill of Rights to the states. Although there is little left to incorporate into the Fourteenth Amendment, the Burger Court has acknowledged that the Eight Amendment prohibition against excessive bail is embraced by the due process clause, has extended *Gideon's* requirement of appointed counsel to include indigents charged with serious misdemeanors, and has found that proof beyond a reasonable doubt is the standard required in criminal trials as a necessity for ordered liberty.[58]

The Effects of Incorporation   In the final analysis, however, Justice Black's victory has been a hollow one. Incorporation of the Bill of Rights into the Fourteenth Amendment has not confined the range of judicial discretion as Black had hoped and predicted. For one thing, most of the justices have refused to accept Black's idea that due process of law means the Bill of Rights and no more. Like the Court of the 1920s, the modern Court has found that constitutional rights cannot be limited to constitutional specifics, and on its own initiative it has created new substantive rights that American government must not infringe.[59] For another thing, Justice Black's position always turned on the unwarranted assumption that the Bill of Rights provisions were specific. That specificity was illusory. Constitutional interpretation has always involved—must necessarily involve—choice. The Fourth Amendment, for example, does not prohibit all searches but only those that are unreasonable. The Sixth Amendment protects the right to counsel but is silent about when that right begins. The Eighth Amendment bans cruel and unusual punishments but makes no mention of the death penalty. Application of these Bill of Rights guarantees to the states does not resolve the hard questions of definition they pose. And last, but certainly not least, the Court's carbon copy application of Bill of Rights prohibitions to the states— not only the provisions themselves but also the rules that have grown up around them through judicial interpretation—may have resulted in diminishing the Bill of Rights.

Throughout the Court's orgy of incorporation during the 1960s, Justice Harlan had warned that the Bill of Rights provisions should not be applied to the states by the same standards required of the federal government. The states, he pointed out, deal with a much greater number and wider variety of criminal offenses than does the federal government. At the same time their resources are much more limited. Requiring the states to meet the same standards as the federal government would, therefore, be unrealistic. For the states to comply with certain Bill of Rights guarantees considerations of public policy would require relaxing the meaning of those guarantees, Harlan predicted. But, if the guarantees were incorporated into the Fourteenth Amendment carbon copy, a later lowering of their standards would, by definition, erode the standards required of the federal government. Harlan's concern seems to have been vindicated by the aftermath of the Court's application of the Sixth Amendment jury trial guarantee to the states.

Before its incorporation into the Fourteenth Amendment, the jury trial provision had been interpreted to require a jury of twelve and a unanimous verdict for conviction. These requirements make the criminal jury slow and cumbersome. Particularly in an era characterized by court congestion and backlogs, it is doubtful that state court systems could realistically operate under such rules. Therefore, Justice Harlan had argued against applying this part of the Sixth Amendment to the states. But the Court ignored Harlan and incorporated the jury trial guarantee into the Fourteenth Amendment, noting in passing that its earlier interpretations of the content of the jury guarantee might be subject to reconsideration.[60] Subsequently, the Court has upheld state experimentation with six-member juries and nonunanimous verdicts,[61] and by the late 1970s some states have begun to use even smaller juries and simple rather than extraordinary majorities for conviction. Such experiments may be desirable. But, if they are held to be constitutional, the Sixth Amendment jury provision ceases to have the meaning it had before its carbon copy incorporation into the Fourteenth Amendment.[62]

CRITICISM OF THE COURT'S POLICIES

The modern Court's decisions affecting federal-state relation have occasioned substantial criticism, some more intelligent than others. In 1958, for example, the Conference of State Chief Justices passed an unprecedented resolution severely condemning the United States Supreme Court, and in 1963 the Council of State Governments proposed three far-reaching constitutional amendments. The first would have undone the reapportionment cases; the second would have permitted state legislatures to amend the Constitution without consideration or discussion of the proposed amendment in any national forum; and the third would have established a Court of the Union, superior to the Supreme Court, consisting of the chief justices of the fifty states, which would have been empowered to reverse the Supreme Court in cases involving federal-state relations. Proponents of these amendments moved so quietly and so quickly that twelve states had ratified one or more of them, before many of even the most informed citizens knew what was happening. Shortly, Chief Justice Warren, in a speech to the American Law

Institute, rebuked the legal profession for its apathy in the matter. Had proposals of such magnitude been made during the early days of the Republic, he noted, a great debate would have resounded throughout the land.

Fortunately, none of the proposed amendments was adopted. They were the product of an ill-advised and hasty reaction and were more unwise than the Supreme Court decisions that had occasioned them. But Chief Justice Warren was correct in calling for a great debate on the question of the relation between the Supreme Court and the principles of American federalism. Even the most nationalistic of the Founding Fathers believed that the jealousies of the sovereign states would serve as a beneficial check on the powers of the central government. Today many Americans from a wide variety of political persuasions are recognizing that the concentration of power in Washington is not a necessary good.

SUMMARY

The principle of federalism contemplates a system in which power is widely dispersed and the individual states are free to adopt different political and legal structures. There are, of course, some limits to this freedom, but the range of permissible state actions is fairly broad. Diversity is the rule, rather than conformity.

That principle notwithstanding, the American states have become ever more similar. The causes of this increasing uniformity have been many: population migration, improvements in transportation systems, and the development of nationwide electronic news media. But, as they have grown alike, the states have also decreased in power. Federal power to regulate domestic matters has been increased at their expense.

Throughout American history, the Supreme Court has clothed these developments with the mantle of constitutional legitimacy. As discussed in chapter 3, for example, it has recognized a presidential power to protect the peace of the United States, a power that may be exercised within a state and contrary to its wishes. As discussed in chapter 4, the Court's broad construction of Congress's powers to regulate interstate commerce and enforce the Reconstruction amendments has had profound implications for the states' control of their internal affairs. At the same time, as this chapter has noted, the Court has narrowly construed state power and strictly limited the scope and meaning of the Tenth Amendment.

But the relationship between Supreme Court decision making and social change is a reciprocal one. The Court has not only acquiesced in these changes; it has also accelerated them by teaching a version of the federal system in which the central government is vastly more powerful than the states and national uniformity of law is desirable.

In the past two decades, the Court itself has aggressively moved to standardize the legislative and judicial structures of the states. Reapportionment has denied the states the power to adopt a wide variety of electoral arrangements. Expansion of the federal courts' habeas corpus jurisdiction and incorporation of the Bill of Rights into the Fourteenth Amendment due process clause have brought must of state criminal procedure under federal scrutiny.

But the lesson of these decisions must surely be that requiring both the state and the federal jurisdictions to march to the same drummer may not be an unmixed blessing. State legal and political processes must be kept fundamentally fair. But that can be achieved without sacrificing the flexibility of federalism.

In the modern era Americans have become accustomed to think of the Bill of Rights, the Fourteenth Amendment, and the Supreme Court as the principal guardians and guarantors of freedom. But it is shallow not to realize that the structure of the American political system has contributed to the preservation of liberty. The Framers knew that human rights were best protected by sound governmental organization, not by paper declarations. Can any interpretation of the Bill of Rights that fails to take due account of the principle of federalism be constitutionally sound?

NOTES

1 New State Ice Co. v. Liebmann, 285 U.S. 262, 280, 311 (1932) (dissenting opinion).

2 14 U.S. (1 Wheat.) 304 (1816).

3 19 U.S. (6 Wheat.) 264 (1821).

4 19 U.S. (6 Wheat.) at 413-14.

5 22 U.S. (9 Wheat.) 1 (1824).

6 17 U.S. (4 Wheat.) 316 (1819).

7 36 U.S. (11 Pet.) 257 (1837).

8 38 U.S. (13 Pet.) 519 (1839).

9 36 U.S. (11 Pet.) 420 (1837).

10 17 U.S. (4 Wheat.) 518 (1819).

11 41 U.S. (16 Pet.) 1 (1842).

12 62 U.S. (21 How.) 506 (1859).

13 53 U.S. (12 How.) 299 (1851).

14 Roscoe Pound, "The Still Small Voice of the Commerce Clause," in *Selected Essays on Constitutional Law,* ed. Association of American Law Schools, 3 vols. (Chicago: Foundation Press, 1938), vol. 3, p. 932.

15 Muller v. Oregon, 208 U.S. 412, 421 (1908).

16 28 U.S.C. secs. 2241-55.

17 344 U.S. 443 (1953).

18 Jones v. Cunningham, 371 U.S. 236 (1963); Townsend v. Sain, 372 U.S. 293 (1963); Fay v. Noia, 372 U.S. 391 (1963).

19 380 U.S. 479 (1965).

20 428 U.S. 465 (1976).

21 401 U.S. 37 (1971). See also Samuels v. Mackell, 401 U.S. 66 (1971).

22 Huffman v. Pursue, Ltd., 420 U.S. 592 (1975).

23 Fuentes v. Shevin, 407 U.S. 67 (1972) ("extrajudicial" proceeding); Steffel v. Thompson, 415 U.S. 452 (1974) (threatened but not yet pending prosecution). See also NLRB v. Nash-Finch Co., 404 U.S. 138 (1971); Mitchum v. Foster, 407 U.S. 225 (1972); Hicks v. Miranda, 422 U.S. 332 (1975); Doran v. Salem Inn, Inc., 422 U.S. 922 (1975).

24 426 U.S. 833 (1976), *reversing* Maryland v. Wirtz, 392 U.S. 183 (1968).

25 Sotirios A. Barber, "National League of Cities v. Usery: New Meaning for the Tenth Amendment?" in *The Supreme Court Review: 1976,* ed. Philip B. Kurland (Chicago: University of Chicago Press, 1977), pp. 164, 174. See also Lawrence H. Tribe, "Unraveling *National League of Cities:* The New Federalism and Affirmative Rights to Essential Government Services," *Harvard Law Review,* 90 (April 1977), 1065-104. Professor Tribe argues, however improbably, that *National League of Cities* must be read as a first step on the part of the Burger Court toward recognition of an affirmative governmental duty to provide certain basic services. This is as optimistic and probably as unrealistic as reading it to be a significant revitalization of the Tenth Amendment.

26 Fry v. United States, 421 U.S. 542 (1975).

27 400 U.S. 122 (1970).

28 Oliver Wendell Holmes, *Collected Legal Papers* (New York: Harcourt, Brace and Howe, 1920), pp. 295-96.

29 Philip B. Kurland, *Politics, the Constitution, and the Warren Court* (Chicago: University of Chicago Press, 1970), p. 57.

30 252 U.S. 416 (1920).

31 U.S. Const. art. VI, sec. 2.

32 Charles A. Lofgren, "Missouri v. Holland in Historical Perspective," in *The Supreme Court Review: 1975,* ed. Philip B. Kurland (Chicago: University of Chicago Press, 1976), p. 93.

33 252 U.S. at 435.

34 U.S., Congress, Senate, Joint Resolution 102, September 14, 1951, *Congressional Record,* 82d Cong., 1st sess., vol. 97, p. 592.

35 Ibid.

36 354 U.S. 1 (1957). See also John C. Ries and Owen S. Nibley, "Justices, Juries, and Military Dependents," *Western Political Quarterly*, 15 (September 1962), 438-48.

37 369 U.S. 186 (1962).

38 377 U.S. 533 (1964).

39 377 U.S. at 562.

40 Martin Shapiro, "Reapportionment: Introduction," in *The Supreme Court and Constitutional Rights*, ed. Martin Shapiro (Atlanta: Scott, Foresman & Co., 1967), p. 82.

41 377 U.S. 713 (1964).

42 Lochner v. New York, 198 U.S. 45, 74, 75 (1905) (dissenting opinion).

43 See, e.g., Gordon v. Lance, 403 U.S. 1 (1971); Mahan v. Howell, 410 U.S. 315 (1973); White v. Regester, 412 U.S. 755 (1973); Gaffney v. Cummings, 412 U.S. 735 (1973).

44 Barron v. Baltimore, 32 U.S. (7 Pet.) 243 (1833).

45 88 U.S. (16 Wall.) 36 (1873).

46 Chicago, B. & Q. R.R. v. Chicago, 166 U.S. 226 (1897).

47 Fiske v. Kansas, 274 U.S. 380 (1927), *anticipated in* Gitlow v. New York, 268 U.S. 652 (1925).

48 See Near v. Minnesota, 283 U.S. 697 (1931) (press); DeJonge v. Oregon, 299 U.S. 353 (1937) (assembly); Cantwell v. Connecticut, 310 U.S. 296 (1940) (free exercise of religion).

49 See O'Neil v. Vermont, 144 U.S. 323 (1892) (cruel and unusual punishment); Maxwell v. Dow, 176 U.S. 581 (1900) (trial by jury); Twining v. New Jersey, 211 U.S. 78 (1908) (self-incrimination).

50 302 U.S. 319, 325 (1937).

51 367 U.S. 643 (1961).

52 Wolf v. Colorado, 338 U.S. 25 (1949).

53 Gideon v. Wainwright, 372 U.S. 335 (1963).

54 See, e.g., Powell v. Alabama, 287 U.S. 45 (1932); Betts v. Brady, 316 U.S. 455 (1942).

55 Malloy v. Hogan, 378 U.S. 1 (1964).

56 See, e.g., Pointer v. Texas, 380 U.S. 400 (1965) (Sixth Amendment, confrontation); Klopfer v. North Carolina, 386 U.S. 213 (1967) (Sixth Amendment, speedy trial); Washington v. Texas, 388 U.S. 14 (1967) (Sixth Amendment, compulsory process); Duncan v. Louisiana, 391 U.S. 145 (1968) (Sixth Amendment, jury trial).

57 395 U.S. 784 (1969).

58 Schilb v. Kuebel, 404 U.S. 357 (1972) (bail); Argersinger v. Hamlin, 407 U.S. 25 (1972) (counsel); *In re* Winship, 397 U.S. 358 (1970) (standard of proof).

59 See, e.g., Griswold v. Connecticut, 381 U.S. 479 (1965) (right to marital privacy); Shapiro v. Thompson, 394 U.S. 618 (1969) (right to interstate travel); Roe v. Wade, 410 U.S. 113 (1973) (right to private choice in matters of procreation).

60 Duncan v. Louisiana, 391 U.S. 145 (1968).

61 Williams v. Florida, 399 U.S. 78 (1970) (six-member jury); Apodaca v. Oregon, 406 U.S. 404 (1972) (ten-to-two verdict).

62 But see Ludwig v. Massachusetts, 427 U.S. 618 (1976), in which the Court upheld a state two-tier procedure affording defendants a jury trial only upon appeal from conviction by a judge, without resolving whether the Constitution would permit a similar system in the federal courts. Speaking for the Court, Justice Blackmun noted that the jury is guaranteed in federal criminal trials not only by the Sixth Amendment but also by article III, which does not apply to the states. However, Callan v. Wilson, 127 U.S. 540 (1888), had held that there is no difference between the article III and the Sixth Amendment guarantees. Justice Powell, who cast the deciding vote in the five-to-four decision, stated in a separate concurrence that *Ludwig* was consistent with his (and the late Justice Harlan's) view that the states are subject to less stringent requirements under the Fourteenth Amendment than the federal government is under the Bill of Rights. *Ludwig*, therefore, may represent a retreat from carbon copy incorporation, at least in the context of jury trials.

SUGGESTED ADDITIONAL READING

Baker, Gordon E. *The Reapportionment Revolution: Representation, Political Power, and the Supreme Court.* New York: Random House, 1966.

Benson, Paul R. *The Supreme Court and the Commerce Clause, 1937-1970.* New York: Dunellen Publishing Co., 1970.

Beth, Loren P. *The Development of the American Constitution, 1877-1917.* New York: Harper & Row, 1971.

Black, Hugo L. *A Constitutional Faith.* New York: Alfred A. Knopf, 1968.

Dixon, Robert G., Jr. *Democratic Representation: Reapportionment in Law and Politics.* New York: Oxford University Press, 1968.

Goldwin, Robert A., ed. *A Nation of States: Essays on the American Federal System.* Chicago: Rand McNally & Co., 1961.

Lewis, Anthony. *Gideon's Trumpet.* New York: Random House, 1964.

Vanderbilt, Arthur T. *The Doctrine of the Separation of Powers and Its Present Day Significance.* Lincoln: University of Nebraska Press, 1953.

THE COURT AND THE INDIVIDUAL

CHAPTER 6

Supreme Court decisions must be read in relation to the character of their political times. Throughout its history the Court has generally reflected the political and intellectual changes occurring within the larger society. Both in the problems brought before it and in its resolution of those problems, it has mirrored the concerns of the politically dominant coalition. This has been true in the modern era no less than in past eras. The post-New Deal Court's decision making has been characterized by judicial approval of government regulation of the economy and by a nationalist spirit. Whether it is interpreting the commerce clause, reviewing state criminal procedures, or sustaining civil rights legislation, the modern Court has shown a preference for legal uniformity across the nation, for solving problems at the federal rather than at the state level; it has also exhibited general suspicion of the quality and motives of state government. At the same time, the Court has manifested a far greater concern for political and civil rights and liberties than in previous eras. This active judicial humanitarianism has in part been the product of the political success of American liberalism and in part been necessitated by the Court's own erosion of the structural checks on governmental power so carefully constructed in the original Constitution. With federalism seriously weakened as a principle of political organization and with congressional power significantly reduced relative to presidential power, the Court had to play a larger and more vigorous role in protecting individual freedoms, in order to maintain the principle of limited government.

During the twentieth century, therefore, and particularly during its middle decades, the Court has been substantially engaged in creating a case law of civil liberties. These Court decisions affecting the relationship between individual and government, have fallen into three principal areas: the constitutional law of criminal procedure, an outgrowth of the "incorporation" cases; the interpretation of the Constitution's guarantee of "equal protection of the laws";[1] and the analysis of the First Amendment.

FIRST AMENDMENT FREEDOMS

The First Amendment decisions are themselves divisible, as is the amendment, into those dealing with the related freedoms of speech, press, and assembly and those interpreting the religion clauses.

The Religion Clauses

While a great deal of constitutional analysis presents complex problems that are difficult to resolve, the First Amendment religion clauses have proved particularly nettlesome. One guarantees the exercise of religious belief free from governmental interference; the other prohibits the establishment of religion. If the meaning of either clause is extended very far, however, it collides with the other. It can be argued, for example, that the armed forces' chaplaincy program or the exemption of conscientious objectors from the draft are (1) constitutionally mandated by the free exercise clause and (2) constitutionally prohibited by the establishment clause as state aid to religious belief. Given this paradoxical situation, the Court's interpretation of the religion clauses has followed a tortuous path characterized by considerable contradiction.

The Free Exercise of Religion   On the one hand, the Supreme Court has found that the free exercise clause constitutes an absolute protection of religious conscience but is not an absolute protection for actions precipitated by religious belief. In other words, one is free to believe anything, but one is not necessarily free to act on those beliefs. Thus, antipolygamy laws or state prohibitions against handling dangerous reptiles do not fall afoul of the First Amendment.[2] On the other hand, the Court has also found that a total, nondiscriminatory ban on door-to-door solicitation could not validly be applied to the peddling of religious tracts, nor was it constitutionally permissible to require licenses, and license fees, of the vendors of such pamphlets.[3] Indeed, a right to make religious solicitations has been recognized even in areas such as a company-owned town, which was clearly posted as private property, and this holding was subsequently extended to protect the right to distribute religious literature on the premises of a United States government installation.[4]

Just as government may not inhibit certain actions inspired by religious belief, it may not usually compel actions odious to religious conviction. During the Second World War, for example, members of the Jehovah's Witnesses objected to public schools' requirements that their children pledge allegiance to the American flag, a ceremony regarded by the Witnesses as contrary to biblical injunction. In the early days of the conflict, the Court sustained the compulsory flag salute.[5] But by 1943 tolerance had increased in direct proportion to the prospects for allied victory, and the Court overturned its original ruling in an eloquent affirmation of the freedom of thought and conscience protected by the First Amendment. "To sustain the compulsory flag salute," wrote Justice Jackson, "we are required to say that a Bill of Rights which guards the individual's right to speak his own mind, left it open to public authorities to compel him to utter what is not in his mind."[6] The Court has since reversed a state denial of unemployment benefits to a Seventh Day Adventist because she refused to accept a job that would have required her to work on Saturdays, and it has held that Amish parents cannot be compelled to send their children to school beyond the eighth grade.[7]

Yet, in contrast, the Court has upheld compulsory vaccination laws in the face of objections based on religious conviction and has allowed the state greater power when dealing with the religiously motivated actions of minors. Thus, while religious pamphlet peddling may not be prohibited, child labor laws may constitutionally prevent such distribution by children; and, while the state may not compel medical treatment for adults when that treatment would violate the tenets of the patient's religion, the state does have the power to order such treatment for minors. In this area the Court has adopted the position that, while adults are free to martyr themselves, they are not free to martyr their children.[8]

The religious liberty protected by the First Amendment, then, does not include the right to commit immoral or criminal acts, even though such acts may be sanctioned or even encouraged by religious doctrine. But neither is the state's power to control behavior absolute. In regulating actions motivated by religious conviction, the state must be pursuing a valid secular purpose that outweighs the individual interest in engaging in the challenged behavior. Moreover, the state must use methods that infringe as little as possible on religiously inspired conduct in order to attain its legitimate secular purpose.

Establishment of Religion   When the Amish are exempted from the full operation of the school attendance laws, when the Jehovah's Witnesses are granted an immunity from license fees, or when an exception to the unemployment compensation laws is carved out to benefit Sabbatarians, governmental preference or benefits are awarded to specified groups on the basis of their religious beliefs. Yet the First Amendment prohibits the establishment of a religion. Does this provision apply to these situations? And, if so, how? In particular, what does the establishment clause have to say about public aid to religion in connection with a nationwide system of compulsory education?

Unfortunately, history does not provide much of a guide. The eighteenth-century proponents of the First Amendment thought of established religion in terms of a state-sponsored and state-supported church. They did not discuss religious establishment in terms of released time programs, textbook loans, and school construction grants. But these are exactly the terms in which the discussion of church-state relations is conducted in the twentieth century.

Since its first authoritative interpretation of the establishment clause in *Everson v. Board of Education* (1947),[9] the Supreme Court has elaborated at least three different, possible ways to read that constitutional provision. At one extreme is the strict "wall of separation" theory. According to that interpretation, the establishment clause prohibits *any* aid whatsoever to churches, parochial schools, and other religious institutions.[10] In light of the patent necessity of providing sectarian buildings with fire and police protection, not to mention sewer service and sidewalks, however, the "no aid" theory breaks down. Pushed to its logical conclusion it would compel ridiculous and socially undesirable results.

At the other extreme is the "benevolent neutrality" thesis, with the emphasis on the benevolent. According to this view, the establishment clause does not prohibit government accommodation of religion, and the free exercise clause virtually requires it. Justice Douglas, who at one time or another endorsed each of the three theories, once put it this way: "We are a religious people whose institutions presuppose a Supreme Being. . . . When the state encourages religious instruction or cooperates with religious authorities . . . , it follows the best of our traditions."[11] Under this theory, a great deal of state aid to religion is constitutionally permissible. For example, Douglas used the theory to sustain a New York program permitting public school students to be released from classes in order to attend religious instruction *off* the school grounds. But except for that instance the Court has used the benevolent neutrality theory only to justify such historically cemented practices as Sunday closing laws and tax exemptions for church-owned property devoted to worship.[12]

The third possible reading of the establishment clause is that the Constitution merely requires government to remain neutral with respect to religion. This is the most generally employed view, though it is by no means so often or so consistently used that it can be regarded as the standard or orthodox interpretation. It holds that neither hostility toward nor encouragement of religion is required or permitted by the First Amendment. Public policy may not be designed to advance or to inhibit religion. But, if an otherwise constitutional program has the incidental effect of indirectly aiding religion, it will not be struck down.

The first and perhaps foremost use of the neutrality theory was Justice Black's opinion for the Court in *Everson*, which upheld the reimbursement to parents of money expended for transporting their children to and from school by means of public transportation. This reimbursement was made to the parents of children attending parochial schools as well as public schools. Justice Black found that nothing in the First Amendment precluded such a policy, for the prohibition against establishment of religion did not, as Black understood it, require people to be deprived of public welfare merely because of their religious beliefs. The reimbursement program was a nondiscriminatory effort to promote the public safety and welfare by encouraging the transportation of school children by public carrier rather than having them walk to school. Since parents have a constitutional right to satisfy the compulsory school attendance laws by sending their children to parochial schools, the state might treat all parents equally in establishing a general program for transportation for educational purposes. The benefit of the program, Black felt, accrued to the children and not to the parochial schools they might attend.

The "child benefit theory" has subsequently been used to sustain textbook loan programs, whereby the state provides books for students in both secular and sectarian schools.[13] But the Court has been unwilling to accept more broad-scale programs for the financial relief of parochial education. Purchase of services contracts, through which the state helps pay the salaries of teachers in sectarian schools, various plans for construction grants to church-related schools, and schemes to provide tax relief for the parents of parochial school students have all been found to entangle the state excessively with religion in violation of the First Amendment.[14] Similarly, devotional services in the public schools, such as the recitation of the Lord's Prayer or reading from the Bible, even if voluntary, have been held to place the state in a nonneutral position with respect to religion.[15] In the most recent cases, only public aid to postsecondary parochial education has been upheld on the grounds—asserted but largely unsubstantiated—that college level students are more mature, more skeptical, and less subject to theological indoctrination, and the religious atmosphere of the school is correspondingly less pervasive.[16]

Freedom of Expression

Like its interpretations of the religion clauses of the First Amendment, the Court's rulings on the amendment's guarantees of freedom of expression have generated an array of complex and often confusing jurisprudential theories. The analytic difficulty arises from the fact that the First Amendment does not prohibit legislation abridging speech or press activities but rather prohibits legislation abridging the *freedom* of speech and of the press. And, since Plato, a great many reasonable and intelligent people have argued that there are some things one is not free to say or to publish. There is no doubt that society, through its government, may regulate socially or individually injurious behavior and may punish such conduct if it does occur. There is also no doubt that expression can produce action, including injurious or undesirable acts, and is often directed at doing so. In light of these facts, the question presented by the First Amendment cases is: How far back into the realm of expression may government control be extended in order to prevent behavior before it takes place?

The Absolutist Position   One answer is: Not at all. The so-called absolute position, often espoused by the late Justice Black, holds that all words, written or spoken, are at all times and under all circumstances protected from all forms of government restraint. This doctrine rests on the premise that the First Amendment is an absolute in the sense that "no law" that "abridges" the "freedom of expression" can be valid. The problem with this premise is that it is constitutionally self-evident. The proposition does not carry the Court very far, since it is still necessary to decide in each case the meaning of words such as "abridge," "law," and "expression."

If the First Amendment is an absolute, how is it that laws forbidding sexual or racial discrimination in employment may be validly applied to newspapers and radio and television stations? The absolutist's usual answer is to distinguish strictly between speech and action. Action, no matter how intimately connected with expression, may be punished; speech may not be. But, in an era of symbolic expression, mass demonstrations, and picketing, such a distinction is either impossible to apply or specious. Like Justice Black's other efforts to arrive at a mechanical jurisprudence, the absolute theory of the First Amendment was and is an illusion, and for that reason it has never commanded a majority of the Court.

The Balancing Test   In determining the constitutionality of restrictions on the freedom of expression, the Supreme Court must strike a balance between competing interests. The balancing formula, often associated with Justice Frankfurter, prescribes that in each case the Court must balance the individual and societal interests in freedom of expression against the social interest sought by the regulation curtailing speech, press, or assembly. In arriving at such a balance, the Court must take into account the relative seriousness of the evil the government seeks to avoid, the social significance of the expression involved, the availability of more moderate controls or less restrictive means than the state has employed, and so forth.

The principal difficulty with the balancing test has been its case-by-case nature. It is too broad, too unstructured, and too ill-defined. Obviously, the Court does and must balance conflicting interests. In actual practice, no right is or can be absolute. But case-by-case balancing provides no standard to guide the Court in reaching its decision. The Court is simply cast adrift to roam at will in striking some sort of balance on the unclarified basis of personal inclination. The balancing test fails to confine the number of potentially relevant values to be balanced or to indicate the relative weight to be given each value. In point of fact, if the Court ever took the balancing test seriously, the factual determinations required would be so enormously difficult and time-consuming that the test would be unworkable. Moreover, the balancing test gives almost conclusive weight to the legislative judgment. After all, in determining to restrict expressive freedoms, the legislature has already done the balancing.

The Clear and Present Danger Test   What is needed, then, is a standard that allows the Court to exercise an independent judgment yet guides the Court in striking a balance consistent with the intention of the First Amendment. Perhaps the most famous effort to create such a rule is Justice Holmes's opinion for the Court in *Schenck v. United States*.[17] During World War I, Congress had enacted an espionage act containing two censorship provisions, one of which made it a felony to attempt to cause insubordination in the armed forces of the United States. Schenck and other members of the Socialist Party had subsequently sent pamphlets to 15,000 draftees urging them to refuse induction and condemning American participation in the war. For this, they were convicted of violation of the espionage act.

On appeal Schenck contended, quite naturally, that the act was an unconstitutional violation of the First Amendment. In reply, Justice Holmes noted that the freedom of speech protected by the Constitution is not an absolute right. It would not, for example, prevent a prosecution against someone for falsely shouting "Fire!" in a crowded theater. Rather, the character of every act depends on the circumstances in which it is done. In order, therefore, to distinguish between permissible and illicit speech, Holmes borrowed the rule of proximate causation from tort law to create the clear and present danger doctrine. "The question in every case," he wrote, "is whether the words used are used in such circumstances and are of such a nature as to create a clear and present danger that they will bring about the substantive evils that [government] has a right to prevent."[18]

Although Schenck's conviction was upheld, Holmes had scotched the old idea that the protection of the First Amendment was very narrow. The *Schenck* opinion committed the Court to a libertarian formula of free expression, for, according to its reasoning, the Constitution did protect any expression that did not present a clear and present danger of the realization of some social or individual injury.

The Bad Tendency Test   During the 1920s the full implications of the clear and present danger test became apparent, and the Court—unwilling to accept this liberal stance—retreated to the more conservative bad tendency test. Holmes joined by Brandeis was consistently in dissent in these cases. While clear and present danger placed the burden of proof on those who would restrict expression and permitted only limited governmental encroachments on expression, the bad tendency test allowed government to cut off expression very early on the road to action. All that was necessary was to show that some expression or publication might have a tendency to produce some socially undesirable outcome. Essentially the difference between the two doctrines was that under clear and present danger the realization of the evil that was feared had to be proximate and actual before government could restrict expression, while under bad tendency it could be merely remote and conjectural.

The Sliding Scale Reformulation   The bad tendency test was so restrictive of expression that the Court abandoned it after 1925.[19] But the Court came very close to reviving the doctrine during the dark days of the cold war. *Dennis v. United States*[20] involved the prosecution of the eleven top Communist leaders in the United States for violation of the Smith Act. This act made it a crime to advocate the overthrow of the United States government by force or violence or to conspire to that end. It had not originally been directed against American Communists at all but had been passed in 1940 as a wartime sedition measure. When the Justice Department began to move against the Communists in 1948, it turned the act to its purposes. But, in *Dennis*, the prosecution did not allege that the defendants had conspired to overthrow the government by force or violence. It merely charged that Dennis and his codefendants in organizing the Communist Political Association, a successor of the Communist Party of the United States, had conspired to form groups that would teach such ideas. Clearly, rigorous application of the clear and present danger test would have made it extremely difficult to sustain the constitutionality of these convictions.

Nevertheless, they were sustained. By the time the *Dennis* case reached the Supreme Court it had become a major national controversy. It had been heard at the circuit court level by Judge Learned Hand, one of the foremost jurists in the world and one of the greatest American judges never to serve on the Supreme Court. In upholding the constitutionality of the Smith Act as applied to the Communist leaders, the Court borrowed liberally from Hand's opinion sustaining the convictions.

Hand had recognized that the First Amendment forbade governmental inroads on free expression unless there was a clear and present danger that the expression would produce some evil that the government otherwise had the power to prevent. But, in Hand's view, a clear and present danger could be said to exist when "the gravity of the 'evil,' discounted by its improbability, justifies such invasion of free speech as is necessary to avoid the danger."[21] In other words, according to Hand's so-called sliding scale reformulation of the clear and present danger test, the greater the evil feared, the more remote the possibility of its happening may be for the government to restrict expression directed toward its realization without violating the Constitution. The Supreme Court in *Dennis* simply endorsed this view. When the evil feared is a small one, the results produced by Hand's test will resemble those of Holmes's doctrine—the danger would have to be very close to occurring. But when the evil feared is a large one, such as the violent overthrow of the government of the United States, the sliding scale test will permit government control of expression much further removed from bringing the danger to fruition. The results then are not unlike those under the bad tendency test.

The Redeeming Social Value Test   With the passing of the McCarthy era, the sliding scale test has become an artifact of constitutional history rather than a rule of constitutional law. Today the clear and present danger doctrine enjoys the primary place, though certainly not the only place, in First Amendment litigation.[22] However, it can still produce results that are considered too libertarian. In order to avoid this situation, while embracing

Holmes's test, the Court has advanced a two-level theory of free expression. According to this thesis, at one level there are expressions that may be odious to majority sentiment or opinion but are of sufficiently redeeming social value that they are entitled to be measured against the clear and present danger standard. At another—and presumably lower—level, there are expressions so superfluous, so utterly lacking in social merit that they require little effort to justify their prohibition.

The mechanism for judicial decision making, thus, becomes quite complex. In judging the constitutionality of any regulation of communication, the social utility of that communication must first be examined. If the communication has no social value, it may be censored. If it has some, the courts must then determine the clarity, proximity, and gravity of the danger that might result from it.

The two-level theory has proved particularly useful to the Court in cases challenging the censorship of allegedly obscene or pornographic publications and films. It has allowed the Court to avoid the potentially embarrassing results that would be produced by applying the clear and present danger test to such regulations of expression. In view of the almost total absence of evidence that exposure to obscene materials results in or contributes to antisocial sexual conduct, statutes and ordinances prohibiting sexually explicit expression probably could not withstand the application of the clear and present danger test. But, by invoking the two-level theory, even during the Warren era, when it very narrowly defined what was obscene, the Court has avoided an outright holding that the censorship of obscenity is unconstitutional.[23]

Press Freedom and the Libel Laws   Ironically enough, the two-level theory originated in the area of libel. It makes little sense to justify antilibel laws in terms of the clear and present danger of the commission of some injurious act, since the libelous expression itself inflicts the injury. Nor was the absolutist position—that the Constitution prohibits all libel laws—socially acceptable or even historically well founded, for it is perfectly clear that the Framers did not intend to prevent libel judgments when they ratified the First Amendment. In order to uphold the constitutionality of libel laws, therefore, the Court hatched the idea that libel might be suppressed because it was socially worthless. The principle was then extended to justify the censorship of obscenity. But, at the very time that this was being done, the Court was working a significant reformation of the constitutional law of libel.

This reinterpretation of First Amendment principles was occasioned by the Court's discovery that government officials might indirectly suppress criticism of their conduct in office through libel suits or the threat of such suits, even though they could not constitutionally suppress the criticism through direct censorship. In *New York Times v. Sullivan*,[24] therefore, the Court ruled that, for a public official to collect in a libel action, the First Amendment required that the official, unlike the private citizen, had to show not merely that the publication had been false and defamatory and had resulted in damage to reputation but also that it had been inspired by malice or broadcast with a reckless disregard for the truth. This rule was later broadened to include public figures as well as public officials.[25]

Indeed, the media's constitutional immunity from libel judgments became so broad under this rule that some critics began to argue that it had reached the point of diminishing social returns. Sensitive people who might be desirable government officials were being discouraged from seeking public office, because they were unwilling to accept the costs to their privacy; or so the critics contended. At the very least, it was argued, since public officials and public figures were denied resort to a libel suit, they had to be given a statutory right to reply. The Court, however, has found that right to reply statutes violate the First Amendment.[26] While the definition of what constitutes a public figure has been adjusted of late,[27] the news media's right to broadcast or publish accounts or criticisms of public officials and public figures remains substantially broader today than it was only a few years ago.

Press Freedom and the Right to a Fair Trial   Unquestionably the modern Court's greatest difficulty with the First Amendment has come when freedom of the press collides head-on with the constitutional right of the criminally accused to receive a fair trial. How should the Court resolve this conflict of constitutional rights? The absolutists adopt the corollary doctrine of the preferred position of the First Amendment, holding that the First Amendment freedoms occupy a favored position above all other constitutional interests. Thus, absolutists argue that any restraint on press coverage of criminal proceedings is constitutionally unwarranted. But, valuable as the freedom of expression is, it is only part of our lives. Why should a criminal defendant's liberty or even life be subordinated to the interest of mass media entrepreneurs in selling newspapers or commercial sponsorship of television news programs?

In attempting a feasible reconciliation between these competing constitutional interests, the Supreme Court has moved with great caution. It has chosen to err, if err it must, on the side of the First Amendment, although it has refused to endorse the journalists' more extravagant claims. Not until 1961 did the Court strike down a criminal conviction solely on the ground of prejudicial pretrial publicity.[28] In the following years, the Court reversed two other convictions achieved on the basis of trial by television.[29] and finally outlined some of the steps trial judges might take to protect the rights of defendants threatened by adverse news coverage.[30] The Court issued these guidelines in overturning the murder conviction of Dr. Sam Sheppard, a conviction obtained after a prolonged campaign by a Cleveland newspaper to induce the authorities to charge Sheppard, a televised inquest, and a trial at which the behavior of the press can only (and most charitably) be characterized as bizarre. The Court held that a trial judge might limit the number of reporters allowed in a courtroom, if their presence was disruptive; witnesses should be insulated before giving their testimony; they should not be interrogated by the news media before they have been questioned by opposing counsel in open court; to control the release of potentially inaccurate, misleading, confusing, or prejudicial rumors, the trial court might use its contempt power to dissuade all parties to the case from "leaking" information to the press; and any reporter or commentator publishing or broadcasting a prejudicial story, particularly one involving material not introduced into evidence, could be and, by implication, should be judicially reprimanded.

The Court, however, stopped short of recognizing a judicial power to control the content of news stories. Trial judges were limited to morally exhorting journalists. What if the press proved recalcitrant? And what control did trial judges have over journalists who, rather than publishing "leaked" information, broadcast evidence uncovered by their own investigations? Although the *Sheppard* decision said nothing about these situations, trial judges on their own initiative shortly began to expand their authority. The so-called gag order increasingly became a staple of American criminal jurisprudence, until the Supreme Court expressed its disapproval in *Nebraska Press Ass'n v. Stuart*.[31] *Nebraska Press* overturned a trial court order prohibiting press reporting of *any* information strongly implicating the accused. But, while the justices unanimously concurred in the result, they required five separate opinions to explain their reasons for doing so. That fact, coupled with the extraordinary breadth of the trial court's order in this case, did not produce a decision that would clarify the principles to govern future cases in this area. At most it can be said that a majority of the Court did not find prior restraints on press reporting in criminal cases inherently unconstitutional, but Chief Justice Burger did suggest that judicial gag orders would be upheld only under the most exceptional circumstances, circumstances that would be lacking in almost all criminal cases.

THE RIGHTS OF THE ACCUSED

The Court's difficulties in the free press–fair trial area have been in part problems of its own making. They have been an outgrowth of the modern

Court's heightened sensitivity to the claims of the criminally accused. This concern for the fairness of the criminal process has resulted in a constitutionalization of American criminal law largely unimagined only a generation ago. Where the decisions have impinged on the practices of police agencies, they have raised a chorus of calumny and vilification of the Court—as well as strong, intelligent, and reasoned criticism.

Search and Seizure

As noted in chapter 5, incorporating the Bill of Rights guarantees into the Fourteenth Amendment contributed little if anything to understanding the actual content of those protections. But it did accentuate the importance of their interpretation, for now they limited the actions not only of a few federal agents but also of every local police officer. For example, the Fourth Amendment, which forms a major component of the constitutional law of criminal procedure, requires that law enforcement officers limit their intrusions on the people's persons, houses, papers, and effects to reasonable searches and seizures. It has further been interpreted to command the suppression at trial of evidence secured in an unreasonable manner. But the difficult task of distinguishing the reasonable from the unreasonable in the myriad fact situations that can arise in real-life police work must be accomplished by the judiciary on a case-by-case basis.

With or Without Warrants   The Fourth Amendment speaks of warrants, but it does not make a search warrant the one and only indication of reasonableness. Some searches are constitutionally invalid even though conducted on the authority of a warrant, because the warrant is found to be legally insufficient for some reason. Conversely, some searches, such as the search of a movable vehicle or a search incident to a valid arrest, cannot in practical terms allow the officers to secure a warrant beforehand. In the former instance, the vehicle may move from the officer's jurisdiction; in the latter, it is necessary for the officer to act quickly in order to protect his person. Finding these considerations compelling, the Supreme Court has recognized the reasonableness, within the meaning of the Constitution, of some warrantless searches.

Scope of the Search   A variety of problems have arisen in connection with these recognized exceptions to the Fourth Amendment's warrant requirement. For example, if there is sufficient time to obtain a warrant to conduct a search incident to arrest or of a movable vehicle, must the officers obtain one for the search to be valid? And what is the permissible scope of a warrantless search, especially a search conducted incident to an arrest? At different times in its history the Court has answered the first question both positively and negatively. Over the decades the Court has dealt with the second problem with varying degrees of strictness. In the leading recent judicial utterance on the subject, *Chimel v. California*,[32] the Court ruled that a search incident to a valid arrest must be confined to the area within the arrestee's immediate control and may not extend beyond the area from which the arrested person might obtain weapons or evidentiary items. The *Chimel* Court, however, did not revive the doctrine that a search warrant must be obtained whenever there is time to do so.

Neither did the Court question the power of the police to search without a warrant at the time of making a valid arrest. While *Chimel* placed some limit on the scope of the area that may be searched incident to arrest, consistent with prior cases, it stated the authority to search the person of the arrestee in exceptionally broad terms and left unresolved whether a search of the area within the arrestee's immediate control was always reasonable or whether it was allowable only when the officer had some reason to believe that weapons or evidence might be found in that area.

In particular, did the *Chimel* statement apply to arrests for minor traffic offenses, where it is unlikely that the arrestee would be armed or where, with rare exceptions, there is no evidence connected with the offense? Yes, the contemporary Court has answered. *United States v. Robinson* and its companion case, *Gustafson v. Florida*,[33] upheld full searches of suspects who had been lawfully arrested and taken into custody for traffic offenses, even though the arresting officers had no basis for believing either that the persons arrested were armed or that seizable objects might be found. The fact of the lawful arrest established the authority to search; no additional justifications were found to be necessary.

Evaluation of the Court's Policy   *Robinson* and *Gustafson* have established a strong presumption of constitutionality for any personal search incident to a valid arrest, and there were compelling reasons for adopting that position. Some have argued the the police should have facts beyond those necessary to justify the arrest in order to validate the search. But such a rule would seriously impair the ability of the officers to respond in situations requiring quick action and would "make each arrest . . . a game of Russian roulette."[34] It is true that traffic offenders as a class are less likely to be armed or to assault an officer than are those arrested for other crimes. But "it is well to remember that in a particular case a policeman is not dealing with a class of offenders but rather one particular offender, and when that person 'stands before the officer, he contains a potential for danger, quantum unknown.'"[35] In a typical year, approximately one hundred police officers are killed or injured in this country while making minor traffic arrests. The danger to the officer lies in the possibility that, unknown to the officer, the traffic offender may be wanted in some other jurisdiction for some more serious offense.

Allowing the police to search individuals who have been taken into custody for minor traffic offenses, however, raises the possibility of arrests whose primary purpose is to justify full-scale searches. Given the facts that in most jurisdictions and for most traffic offenses the determination of whether to issue a citation or make an arrest is within the officer's discretion and that very few drivers can traverse any appreciable distance without violating some traffic regulation, this is a real threat. Just as *Chimel* presented the problems resolved in *Robinson* and *Gustafson*, these cases in turn have created the problem of the "pretext arrest" with which the Court must deal at some time in the immediate future.

While the results in *Robinson* and *Gustafson* were reasonable, practical, and not inconsistent with *Chimel*, they were not dictated by that prior holding. Their permissive attitude toward police power is one of many Burger Court retrenchments from the more advanced positions staked out by the Warren Court in the area of criminal suspects' rights. Some have argued that a Court comprised of four Nixon appointees and a Ford appointee have aimed for, if not achieved, a general reversal of the Warren Court's liberal legacy.[36] On closer inspection, however, this does not appear to have been the case, *with the exception of the decisions affecting the practices of law enforcement.*[37] Here, without question, the decision making of the 1970s has been in marked contrast with that of the 1960s. In particular, this has been apparent in the gelding of *Miranda v. Arizona.*[38]

Custodial Interrogation

Since the 1930s the Supreme Court had been concerned with the potential for abuse inherent in police interrogation of suspects in their custody. Convictions based on statements, admissions, or confessions extracted from an accused by means of police coercion are objectionable both because they offend the sense of justice and because they are unreliable. An innocent suspect may confess to a crime in the hope that the officers will desist from their strong-arm tactics. But to convict the innocent is not only individually unjust but also socially undesirable; for, if the innocent are convicted, the guilty are left free to prey upon more victims. The Court, therefore, had adopted the rule that coerced confessions or other statements, whether inculpatory or exculpatory, were constitutionally inadmissible at trial.

The Court then necessarily set about the task of defining coercion. Physical brutality and torture clearly amounted to coercion, but psychological pressures short of violence might also be coercive. In order to distinguish the coercive from the noncoercive, the Court established the rule that, in determining whether to admit or exclude the defendant's statements, the trial court must examine the totality of circumstances surrounding the interrogation at which it was secured, including the length of the interrogation, the demeanor of the officers, the suspect's age and intelligence, and so forth. Based on all the circumstances, if the statements could be said to have been voluntarily given, they were admissible at trial.[39]

The *Miranda* Warnings   *Miranda*, however, abandoned this rule in favor of a more objective standard. By the narrowest of margins, five to four, the *Miranda* Court required that, whenever a suspect is subjected to custodial interrogation, the police must advise the suspect before the questioning that he has the right to remain silent. The suspect must be told that anything he says may be used against him at trial. He must be made aware that he has a right to consult with counsel and the right to have an attorney appointed for him at state expense, if he is too poor to afford counsel. If the suspect indicates a desire to remain silent, the interrogation must cease. If he asks to talk with an attorney, the interrogation must be suspended until counsel arrives or until a lawyer has been appointed to represent an indigent suspect. If the interrogation does continue in the absence of defense counsel, and a statement is taken, a heavy burden will rest on the prosecution to show that the defendant knowingly and intelligently waived his rights. Thus, while waiver is still possible, the prosecution must demonstrate that adequate procedural safeguards were applied at the interrogation to protect the accused's privilege against self-incrimination. Otherwise, none of his statements may be introduced into evidence at trial.

Criticisms of *Miranda*   To say that *Miranda* constituted a radical departure from the previous constitutional law governing the admissiblity of confessions would be an understatement. To say that it provoked a rash of hostile criticism would be repeating the obvious. And to say that the majority's position rested on very questionable empirical premises, that it was logically self-contradictory, that it was untimely as a matter of policy, and that its long-term effect on the administration of the criminal law has apparently been negligible would also be accurate.

If the *Miranda* majority was concerned that some confessions were coerced while others were not, the old voluntariness test was adequate. Obviously, the Court's blanket requirement of prequestioning warnings in all interrogations could only rest on the premise that custodial interrogation was inherently coercive. On what basis had the majority arrived at this conclusion? By surveying a series of manuals or texts used in police department training courses. These police science manuals advocated a number of psychological tactics that the majority found to be coercive if not downright dishonest. But, as Justice White pointed out in dissent, the most recent of the manuals relied on by the majority was five years out of date, and the majority had produced no evidence that the texts had any influence on or correlation with actual police practice.

Also in dissent, Justice Harlan noted that reform of the criminal justice system could not wisely be accomplished piecemeal. At the time *Miranda* was announced, the American Bar Association, the American Law Institute, the Institute of Criminal Law and Procedure at Georgetown University School of Law, and the President's Commission on Law Enforcement and the Administration of Justice were all engaged in extensive, well-financed studies of American criminal procedure. Unlike the Court, which is confined by the facts of a particular case, these groups had the ability and resources to study the system in all its interrelationships. If the Court were truly interested in sound and enduring reform of the criminal process, Harlan suggested, it should have waited until these groups had had a chance to issue their conclusions and proposals.

Besides, the majority's position was illogical. If the atmosphere of custodial interrogation was inherently coercive, how could waiver still be possible? A waiver of one's constitutional rights must be freely given to be effective. Coerced waivers are no waivers. The *Miranda* majority found that the very nature of the custodial interrogation situation was so coercive that a suspect could not voluntarily give statements to the police until apprised of his constitutional rights. But, if that is true, how could a suspect ever waive his rights in such a situation? Once the warnings are read and the suspect is asked if he wishes to waive, how has the coercive nature of the situation diminished? If it has not, then the waiver by definition is coerced and constitutionally ineffective. On the other hand, if the situation is not sufficiently coercive to render the waiver ineffective, why is it so coercive that it renders unwarned statements involuntary?

The Effects of *Miranda* All of the justices, both the majority and the minority, assumed that *Miranda* would significantly affect law enforcement. So, too, did the Court's critics and defenders. All believed that, if criminal suspects were advised of their constitutional rights to counsel and silence, the percentage of those who would talk to the police would diminish significantly.

Empirical studies done in the aftermath of *Miranda*, however, presented a quite different picture. Almost without exception, researchers found that the police have been no less effective in securing statements and admissions from suspects after *Miranda* than they were before. In part, but only in part, this has been attributable to police noncompliance with *Miranda*. However, even when the officers do give adequate and effective warnings, a surprising number of criminal suspects fail to understand either the warnings or their importance for themselves. And, even when the warnings are given and understood, a significant percentage of suspects choose to talk anyway, either out of a hope that cooperation will induce leniency from the prosecutor or the judge or out of a compulsion to expiate their guilt.[40]

Burger Court Developments in Criminal Procedure

Just as *Miranda* produced howls of outrage from the Right, so the Burger Court's qualification of that decision has raised anguished cries from the Left. The contemporary Court has not seen fit to overrule *Miranda*, and perhaps will never do so, but it may distinguish it to death. The Court has held, for example, that statements secured in the absence of *Miranda* warnings, though inadmissible as direct evidence of guilt, may be used to impeach the credibility of the defendant, if his testimony at trial contradicts the information he gave the officers.[41] Similarly, the Court has upheld the admissiblity of evidence derived from an interrogation in which the suspect was informed of all of his rights except the right to appointed counsel.[42] While these decisions may strain legal logic to the breaking point, they do not appear especially critical as policy changes in view of *Miranda's* limited impact.

The contrast between the decision making of the Warren and the Burger Courts has not been as clear-cut as it is often presented, even in the area of criminal procedure. For one thing, the Warren Court was not the thoroughgoing "criminal coddler" it has been pictured. It did hold that a criminal suspect had a right to the presence of defense counsel at a lineup,[43] but it declined to recognize a constitutional right to refuse to participate in such identification procedures, and it upheld the conviction of a drunken motorist based on a blood sample extracted over the motorist's objections.[44] It did find that wiretapping and electronic eavesdropping were searches within the meaning of the Fourth Amendment,[45] but it refused to rule that technological surveillance was inherently unreasonable, and it even suggested some of the means necessary to draft a constitutionally sufficient warrant to permit such evidence gathering.[46] It did promulgate standards to govern police conduct in "stop-and-frisk" situations,[47] but, in so doing, it recognized the police power to conduct limited, constitutionally valid searches on the basis of evidence short of that necessary to establish probable cause as required by the Fourth Amendment.

Nor has the Burger Court uniformly sustained police and prosecution claims. In *Brown v. Illinois*[48] it rejected the theory that giving the *Miranda* warnings removed any taint of illegality from a conviction following an unlawful arrest. In *United States v. Hale*[49] it found impermissible a prosecutor's attempt to impeach the credibility of Hale's alibi defense by forcing him to concede that he had remained silent at his interrogation after hearing the *Miranda* warnings. In *United States v. United States District Court*[50] it unanimously rebuffed the Nixon administration's claims that the president had the power to authorize warrantless electronic surveillance for national security purposes. Among its other rulings in the area are these: the right to appointed counsel announced in *Gideon* has been extended to include indigents tried for any offense, even a misdemeanor, that is punishable by imprisonment;[51] no convicted defendant may be jailed for failure to pay a fine;[52] and a parolee has a right to a full evidentiary hearing *before* parole may be revoked.[53] Indeed, as one moves through the criminal process from investigation to trial to corrections, the Burger Court's decisions become less and less conservative.

To be sure, Burger Court decision making has not capitulated to the most extreme libertarian claims. Doubtless influenced by policy considerations, it has not accepted the idea that the practice of plea bargaining violates a defendant's constitutional rights,[54] but it has ruled that the prosecution may not renege on a bargain once struck.[55] Taking judicial notice of public opinion polls, it has not struck down capital punishment as unconstitutionally cruel and unusual on its face,[56] but it has endeavored to confine discretion in applying the death penalty, while mitigating the harshness of mandatory sentences.[57]

EQUAL PROTECTION

The third and perhaps most socially significant area of the modern Court's decision making affecting the civil rights of the individual has involved the concept of equality and its constitutional meaning. After 1937, when the reconstituted Supreme Court minimized due process as a substantive safeguard for property rights, equal protection entered a period of tremendous growth, highlighted in 1954 by the Court's decision abolishing racial segregation in public schools.

Judicial Response to the Fourteenth Amendment

One of the most persistent ideas attending the proposal and ratification of the Fourteenth Amendment had been that the states that had been defeated in the Civil War should be constitutionally deprived of their power to discriminate against the newly emancipated blacks. But, as the years passed, northern ardor for a program of reconstruction in the South cooled and eventually completely subsided with the Hayes-Tilden Compromise of 1877. Deprived of legislative and executive support, black Americans turned to the courts. But the judiciary, as a mirror of the dominant political and social trends of the time, validated the northern abandonment of the former slaves. In the *Slaughter-House Cases* (1873),[58] despite much ringing language, the Court construed the Fourteenth Amendment so narrowly that it rendered the privileges and immunities clause a nullity. The majority did indicate that the primary if not sole purpose of the equal protection clause was to ensure equal rights for blacks, but that clause was then seriously diluted by the decision in the *Civil Rights Cases* (1883),[59] declaring the federal Civil Rights Act of 1875 unconstitutional. This act had provided that all persons regardless of race were to enjoy full and equal access to a variety of specified public accommodations. Taking the text literally, the Court reasoned that the Fourteenth Amendment prohibited only discrimination involving some state action. Private discrimination was not touched by the amendment, and thus Congress lacked power to outlaw such private acts through legislation enforcing the Fourteenth Amendment. In essence the *Civil Rights Cases* said that the system of white supremacy was mainly beyond federal control.

The Separate But Equal Doctrine

Southern whites, taking their cue from these decisions, then moved to protect their segregated social system by enacting legislation requiring the separation of the races in all manner of public and private facilities—businesses, recreation, and most significantly, in view of subsequent constitutional developments, education. To sustain this institutionalized racism the South advanced the principle of "separate but equal" facilities, a legal formula endorsed by the Supreme Court in *Plessy v. Ferguson* (1896).[60] According to *Plessy*, state-imposed separation of the races did not violate the equal protection clause, because there was no discrimination; both races were equally separated from one another. As for the contention that such a classification stamped blacks with a badge of inferiority, Justice Brown observed that, "if this be so, it is not by reason of anything found in the act, but solely because the colored race chooses to put that construction upon it."[61]

Thus, while the majority in *Slaughter-House* had argued that the equal protection clause was the constitutional device to guarantee blacks equality under the law, the Court in *Plessy* interpreted that clause in a manner that thoroughly discredited it as a limitation on racial discrimination. In the following years, the Court continued to accept the separate but equal doctrine, although that formula ceased to have any meaning because the Court refused to look behind lower court determinations of fact to find if the segregated facilities actually were equal—which they invariably were not.

Educational Equality

Not until 1938 did the Supreme Court move to undermine the systematic racial segregation in education that had been created under the umbrella of *Plessy*. Then, for the first but certainly not the last time, it compelled the admission of a black to a previously all-white school.[62] Lloyd Gaines, a graduate of Missouri's all-black university, sought admission to the University of Missouri Law School. Missouri had no law school for blacks, but it offered to finance Gaines's legal study at the law school of any neighboring state that admitted members of his race. Gaines quite appropriately refused this offer and was sustained by the Supreme Court. The Court ruled that, if facilities were provided for one race, they must be provided for the other. To provide facilities for only one race amounted to unconstitutional discrimination. In other words there was a lack of substantially equal facilities. Since there was no black law school in Missouri, the state had no choice but to admit Gaines to the only law school it maintained.

On its face *Gaines* was not an attack on the merits of the separate but equal doctrine. That theory still remained the appropriate constitutional test. But careful observers concluded that the Court's emphasis was beginning to shift from separate to equal, in which case the South's entire system of legally enforced school segregation was in trouble, given the notorious inequality of the black schools.

This implication was heightened by two cases decided on the same day in 1950. In the first, *McLaurin v. Oklahoma State Regents*,[63] involving an incredible campaign of in-class discrimination, the Court ruled that the equal protection clause required that all students receive the same treatment on admission to an institution of public education. In the second, *Sweatt v. Painter*,[64] the Court supported Herman Sweatt's demand to be admitted to the University of Texas School of Law, rather than attend Texas's law school for blacks. Sweatt's refusal to attend the black law school, the Court found, was constitutionally protected, because of that school's inequality.

As in *Gaines*, the Court simply found a lack of substantial equality in the segregated facilities. But the importance of *McLaurin* and *Sweatt* rested in the fact that, in determining equality, the Court did not just look to physical factors but considered psychological elements as well. *McLaurin* noted that the in-class discrimination impaired McLaurin's "ability to study, to engage in discussions and exchange views with other students, and, in general, to learn his profession."[65] *Sweatt* emphasized the inequality between the white and the black law schools in terms of such intangibles as the prestige of the faculties and the influence and position of the alumni. Judicial thinking seemed to be moving toward the conclusion that it was impossible for the states to comply with the mandate of separate but equal.

The *Brown* Decision   In 1954 this was explicitly recognized in *the* landmark of modern constitutional jurisprudence, *Brown v. Board of Education.*[66] Moving with exceptional, though understandable, caution, after extensive briefing and rebriefing and protracted oral argument, the Court finally rejected the doctrine of separate but equal. Relying heavily on social scientists' research, *Brown* bluntly ruled, "In the field of public education the doctrine of 'separate but equal' has no place. Separate educational facilities are inherently unequal."[67] The Court was convinced that, even though the physical facilities and other tangible factors might be equal, segregation on the basis of race gave minority group children a sense of inferiority that so damaged their motivation to learn as to deprive them of equal educational opportunity.

The Deliberate Speed Requirement   Well aware of the momentous consequences of this decision, the Court dealt separately with the question of implementing desegregation in a subsequent opinion delivered the following year. It concluded that flexibility should be the governing principle, and it therefore directed the federal district courts to supervise the dismantling of segregated schooling "with all deliberate speed."[68] In retrospect, it is easy to criticize this gradualist approach and to argue that the Court should have treated *Brown* as just another lawsuit, requiring the immediate implementation of its decision. But in 1955 the justices could hardly have foreseen the massive, often violent, resistance that desegregation would provoke. Nor could they have anticipated that it would take nearly a decade before a policy of racial integration enjoyed the full support of Congress and the White House.

For years southern school districts resisted the implementation of *Brown v. Board of Education* through a variety of techniques, ranging from the establishment of "private" educational systems through pupil placement laws to outright physical force. Not until 1963, with the admissions of Vivian

Malone and James Hood to the University of Alabama, was the last public institution of *higher* education desegregated, and as late as 1968 the vast majority of black pupils in the southern states still attended racially identifiable schools.

This effort to inhibit the implementation of *Brown* is in some ways reminiscent of the behavior of the post-Civil War South. Perhaps segregationists believed that, if this policy, like Reconstruction, could be forestalled long enough, the federal government would lose heart. But such was not the case. With increasing frequency and intensity of commitment, the presidency, Congress, the Justice Department, the Department of Health, Education, and Welfare, and when necessary the United States Army came to the assistance of the Supreme Court's desegregation policy. Buoyed by these alliances, the Court itself became ever less tolerant of evasions of the *Brown* mandate and finally abandoned the "all deliberate speed" formula.[69]

Acceptable Desegregation Plans   With this decision the focus of the integration debate changed radically. For fifteen years the United States had been arguing over when desegregation must occur. Now continued operation of segregated schools was no longer constitutionally permissible. Every affected school district was under an obligation to terminate racially separate school systems at once and to adopt an acceptable desegregation plan. No more was the question *when* to desegregate (that had been resolved) but *what* must be done to achieve "acceptable" desegregation.

Owing to this shift of focus, in the 1970s Supreme Court decisions on educational desegregation have primarily concerned the remedial devices necessary to achieve racially unitary school systems. The Court has approved court-ordered busing as one means, although it is important to note that the Court did not compel busing or indicate that it thought this the best means to achieve desegregation. It merely held that busing was a means that lower courts might employ to implement *Brown*.[70]

Similarly, the Court has refused to countenance the formation of new school districts that might impair the transition from segregation to desegregation.[71] On the other hand, the Court emphatically rejected the amalgamation of existing urban and suburban school districts into a single, metropolitan district to be administered by a federal district court as a device to achieve desegregated education.[72]

The contemporary Court has extended Brown's policy beyond the Mason-Dixon line, finding various northern school districts in need of desegregation.[73] But the Court has continued to adhere to the distinction between *de jure* segregation (segregation in the public schools required by law and unconstitutional under *Brown*) and *de facto* segregation (segregation in the schools resulting coincidentally from racial housing patterns and not touched by the ruling in *Brown*). If this doctrinal path charted by the Court seems tortuous—and it does—it has arisen from the fact that the Court, like the country, has exhibited some confusion over the ultimate objectives of integration and has, therefore, been uncertain about the degree to which other values should be sacrificed in order to achieve it.

"Benign" Racial Classifications

Contemporary constitutional law has witnessed a significant rethinking of *Brown* and some of its implications. Although *Brown* emphasized the importance of education, subsequent decisions eventually dropped that emphasis, noting only that segregated facilities were inherently unequal, however trivial their psychic effect might be. Segregated recreational facilities, antimiscegenation laws, and the like all uniformly failed to pass constitutional muster. By the late 1960s, therefore, it appeared that *Brown* and the decisions that followed it had fashioned a subsidiary doctrine of equal protection law: the rule that race was never a valid classification.

At this very same time, the argument was increasingly heard that equality of educational opportunity was not enough; there must be equality of result as well. One of the policy consequences of such a theory was the adoption of programs of reverse or "benign" discrimination, allocating specified quotas to minority applicants in admissions to graduate and professional schools. If race was *never* a valid classification, however, such preferential treatment was unconstitutional.

Through an exceptionally strained interpretation of the mootness doctrine, the Court managed to avoid its initial brush with this thorny problem.[74] At the time of this writing, however, a second case raising the question of the constitutionality of remedial discrimination is before the Court.[75] Since the lower courts have differed sharply in their resolution of that question, the Supreme Court probably cannot long postpone a decision on the matter. Whichever way that decision may go, one conclusion is inescapable: What seemed to be such a simple, moral question in *Brown* has proved a much more complex issue than anyone, including the Court, ever anticipated.

Other Classifications

In its decision making on the subject of racial discrimination, the Supreme Court was fashioning constitutional law with implications far beyond that original context.[76] Because of its necessary generality, every interpretation of the Constitution does more than resolve the case immediately before the Court; it constitutes a statement of meaning with consequences for future unforeseen circumstances. Because virtually every public policy classifies people in some way—treating one group (for example, convicted felons) differently from another (such as the law-abiding)—a strict interpretation of the equal protection clause would render government almost powerless.

Over the years, therefore, the Court had adopted a very narrow understanding of the equal protection guarantee. The Constitution did not require that all persons be treated the same but only that persons similarly situated be treated identically. Classification itself did not deny equal protection of the laws—only classifications that were arbitrary, unreasonable, capricious, or invidious. While a legislature might not arbitrarily select certain individuals for the operation of its statutes, the Constitution did not preclude the legislature from recognizing differences in relevant circumstances. Thus, penal sanctions, graduated taxation, distinctions drawn on the basis of age, and so forth were constitutionally permissible.

The Rational Relationship Test   During the 1940s in particular, influenced no doubt by the grievous results produced by the old Court's use of the due process clause as a substantive bar to legislation, the Supreme Court allowed legislatures wide discretion in their selection of statutory classifications.[77] All that was necessary for a classification to be valid was that it be rationally related to some legitimate state interest. Like its due process and commerce clause decision making, the Court's understanding of what constituted a rational relationship was broad and flexible indeed.

The Compelling State Interest Test   As the Court labored to eradicate all vestiges of state-inspired racial discrimination, however, it created a second and alternative equal protection test. Like most other rules of constitutional law, this new standard was not adopted in one piece but evolved through interpretation, as the Court molded and remolded the case law. What eventually did emerge was a test calling for a much stricter judicial scrutiny of legislative classifications. According to this new standard of active review, a statutory classification involving an inherently suspect category or touching on a fundamental right had to advance a compelling state interest in order to pass the test of constitutionality. No longer was it sufficient for legislation to be rational; it had to serve a compelling purpose. This test naturally raised the question, Compelling to whom? Since in the final analysis the answer must be, compelling to five or more justices, this test has been severely criticized as encouraging the kind of subjective discretion exercised by the laissez-faire Court in interpreting substantive due process.[78] Nevertheless, the Court has not seen fit to abandon active equal protection review. As a consequence, a variety of groups have pressed for the recognition of categories other than race as constitutionally suspect.

Discrimination on the Basis of Sex   In particular, it has been urged with great vehemence that classifications based on gender merit strict scrutiny. So far a majority of the Court has resisted these claims, and sex has not been found to be a constitutionally suspect category. But the outcomes of the recent sex discrimination cases have formed such a consistent pattern that it is difficult to read those decisions without concluding that the Court and the Constitution have become especially sensitive to sex as a basis for drawing legislative lines.

Reed v. Reed[79] struck down a provision of the Idaho probate code giving men a mandatory preference over women in the appointment of administrators of estates. *Frontiero v. Richardson*[80] overturned a congressional policy distinguishing between male and female armed service personnel in the payment of fringe benefits. On the other hand, *Schlesinger v. Ballard*[81] upheld naval discharge provisions that favored female officers, and *Kahn v. Shevin*[82] sustained a Florida tax exemption granted to widows but denied to widowers. And, under the umbrella of due process, the Court has created a qualified right for women to exercise unencumbered private choice in the matter of terminating pregnancy.[83]

Justice Stewart has incurred the hostility of feminists for his informally expressed view that the Fourteenth Amendment allows the "female of the species" the "best of both worlds" in that she can "attack laws which unreasonably discriminate against women, while saving some ... which favor them."[84] Whatever one's evaluation of Stewart's statement and the sentiments that fostered it, as a factual observation his position appears unassailable. In terms of the constitutional meaning of equal protection, however, these decisions taken together have been more enigmatic than enlightening. The Court has appeared to be marking time, waiting for the ratification of the Equal Rights Amendment.[85] But if that amendment fails the Court will have to return to the task of fashioning a coherent equal protection law of sex-based discrimination.

Discrimination on the Basis of Wealth   Discriminations based on wealth have also been argued to constitute suspect classifications similar to those based on race. Here, too, the Court has tended to set its face against these arguments. *Griffin v. Illinois*[86] did uphold the contention that, to comply with equal protection, indigents had to be provided with transcripts of their trials free of charge if such records were necessary to secure full, direct appellate review of their convictions. "There can be no equal justice where the kind of trial a man gets depends on the money he has," opined Justice Black for the Court.[87] That principle was used in a later case to require state payment for appellate counsel.[88] In a related matter, *Shapiro v. Thompson*[89] struck down residence requirements for the receipt of welfare benefits.

On closer analysis, however, it can be seen that *Shapiro* turned on the state-imposed burden the requirement laid on exercise of the right to travel interstate. The residence requirement did not discriminate against the poor in favor of the well-to-do; it created two groups of the needy, distinguishable only in that one group had recently exercised a fundamental (though judicially created) right to travel from one state to another. Similarly, while *Griffin* did apply active equal protection review to a wealth-based discrimination, it involved a total deprivation of the right to appeal. As such, these holdings were distinguishable from a situation in which a legislative classification neither completely deprived the poor of a state service nor touched on a constitutional right.

Perhaps the most important decision in this area has been *San Antonio Independent School Dist. v. Rodriguez*,[90] in which the Court declined to hold that the use of local property taxation to finance public education violated the equal protection clause, even though such a financing system results in substantial differences in per-pupil expenditures. Property-rich districts may spend more than twice as much per pupil as property-poor districts, while actually maintaining a lower tax rate than the poorer districts! Nevertheless, the Supreme Court noted that this was not a wealth-based discrimination, since in most states there is no correlation between the value of taxable property in a school district and the median income of families residing in that district. Indeed, the very poor often live in commercial and industrial areas with large property tax bases. Moreover, the Court observed, there was no federal constitutional right to education, and in *Rodriguez* there was no evidence that the state of Texas was failing to provide a minimally adequate education in even its poorest school districts. Thus, there was no total deprivation, and *Griffin* was not a controlling precedent.

Rodriguez, in fact, was anticipated by *Dandridge v. Williams*.[91] *Dandridge* sustained a state-imposed maximum limit on the amount of public assistance a family might receive under the Aid to Families with Dependent Children program. Although such a welfare ceiling discriminated against large families, which then received less per child than small families, the Court felt that the limitation was not unreasonable, capricious, or arbitrary.

From a policy perspective, *Dandridge* and *Rodriguez* are certainly understandable. The maximum welfare limit was necessary to maintain the fiscal integrity of the program in allocating the limited amount of funding available. Likewise, the restructuring of taxation schemes for school financing is an exceptionally complex matter with potentially very costly consequences. And education experts do not all agree that the quality of a child's education is significantly improved simply by spending more money on it. In view of the contradictory and confusing evidence, the Court was persuaded that it was wiser to leave the states free to work out their own solutions through their individual legislative and judicial processes.

THE DOUBLE STANDARD: "HUMAN" RIGHTS VERSUS "PROPERTY" RIGHTS

Ironically, however, the doctrine relied on to arrive at these decisions was that mainstay of liberal jurisprudence, the distinction between human rights and property rights.[92] In *Dandridge* the majority found that, because the welfare grant regulation was an economic matter, the appropriate equal protection test to use was the traditonal rationality standard. This approach was continued in *Rodriguez*.

The double standard of constitutional protection postulates a difference between so-called human rights and so-called property rights and accords a much more rigorous judicial protection to the former. It has become so familiar during the past two generations that most Americans accept it without question. Human rights are felt to be good; property rights are at best suspect, to be defended apologetically.

As a matter of case law the double standard is traceable to a footnote in Justice Harlan Fiske Stone's opinion for the Court in *United States v. Carolene Products Co.*[93] Stone's doctrine, though somewhat ambiguous, appears to rest on three interrelated propositions. First, the presumption of constitutionality that normally attaches to legislation is reversed in civil liberties cases. When a value protected by a Bill of Rights guarantee is threatened by legislation, it is the value that commands respect; on the other hand, when property is threatened, it is the legislative judgment that commands judicial respect. Secondly, legislation affecting political processes that are basic to a democratic system must also be subjected to stricter judicial scrutiny than is legislation affecting economic processes. Thirdly, Stone suggested that small and often unpopular groups are the particular constituency of the Court. Unlike economic interests, these religious, national, or racial minorities might need special judicial protection.

Justifications of the Policy

In the decades following *Carolene Products*, the Court viewed legislative efforts in the area of personal rights with increasing suspicion. It actively promoted its liberalized interpretations of the content of the Bill of Rights and applied those interpretations to the states through the process of selective incorporation described in chapter 5. At the same time, however, as already noted, the Court adopted a posture of extreme deference to governmental economic regulation. Regulatory legislation in the realm of property came to enjoy an almost irrebuttable presumption of constitutionality. Just why the enjoyment of one's property was not a personal right the Court never took the time to explain.

The Constitution Is Clear

One possible justification for the human rights-property rights double standard is that the Constitution speaks with greater clarity about noneconomic rights than it does about property interests. Though such an argument is often advanced by academic defenders of the double standard, it will not withstand analysis.[94] For one thing it neglects the several constitutional expressions of the Founders' solicitude for private property, some of them fairly explicit. There is the Third Amendment protection of the household and its uses. The Fourth Amendment speaks of "the right of the people to be secure [not only] in their persons, [but also in their] *houses, papers, and effects*." (Emphasis added.) The Fifth Amendment shields private property not only from being taken without due process but also against confiscation for public use without just compensation. There are few, if any, provisions more explicit than the Seventh Amendment guarantee of jury trials in civil suits. Moreover, it is noteworthy that, in the body of the original, unamended Constitution submitted for ratification, there are few protections of human rights but several of economic or proprietarian interests, such as the denial to the states of the power to coin money, emit bills of credit, impair the obligation of contracts, or lay customs duties.

On the other hand, the language of the Constitution governing human rights is less than crystalline. The Framers of the due process clauses of the Fifth and Fourteenth Amendments did not spell out "property" except for stating that one should not be deprived of it without due process of law, but neither did they spell out "liberty." The interpretation of these and other amendments in the Bill of Rights has proved extraordinarily difficult over the years. Were they as explicit as some claim, their interpretation could hardly have proved so troublesome. The difficulty of justifying active, aggressive judicial review by relying on such moral adjurations has disturbed some of America's leading jurists, among them Judge Learned Hand and Justice

Robert Jackson.[95] These judges expressed, often eloquently, grave misgivings about the judicial capacity to enforce such inexplicit admonitions in the field of either property or personal rights. Judge Hand carried his doubts to a rather extreme degree, advocating total judicial abstinence, but one need not accept his prescription in order to agree with him that the double standard is not justified by explicit language in the Bill of Rights.

The Judicial Expertise Argument   Hand's reservations, were occasioned not only by the inexactitude of the Constitution but also by his views on the limits of judicial expertise. Conversely, defenders of the double standard argue that a second possible justification for its existence is the appropriate expertise of the judiciary. They contend that, on the one hand, the Supreme Court is peculiarly ill-equipped to deal with questions of economic regulation and that, on the other, "no other agency or institution of the United States government has proved itself either so capable of performing, or so willing to undertake, the necessary role of guardian of our basic rights."[96]

The second half of this proposition, however, is belied by our constitutional history. Until quite recently, the Court rarely concerned itself with civil liberties issues, and when it did, it often failed to distinguish itself. From Marshall's opinions on debtor relief legislation through *Dred Scott*, the *Civil Rights Cases*, *Plessy v. Ferguson*, the post-World War I sedition cases, and the Japanese-American internment of World War II, to the contemporary obscenity rulings, the Court's record as guardian of our basic rights has been a checkered one. It is equally difficult to understand how a Court whose membership has historically been recruited primarily from among corporation lawyers would possess less expertise in the area of property than in the area of civil rights.

That is not to defend the proposition that the Court is uniquely well qualified to pass judgment on economic regulatory legislation. In fact, the assertion that such matters are ill-suited to judicial resolution is superficially attractive to anyone acquainted with the Court's history. The legal labyrinth that the Court created and in which it trapped itself by attempting to supervise government economic regulation is enough to raise serious questions of judicial competence in this area. But it is a somewhat different thing to argue that this history supports the double standard of judicial review.

Virtually every question that reaches the level of the Supreme Court involves subtle complexities. That fact, standing alone, does not warrant judicial abandonment of the field, unless the Court is to abandon all fields equally. But that is not what the double standard advocates. Rather, it contends that the Court should abstain from passing on questions of economic regulation because of its limited expertise but that it need not abstain from judging other difficult issues. All questions that reach the Court are not of equal difficulty, however. Some perhaps are so complex that they are inappropriate for judicial decision, but others are not. How can a blanket rule of judicial abstinence be fashioned for all economic matters? And, even if one could be fashioned, how would that justify judicial resolution of human rights issues that are no less opaque? "In short, while doubts about judicial expertise and power may warrant withdrawal from some economic questions, they cannot justify withdrawal from all such questions, unless the doubter is willing to go the full distance with Learned Hand and give up most of the residue of modern judicial review."[97]

Frankfurter's Open Society   Sensitive to this problem, Felix Frankfurter attempted to construct yet a third justification for the double standard by emphasizing the crucial nature of basic human freedoms. Justice Frankfurter argued that the Court should be more vigilant in its scrutiny of legislation affecting the freedom of inquiry than in the area of economics, because of the relative social utility of the different kinds of freedom. Differential judicial treatment of property rights and of personal rights is justified because, to quote Frankfurter, "those liberties of the individual which history has attested as the indispensable conditions of an open society as against a closed society come to this Court with a momentum for respect lacking when appeal is made to liberties which derive merely from shifting economic arrangements."[98]

Modern scholarship has cast serious doubt on the proposition that history speaks as clearly on these subjects as Frankfurter believed. Nevertheless, the champions of the double standard have enthusiastically embraced the relative social utility thesis with its emphasis on an "open society." Certain rights are so fundamental, they argue, that without these rights none of the other rights in a democratic political system could exist. Without them, other interests, including property rights, cannot possibly be protected; with them, they may.

The argument actually has two facets, the individual and the social. The individual-centered focus rests on the perception that the human personality is more grievously offended by governmental regulation of thought and expression than by control of economic liberty. The individual has a constitutionally justifiable expectation of personal privacy; in particular, a person has a legitimate interest in the freedom of intellectual and spiritual choice.

The protection of this freedom of choice has a larger, societal benefit as well. A viable democracy depends on the protection of voting rights, but this is not enough. Popular decision making must be intelligent and informed. For the people of a democracy to govern themselves properly, they must be fully informed, and this is impossible if the state regulates the flow of information.

In the marketplace of ideas, enlightenment and truth will ultimately emerge victorious, and the society that is governed by such principles is of necessity a well-governed society. Thus, the individual freedom of intellectual and spiritual choice is vitally related to the democratic process of self-government.

The Relationship of Property to Freedom   There can be no doubt that in a liberal society this analysis has a certain attraction. But as a justification for the double standard it seriously begs the question. It may support the validity of judicial activism to protect individual freedom of thought and expression, but it says very little about the appropriate judicial role in the realm of economic liberty. Instead, it rests on the undocumented assertion that property is of lesser importance, both individually and societally.

The contemporary success of socialism surely suggests that, given the choice between political freedom and economic security, the vast majority of people will opt for the latter. Disregard of the fact by the judiciary is not adequately justified by insistence on the importance of political freedom. The regulation of one's livelihood may be as constraining as the regulation of one's mind.

Indeed, one consequence of emphasizing the importance of human rights has been a failure to perceive that the protection of private property is also related to the maintenance of a free society. Even writers of the contemporary Left have acknowledged, though grudgingly, the relationship between property and freedom in the era of the welfare-warfare state. Thus, C. Wright Mills, not a noted friend of economic conservatism argued that the manipulable mass society that he both detested and feared was the product of changes in the economic structure.[99] The old middle class, Mills postulated, was based on wealth and composed of small property owners. The rise of the corporation and the increasing bureaucratization of economic life displaced the old middle class with its proprietarian base. In its place appeared a new middle class of white-collar workers, clinging frantically to the prestige of the old middle class, but without its economic foundation. This class, having no tradition, no organization, no unity, no values, *and no property*, was the most easily controlled group in society. Its very existence provided a fertile field for potential government exploitation. Its lack of a property-based status, in other words, presented a significant threat to freedom.

The Double Standard and Majority Rule   Participation in the political process is surely an important means for securing and protecting one's freedom. But it has never been an absolutely certain means. Bias, prejudice, oppression, and injustice are not necessarily antithetical to democracy, depending on one's understanding of that term. No disparagement of the democratic process is intended by these observations. But it must be remembered that historically the democratization of political systems has seldom, if ever, been viewed as an end in itself. Rather, it has been seen as a means to the end of securing certain inalienable rights, among which have been liberty, life, fraternity, the pursuit of happiness, equality, and *property*.

The open society justification of the double standard rests on a commitment to majority rule that is quite at odds with the tradition of American politics. The argument seems to run like this: A citizen who has participated in the decision-making process and lost can have no fundamental objection to the majority's decision, no matter how grievous its effects on that citizen, so long as he or she still has the right to attempt to persuade the majority to change its mind. But the basic tenets of American constitutionalism do not support the notion that majority rule and justice are synonymous, even if the minority does retain the theoretical right to convince the majority of its error. Undoubtedly denial of that right would multiply the injustice, but its acknowledgment does not minimize the original wrong. The purpose of the Constitution, as Justice Jackson noted in the flag-salute case, was to remove certain fundamental subjects from the vicissitudes of majority rule. It could be argued that property should not be such a fundamental subject. But in theory that shifts the basic focus of the argument, and in practice it would require constitutional amendment.

Judicial Protection of Politically Isolated Minorities The most striking aspect of the open society justification for the double standard, however, is that it fundamentally conflicts with yet a fourth justification sometimes advanced on behalf of the double standard. That argument notes the fact that minority groups, which are themselves often unpopular, do not enjoy significant access to the political process; therefore, the Supreme Court must actively intervene on their behalf. But the Court need not crusade on behalf of economic- or property-interest groups, since they are more capable of success in the legislative and administrative process. This justification, based on the discrepancy of access to the political process, is in some respects more attractive than the open society argument. (It is strange indeed that a doctrine whose fundamental, but tacit, presumption was a commitment to majority rule should place such confidence in an unelected, life-tenured Court.) But the thesis that political, ethnic, and religious minority groups need special judicial protection is open to other challenges.

The first objection proceeds from a concern for basic judicial fairness. It is true that in democratic bodies, such as the legislative and executive branches of American government, groups with limited political resources do not usually enjoy prospects of success. By shifting the arena of the political struggle from the legislature to the judiciary, these groups can equalize that struggle. In court they have a chance to neutralize their opponents' strengths. This is because the judiciary, especially the federal judiciary, is organized on fundamentally different political and constitutional principles than the legislature. Before the courts, numbers and money are of less significance in determining outcomes.

Must the courts go further, however, than providing a forum in which groups of differing political strengths can compete on the basis of relative equality? Must they adopt an attitude of special concern for groups that are disadvantaged in the political process? Was the error of the old, laissez-faire Court the adoption of a protective attitude toward a group that already enjoyed "sufficient" strength in legislative and executive councils? Or did the error lie in the Court's adopting a special solicitude for any group?

A second difficulty with according greater judicial protection to "personal" rights than to "property" rights, is that, if the distinction is to have some meaning as a general principle, if it is to be more than a shorthand euphemism for arbitrary judicial decision making, it cannot be confined—it must apply to all cases of property rights. No tears need be shed for the multibillion-dollar, conglomerate, multinational corporation. But isolated wage earners as well will have to be told to protect their property or their occupational freedom by means of political action. Their power to do so is an amiable fiction.

Modern Consequences of the Double Standard

The distinction between human rights and property rights, then, rests on mere assertion rather than reasoned analysis. The Court and the country are left with a series of arguments that might justify a minimal judicial role in all cases but will not support differing levels of review depending on the subject matter at issue. Nevertheless, repetition creates belief; after nearly four decades, the distinction, with its corollary of different standards of constitutional scrutiny for "human" rights and "property" rights, has become an accepted article of American political faith both on the Court and off.

In practice, however, economic interests cannot be so easily separated from other interests and liberties. The irony of the double standard in contemporary times is that, when applied to the "property" of welfare recipients, arguably a despised minority group, it is self-defeating. As *Dandridge v. Williams* so aptly illustrated, a rule of judicial decision making that was originally conceived to promote liberal ends now works to produce quite different results in cases challenging social welfare administration.

Speaking for the Court in *Dandridge*, Justice Stewart explicitly recognized that, as a factual matter, there was a difference of degree between state regulation of business and state welfare assistance. But, as a constitutional matter, he could not see any qualitative difference between the two that was sufficient to justify the use of different standards to review the constitutionality of legislation in the two areas. Both involved economics.

Justice Stewart, therefore, stated that the stricter compelling state interest test would be used only in cases involving classifications infected with racially discriminatory purposes or effects. All other cases were to be reviewed under the more lax, traditional, simple rationality test. It is this formulation that the Court has since followed in its application and interpretation of the Constitution's equal protection guarantee.

SUMMARY

The Supreme Court's record as a civil libertarian has been uneven. The Court has scored some notable and applaudable victories for individual rights. But there is another and darker side of the ledger. Recent experience has tended to obscure this historical truth. Judicially mandated racial integration, the constitutionalization of criminal procedure, ever-widening expressive freedoms, the abortion cases—all have cast the Court in the role of defender of the defenseless, and this is its image in the public eye. But it is largely a mythological view. The modern Court's adoption of an active libertarianism has arisen from a combination of structural necessities and the temper of the times. The decline, much of it Court-aided, of many of the constitutional checks designed to restrict the scope and vigor of government activity impelled some agency to restrain the exercise of public power, in order for the tradition of limited government to survive. For a variety of reasons, it fell to the Supreme Court to deal with many of these problems through the vehicle of constitutional adjudication. The modern American mind tolerated, if it did not actually support, this assumption of responsibility. Reformation of the judicial function has not been based on a well-reasoned, coherent theoretical foundation, however, and much of the modern Court's record— *Miranda*, the double standard of equal protection analysis, the two-level free speech theory—has been based on very questionable premises and logic. Can such judge-made policy be sound? The more tenuous the holding, the more it is subject to qualification, modification, or reversal.

One of the less desirable consequences of the modern Court's liberal activism has been to encourage the belief that all Americans need do to protect their civil rights and liberties is to rely on the Court. But, even if the justices were so inclined, can the Supreme Court save us from ourselves?

NOTES

1 U.S. Const. amend. XIV, sec. 1. See also Bolling v. Sharpe, 347 U.S. 397 (1954).

2 Reynolds v. United States, 98 U.S. 145 (1878) (antipolygamy laws); Cantwell v. Connecticut, 310 U.S. 296, 306 (1940) (fraud). See also Harden v. State, 188 Tenn. 17 (1949) (snake handling). But compare United States v. Ballard, 332 U.S. 78 (1944).

3 Murdock v. Pennsylvania, 319 U.S. 105 (1943); Martin v. Struthers, 319 U.S. 141 (1943); Follett v. McCormick, 321 U.S. 573 (1944).

4 Marsh v. Alabama, 326 U.S. 501 (1946) (company town); Tucker v. Texas, 321 U.S. 517 (1946) (government facility).

5 Minersville School Dist. v. Gobitis, 310 U.S. 586 (1940).

6 West Virginia State Bd. of Educ. v. Barnette, 319 U.S. 624, 634 (1943).

7 Sherbert v. Verner, 374 U.S. 398 (1963) (unemployment compensation); Yoder v. Wisconsin, 406 U.S. 205 (1972) (Amish children).

8 See, e.g., Jacobson v. Massachusetts, 197 U.S. 11 (1905) (compulsory vaccination); Prince v. Massachusetts, 321 U.S. 158 (1944) (child labor); Application of Georgetown College, 331 F.2d 1000 (D.C. Cir.), *cert. denied,* 377 U.S. 978 (1964) (compulsory blood transfusion).

9 330 U.S. 1 (1947).

10 See McCollum v. Board of Educ., 333 U.S. 203 (1948).

11 Zorach v. Clauson, 343 U.S. 306, 313-14 (1952).

12 McGowan v. Maryland, 366 U.S. 420 (1961) (Sunday closing); Walz v. Tax Comm'n, 397 U.S. 664 (1970).

13 Board of Educ. v. Allen, 392 U.S. 236 (1968).

14 See Lemon v. Kurtzman, 403 U.S. 602 (1971); Levitt v. Committee for Pub. Educ., 413 U.S. 472 (1973); Committee for Pub. Educ. v. Nyquist, 413 U.S. 756 (1973); Sloan v. Lemon, 413 U.S. 825 (1973); Meek v. Pittenger, 421 U.S. 349 (1975).

15 Engel v. Vitale, 370 U.S. 421 (1962) (prayer); Abington School Dist. v. Schempp, 374 U.S. 203 (1963) (Bible reading).

16 See Tilton v. Richardson, 403 U.S. 672 (1971); Hunt v. McNair, 413 U.S. 734 (1973); Roemer v. Board of Pub. Works, 426 U.S. 737 (1976).

17 249 U.S. 47 (1919).

18 249 U.S. at 52. Although Holmes spoke of "Congress," ever since the incorporation of the First Amendment into the Fourteenth (as discussed in chapter 5), the test would apply to state as well as to federal efforts to curtail expression.

19 See Gitlow v. New York, 268 U.S. 652 (1925).

20 341 U.S. 494 (1951).

21 341 U.S. at 510, quoting 183 F.2d at 212.

22 See, e.g., Brandenburg v. Ohio, 395 U.S. 444 (1969). See generally Frank R. Strong, "Fifth Years of 'Clear and Present Danger': From Schenck to Brandenburg—and Beyond," in *The Supreme Court Review: 1969,* ed. Philip B. Kurland (Chicago: University of Chicago Press, 1969), pp. 41-80.

23 See generally Richard Funston, "Pornography and Politics: The Court, the Constitution, and the Commission," *Western Political Quarterly*, 24 (December 1971), 635-52.

24 376 U.S. 254 (1964).

25 See, e.g., Curtis Publishing Co. v. Butts, Associated Press v. Walker, 388 U.S. 130 (1967); Rosenbloom v. Metromedia, Inc., 403 U.S. 29 (1971).

26 Miami Herald Publishing Co. v. Tornillo, 418 U.S. 241 (1974).

27 See Gertz v. Robert Welsh, Inc., 418 U.S. 323 (1974).

28 Irvin v. Dowd, 366 U.S. 717 (1961).

29 Rideau v. Louisiana, 373 U.S. 723 (1963); Estes v. Texas 381 U.S. 532 (1965).

30 Sheppard v. Maxwell, 384 U.S. 333 (1966).

31 423 U.S. 1327 (1976).

32 395 U.S. 752 (1969).

33 United States v. Robinson, 414 U.S. 214 (1973); Gustafson v. Florida, 414 U.S. 260 (1973).

34 Note, "The Supreme Court, 1973 Term," *Harvard Law Review*, 88 (November 1974), 184.

35 Wayne R. LaFave, " 'Case-by-Case Adjudication' versus 'Standardized Procedures': The Robinson Dilemma," in *The Supreme Court Review: 1974*, ed. Philip B. Kurland (Chicago: University of Chicago Press, 1975), p. 151, quoting 471 F.2d 1082, 1118 (D.C. Cir. 1972) (Wilkey, J., dissenting).

36 E.g., Louis H. Kohlmeier, *"God Save This Honorable Court!"* (New York: Charles Scribner's Sons, 1972); James F. Simon, *In His Own Image: The Supreme Court in Richard Nixon's America* (New York: David McKay Co., 1973); Leonard Levy, *Against the Law: The Nixon Court and Criminal Justice* (New York: Harper & Row, 1974).

37 See Richard Funston, *Constitutional Counterrevolution? The Warren Court and the Burger Court* (Cambridge, Mass.: Schenkman Publishing Co., 1977); Stephen L. Wasby, *Continuity and Change: From the Warren Court to the Burger Court* (Pacific Palisades, Calif.: Goodyear Publishing Co., 1976); Robert J. Steamer, "Contemporary Supreme Court Directions in Civil Liberties," *Political Science Quarterly*, 92 (fall 1977), 425-42; Gerald Gunther, "The Supreme Court, 1971 Term—Foreword: In Search of Evolving Doctrine on a Changing Court: A Model for a Newer Equal Protection," *Harvard Law Review*, 86 (November 1972), 1-48; Harry Kalven, Jr., "The Supreme Court, 1970 Term—Foreword: Even When a Nation Is at War—," *Harvard Law Review*, 85 (November 1971), 3-36.

38 384 U.S. 436 (1966).

39 See, e.g., Brown v. Mississippi, 297 U.S. 278 (1936); Chambers v. Florida, 309 U.S. 227 (1940); Spano v. New York, 360 U.S. 315 (1959).

40 See Note, "Interrogations in New Haven: The Impact of *Miranda*," *Yale Law Journal*, 76 (July 1967), 1519-648; Richard J. Medalie, Leonard Zeitz, and Paul Alexander, "Custodial Interrogation in Our Nation's Capital: The Attempt to Implement Miranda," *Michigan Law Review*, 66 (May 1968), 1347-422.

41 Harris v. New York, 401 U.S. 222 (1971); Oregon v. Hass, 420 U.S. 714 (1975).

42 Michigan v. Tucker, 417 U.S. 433 (1974). However, one of the factors influencing the decision in *Tucker* was that, although Tucker's trial occurred after the decision in *Miranda* and was, therefore, governed by *Miranda*, the faulty interrogation had taken place before *Miranda* had been announced.

43 United States v. Wade, 388 U.S. 218 (1967); Gilbert v. California, 388 U.S. 263 (1967).

44 Schmerber v. California, 384 U.S. 757 (1966).

45 Katz v. United States, 389 U.S. 347 (1967).

46 Ibid.; Berger v. New York, 388 U.S. 41 (1967).

47 Terry v. Ohio, 392 U.S. 1 (1968).

48 422 U.S. 590 (1975).

49 422 U.S. 171 (1975).

50 407 U.S. 297 (1972). See also United States v. Giordano, 416 U.S. 505 (1974); United States v. Chavez, 416 U.S. 562 (1974).

51 Argersinger v. Hamlin, 407 U.S. 25 (1972). See also Mayer v. Chicago, 404 U.S. 189 (1971).

52 Tate v. Short, 401 U.S. 395 (1971). See also Williams v. Illinois, 399 U.S. 235 (1970).

53 Morrissey v. Brewer, 408 U.S. 471 (1972).

54 See Brady v. United States, 397 U.S. 742 (1970); Parker v. North Carolina, 397 U.S. 790 (1970). Compare Note, "The Unconstitutionality of Plea Bargaining," *Harvard Law Review*, 83 (April 1970), 1387-411.

55 Santobello v. New York, 404 U.S. 257 (1972).

56 Furman v. Georgia, 408 U.S. 238 (1972). Compare Arthur J. Goldberg and Alan M. Dershowitz, "Declaring the Death Penalty Unconstitutional," *Harvard Law Review*, 83 (June 1970), 1773-819.

57 Gregg v. Georgia, 426 U.S. 918 (1976); Jurek v. Texas, 428 U.S. 262 (1976); Proffitt v. Florida, 428 U.S. 242 (1976); Woodson v. North Carolina, 428 U.S. 280 (1976); Roberts v. Louisiana, 428 U.S. 325 (1976).

58 83 U.S. (16 Wall.) 36 (1873).

59 109 U.S. 3 (1883).

60 163 U.S. 537 (1896).

61 163 U.S. at 551.

62 Missouri *ex rel.* Gaines v. Canada, 305 U.S. 337 (1938).

63 339 U.S. 637 (1950).

64 339 U.S. 629 (1950).

65 339 U.S. at 641.

66 347 U.S. 483 (1954).

67 347 U.S. at 495. As discussed in chapter 4, Bolling v. Sharpe, 347 U.S. at 497 (1954), a separate decision rendered with *Brown*, found an equal protection component in the Fifth Amendment due process clause that was sufficient to prohibit segregated education in the District of Columbia, which is governed by Congress and therefore outside the reach of the Fourteenth Amendment.

68 Brown v. Board of Education, 349 U.S. 294 (1955).

69 Alexander v. Holmes County Bd. of Educ., 396 U.S. 19 (1969). See also Green v. County School Bd., 391 U.S. 430 (1968).

70 Swann v. Charlotte-Mecklenburg Bd. of Educ., 402 U.S. 1 (1971).

71 Wright v. Council of the City of Emporia, 402 U.S. 451 (1972).

72 Milliken v. Bradley, 418 U.S. 717 (1974).

73 See, e.g., Keyes v. School Dist. No. 1, Denver, 413 U.S. 189 (1973).

74 Defunis v. Odegaard, 416 U.S. 312 (1974), discussed at p. 25.

75 Baake v. Regents of Univ. of Cal., 18 Cal.3d 34 (1976), *cert. granted*, ___ U.S. ___, 97 S. Ct. 1098 (1977).

76 See generally "Developments in the Law—Equal Protection," *Harvard Law Review*, 82 (March 1969), 1065-192.

77 See, e.g., Goesart v. Cleary, 335 U.S. 464 (1948); Railway Express Agency, Inc. v. New York, 336 U.S. 106 (1949).

78 See, e.g., Gunther, "The Supreme Court, 1971 Term"; Wallace Mendelson, "From Warren to Burger: The Rise and Decline of Substantive Equal Protection," *American Political Science Review*, 66 (December 1972), 1226-33.

79 404 U.S. 71 (1971).

80 411 U.S. 677 (1973).

81 419 U.S. 498 (1975).

82 416 U.S. 351 (1974).

83 Roe v. Wade, 410 U.S. 113 (1973); Doe v. Bolton, 410 U.S. 179 (1973). See also Planned Parenthood of Cent. Mo. v. Danforth, 428 U.S. 52 (1976) (statutory requirement of husband's consent to abortion held unconstitutional).

84 *Harvard Law Record*, March 23, 1973, p. 15. Compare Ruth Bader Ginsburg, "The Need for the Equal Rights Amendment," *Women Lawyers Journal*, 60 (winter 1974), 4-15.

85 See also Geduldig v. Aiello, 417 U.S. 484 (1974); Stanton v. Stanton, 421 U.S. 7 (1975); General Elec. Co. v. Gilbert, 429 U.S. 125 (1976); Matthews v. de Castro, 429 U.S. 181 (1976); Craig v. Boren, 429 U.S. 191 (1976); Dothard v. Rawlinson, ___U.S. ___, 97 S. Ct. 2720 (1977). See generally Ruth Bader Ginsburg, "Gender in the Supreme Court: The 1973 and 1974 Terms," in *The Supreme Court Review: 1975*, ed. Philip B. Kurland (Chicago: University of Chicago Press, 1976), pp. 1-24; Julius G. Getman, "The Emerging Constitutional Principle of Sexual Equality," in *The Supreme Court Review: 1972*, ed. Philip B. Kurland (Chicago: University of Chicago Press, 1973), pp. 157-80.

86 351 U.S. 12 (1956).

87 351 U.S. at 19.

88 Douglas v. California, 372 U.S. 353 (1963) (appellate counsel).

89 394 U.S. 618 (1969).

90 411 U.S. 1 (1973).

91 397 U.S. 471 (1970).

92 See generally Richard Funston, "The Double Standard of Constitutional Protection in the Era of the Welfare State," *Political Science Quarterly*, 90 (summer 1975), 261-87; Robert G. McCloskey, "Economic Due Process and the Supreme Court: An Exhumation and Reburial," in *The Supreme Court Review: 1962*, ed. Philip B. Kurland (Chicago: University of Chicago Press, 1962), pp. 34-63.

93 304 U.S. 144, 152 n. 4.

94 The best marshaling of the justifications for the double standard is Henry J. Abraham, *Freedom and the Court: Civil Rights and Liberties in the United States*, 3d ed. (New York: Oxford University Press, 1977), pp. 9-32.

95 See Learned Hand, *The Bill of Rights* (Cambridge: Harvard University Press, 1958); Robert H. Jackson, *The Supreme Court in the American System of Government* (Cambridge: Harvard University Press, 1955).

96 Abraham, *Freedom and the Court*, p. 28.

97 McCloskey, "Economic Due Process," pp. 53-54.

98 Kovacs v. Cooper, 336 U.S. 77, 95 (1949) (concurring opinion). See also American Fed'n of Labor v. American Sash & Door Co., 335 U.S. 538, 544 (1949) (Frankfurter, J., concurring).

99 See C. Wright Mills, *The Power Elite* (New York: Oxford University Press, 1956); id., *White Collar* (New York: Oxford University Press, 1951); id., *The New Men of Power* (New York: Harcourt, Brace & Co., 1948). See also Eugene V. Schneider, "The Sociology of C. Wright Mills," in *C. Wright Mills and the Power Elite*, ed. G. William Domhoff and Hoyt B. Ballard (Boston: Beacon Press, 1968), pp. 12-21.

SUGGESTED ADDITIONAL READING

Abraham, Henry J. *Freedom and the Court: Civil Rights and Liberties in the United States.* 3d ed. New York: Oxford University Press, 1977.

Berger, Raoul. *Government by Judiciary: The Transformation of the Fourteenth Amendment.* Cambridge, Mass.: Harvard University Press, 1977.

Emerson, Thomas I. *The System of Freedom of Expression.* New York: Random House, 1970.

Funston, Richard. *Constitutional Counterrevolution? The Warren Court and The Burger Court: Judicial Policy Making in Modern America.* Cambridge, Mass.: Schenkman Publishing Co., 1977.

Graham, Fred P. *The Due Process Revolution: The Warren Court's Impact on Criminal Law.* New York: Hayden Book Co., 1970.

Grimes, Alan P. *Equality in America: Religion, Race and the Urban Majority*. New York: Oxford University Press, 1964.

Levy, Leonard. *Against the Law: The Nixon Court and Criminal Justice*. New York: Harper & Row, 1974.

Murphy, Paul L. *The Constitution in Crisis Times, 1918-1969*. New York: Harper & Row, 1972.

Sigler, Jay A. *American Rights Policies*. Homewood, Ill.: Dorsey Press, 1975.

Sorauf, Frank J. *The Wall of Separation: The Constitutional Politics of Church and State*. Princeton, N.J.: Princeton University Press, 1976.

Wasby, Stephen L. *Continuity and Change: From the Warren Court to the Burger Court*. Pacific Palisades, Calif.: Goodyear Publishing Co., 1976.

THE COURT AND AMERICAN SOCIETY

CHAPTER 7

The Supreme Court, as an institution of government, and the individual justices, as public actors, should be no more exempt from scrutiny and criticism than are other governmental institutions and public actors. It is proper that the justices be kept aware of their limitations, but it is only fair that critics should recognize the difficulties inherent in the task of judging. The Court should be subjected to vigorous and candid criticism, but by those who take the trouble to understand it. In retrospect what is remarkable is not that the Court has occasionally failed the Republic, but that it has so often made a positive contribution to the development of American constitutionalism. "On the whole it has been successful in providing legal resolution for a significant area of political controversy and in elevating the quality of American political life."[1] Largely because of that, today the Court's claim to be the ultimate interpreter of the Constitution commands more nearly universal respect than at any previous time in the nation's history.

CONSTITUTIONAL INTERPRETATION

Judicial prestige tends to give the impression that the Court's decisions are not only authoritative but also final. This should be dismissed for the illusion it is. American constitutional law is not a fixed body of truth but rather a mode of social adjustment. The Constitution may be what the Supreme Court says it is, but in working out the terms of that adjustment the Court tends to be guided by the politically dominant values and mores of the era. Constitutional law is evolutionary, a function of time, place, and circumstance. To observe that the Supreme Court follows the election returns not only is accurate but also draws attention to the fact that most of the time the Court does not exercise a will independent of society.

The Court as Reflection of Society

Society, then, must share responsibility for the present shape of the constitutional system. The Court has acquiesced in the strong presidency, eroded the principle of federalism, abandoned the protection of property, and elevated individual self-realization to a place of primacy in the pantheon of constitutional values. In doing so, it has tended to reflect choices made by the larger society. At most the Court has been a catalyst for change, not a causative agent. In its nationalism the Court has fulfilled the Framers' expectations of its role in relation to the states. But the United States now approaches a political situation in which it could be argued that that expectation has been overfulfilled.

Similarly, the Framers intended the Court to resist Congress. But, given the democratization of the presidency, it has not resisted the democratic principle. Thus, in order to protect individual liberty, the modern Court has increasingly intervened in the policy processes. But even the Warren Court's libertarianism, and especially its egalitarianism, were reflections of liberal attitudes that had dominated American politics since the New Deal. Today, however, with liberalism in decline or—as the present euphemism puts it—being redefined, many are beginning to realize that the Supreme Court, operating under serious handicaps, is a very weak reed on which to pin hopes for a just society.

The Error of Absolute Jurisprudence

During short-run transitional phases of partisan realignment, the Court sometimes loses its way. The usual result is a judicial effort to elevate some passing value to the status of a constitutional absolute. The laissez-faire Court of the late nineteenth and early twentieth centuries, for example, saw property as having a mystical, quasi-religious character. Property became an absolute value, superior to all other legal and political values, different from all other values protected by the Constitution, not subject to adjustment or modification in the light of changed social or economic circumstances, to be defended at all costs through a substantive reading of the due process clauses of the Fifth and Fourteenth Amendments. Indeed, one can argue that it was not Justice Stone who introduced the notion that property rights were separable from other forms of liberty; by 1937 that was already an implicit constitutional doctrine. In *Carolene Products*, Stone merely stood that doctrine on its head, holding property to be a lesser, rather than a greater, value.

The difficulty with the jurisprudence of the age of enterprise was probably not its protection of property through the judicial process but its elevation of property to the level of an absolute value. Despite this lesson, there are some today who call for the elevation of various "human" rights to the lofty plane of the absolute. To protect these "absolutes," contemporary justices have even developed the habit of writing constitutional opinions that more closely resemble legislative codes. "We must never forget," Chief Justice Marshall adjured his successors, "it is *a constitution* we are expounding."[2] Yet it could be argued that the modern Court, under both Chief Justice Warren and Chief Justice Burger, has forgotten exactly that. In their attention to specificity, holdings such as *Miranda*,[3] the abortion cases,[4] and the decisions requiring "fair" hearings in administrative procedures[5] are far removed from the Great Chief Justice's view of the Constitution as a document tracing the broad outlines of government and leaving society to fill in the details through its elected representatives.

Usually, if exercises of judicial power are at odds with the dominant societal norms, they are put right by the normal processes of death or retirement. But, if the American people are not willing to allow nature to run its course, they have the power to correct the situation. They are not saddled with the present as an inevitable, unchanging condition. In the modern era, the Supreme Court has increasingly taught centralization of government power and executive leadership. But these were lessons that the American public wanted taught. If the people desire other lessons, the Court can teach those too.

Limits on the Court's Flexibility

This blunt statement grossly oversimplifies the Court's function, however. For all its openness, the Constitution is not written on the wind. It has some meaning! While the Court's work has a highly political character, the Court's choices are not unlimited. A government of laws and not of men is a significant human aspiration, and the Constitution of the United States represents a singular achievement in the establishment of the rule of law. Constitutional interpretation does call "for a range of talent well outside that of traditional legal analysis.... Yet it remains one branch of legal analysis, and the Court's success in its unique endeavor is intimately tied to its performance as a court of law."[6] Only within these bounds may the Court exercise discretion. In exercising it, however, the Court must be attentive to its political support: it "should be conversant with public opinion, and imbibe the spirit of the times."[7]

This is a fine line to walk, and Tocqueville captured its difficulty:

> The power of the Supreme Court Justices is immense, but it is power springing from opinion. They are all-powerful so long as the people consent to obey the law; they can do nothing when they scorn it. Now, of all powers, that of opinion is the hardest to use, for it is impossible to say exactly where its limits come. Often it is as dangerous to lag behind as to outstrip it.
>
> The federal judges therefore must not only be good citizens and men of education and integrity, qualities necessary for all magistrates, but must also be statesmen; they must know how to understand the spirit of the age, to confront those obstacles that can be overcome, and to steer out of the current when the tide threatens to carry them away, and with them the sovereignty of the Union and obedience to its laws.[8]

THE EDUCATIONAL DIALOGUE

Some assert that acceptance of the idea of an evolving Constitution "would go far to undermine the postulates of judicial review."[9] For the Court to play a legitimate role in the constitutional system, they claim, it is necessary that the Constitution be interpreted as a collection of absolute rules whose meaning is irrevocably fixed by language and history. This view allows for only two choices in constitutional adjudication. Either the Court must be able to deduce its findings automatically from a text that is inescapably clear, or the Court must be seen as a third, unelected house of Congress, governing by fiat, yet beyond popular control.

This vision of unrestrained judicial subjectivity is as unrealistic as the idea of a neutral Court intervening against a purely democratic process to protect individual liberty by upholding an absolute constitutional text. The choice is not between "no standards or clear standards but between better or worse standards for public life."[10] And in making these choices the Supreme Court is engaged in an educative dialogue with the American people, a dialogue between participants both operating under certain constraints.

Constitutional interpretation involves the Court with basic and enduring questions of political philosophy. Indeed, the Court's function in this respect resembles the procedure that the philosopher John Rawls claims is inherent in establishing the very principles of justice.[11] A citizen or group of citizens asserts that it has a legitimate complaint against its established institutions. Such complaints are perfectly natural in any normal society. In the United States the Constitution enunciates the principles by which these complaints are to be judged. But the Constitution's principles are not entirely clear. Each side advocates that interpretation of the principles on which it wishes the complaint to be tried. *But* all involved—the complainants, the respondents, their advocates, and the Court—understand that the interpretation adopted on this occasion will be binding on all similar, future occasions. Each side, therefore, is wary of proposing an interpretation of constitutional principle that would give it a peculiar advantage in the present case; in future cases, whose circumstances are unknown, that interpretation might work to its peculiar disadvantage. The Court's resolution of this contest of competing interpretations of principle might then be likened to "this highest order 'game' of adopting... principles of argument for all coming particular 'games' whose peculiarities one can in no way foresee."[12] At its best, the Court does so through reasoned opinions that justify its claim to be the resident philosopher of the American constitutional system.

No philosopher theorizes in a vacuum, however. In selecting from the infinite diversity of reality those elements deemed important to the advancement of theoretical understanding, in the logical processes by which those elements are related one to another, and in the values that are used to appraise the conclusions reached, philosophers are guided by the spirit of the age in which they live. "In the United States the history of political theory since the founding of the Republic has resided in the Supreme Court. *The future of political theory lies there too.*"[13] In shaping that theory, the value structures dominant on the Court will tend to correspond closely with those dominant in the elected branches. The Court's Constitution, therefore, will normally accommodate Congress's statutes and the President's acts. As a result, most of the time the Court will declare legitimate the actions of the popular branches. But, in so doing, the Court will detail the underlying principles of American government and teach the people of the larger, philosophic ramifications of their acts.

This concept of the Court—as a legitimating institution, bringing the nation's short-run, expedient means into accord with its long-run ends or principles—is also a ground for justifying the Court's power of judicial review, its power to declare acts of Congress unconstitutional. For what would be the good of a declaration of legitimacy from an institution that had no choice but to validate everything that was brought before it? It is only because the Court has the power to annul that its validation is worthwhile.

THE COURT AS SYMBOL OF NATIONHOOD

As guardian of constitutional legitimacy, the Supreme Court provides the United States with the symbol of nationhood that all viable polities apparently require. This country's national continuity is made manifest in the persons of the justices. "Here the human chain goes back unbroken in a small, intimate group to the earliest beginnings," wrote Alexander Bickel.

> Senior members of the Court are witnesses to the reality and validity of our present—distracted improbable, illegitimate as it often appears—because in their persons they assure us of its link to the past which they also witnessed and in which they were themselves once the harbingers of something outrageously new. . . . When the great Holmes, who was wounded at Ball's Bluff and Antietam, retired in 1932, being past ninety, the emotional public response was not due wholly to his undoubted greatness. It was also that his years, his years alone, fulfilled one of the functions of the Supreme Court.[14]

Holmes's assessment of Marshall, then, may be extended to the Court as an institution: Its significance is essentially symbolic.[15] Its most striking power, judicial review, is largely, if not solely, symbolic and is merely the logical corollary of its power to legitimate. As Lord Bryce put it, the Court derives its authority by being "the living voice of the Constitution, the unfolder of the mind of the people."[16] Its decisions are generally reflections of deeper currents in the national thought.

This view again emphasizes the relation between the conditions of freedom and a people's civic culture. As Justice Jackson so cogently stated the matter:

> It is not idle speculation to inquire which comes first, either in time or importance, an independent and enlightened judiciary or a free and tolerant society. Must we first maintain a system of free political government to assure a free judiciary, or can we rely on an aggressive, activist judiciary to guarantee free government? While each undoubtedly is a support for the other, and the two are frequently found together, it is my belief that the attitude of a society and of its organized political forces, rather than its legal machinery, is the controlling force in the character of free institutions.[17]

To maintain that the Court can mold the national mind presupposes at the very least, an educable public. For the Court to perform as a national seminar in political theory there must first be a society willing to listen to the Court. "This in turn rests on a general societal commitment to the principles of reasonableness, fairness, and justice, [and] on the quality of debate in interpreting these commitments."[18] In its interpretation of American law and especially the law of the Constitution, the Supreme Court can play a major role in this debate, shaping and articulating fundamental principles. But, to borrow again from the wisdom of Holmes:

> I have no belief in panaceas and almost none in sudden ruin. I believe with Montesquieu that if the chance of a battle—I may add, the passage of a law—has ruined a state, there was a general cause at work that made the state ready to perish by a single battle or law.[19]

The Supreme Court cannot ensure racial equality in the absence of a societal commitment to racial justice. There can be no hope for the First Amendment without popular acceptance of the idea that freedom of expression is socially necessary and beneficial. Whether *Miranda* remains the law is far less important than whether Americans respond to the call for improved police procedures. Those who would discount the importance of these observations would do well to recall one last piece of Holmesian advice:

> [A]t this time we need education in the obvious more than the investigation of the obscure.[20]

NOTES

1 Sylvia Snowiss, "The Legacy of Justice Black," in *The Supreme Court Review: 1973*, ed. Philip B. Kurland (Chicago: University of Chicago Press, 1974), p. 252.

2 McCulloch v. Maryland, 17 U.S. (4 Wheat.) 316, 407 (1819).

3 Miranda v. Arizona, 384 U.S. 436 (1966).

4 Roe v. Wade, 410 U.S. 113 (1973); Doe v. Bolton, 410 U.S. 179 (1973).

5 See, e.g., Goldberg v. Kelly, 397 U.S. 254 (1970) (welfare termination); Bell v. Burson, 402 U.S. 535 (1971) (automobile license suspension); Morrissey v. Brewer, 408 U.S. 471 (1972) (parole revocation proceedings); Perry v. Sindermann, 408 U.S. 593 (1972) (government employment termination); Wolff v. McDonnell, 418 U.S. 539 (1974) (prison discipline); Goss v. Lopez, 419 U.S. 565 (1975) (public school suspension).

6 Snowiss, "Legacy of Justice Black," p. 252.

7 U.S., Congress, Senate, remarks of Senator Harper, April 14, 1826, *Register of Debates in Congress*, 19th Cong., 1st sess., II, pt. I, col. 554.

8 Alexis de Tocqueville, *Democracy in America*, trans. George Lawrence (New York: Harper & Row, 1966), p. 137.

9 Alfred H. Kelly and Winfred A. Harbison, *The American Constitution: Its Origins and Development*, 4th ed. (New York: W. W. Norton & Co., 1970), p. 755.

10 Snowiss, "Legacy of Justice Black," p. 249.

11 See John Rawls, "Justice as Fairness," in *Contemporary Political Theory*, ed. Anthony de Crespigny and Alan Wertheimer (New York: Atherton Press, 1970),

pp. 192-216. See generally id., *A Theory of Justice* (Cambridge, Mass.: Harvard University Press, 1971).

12 Rawls, "Justice as Fairness," p. 201.

13 Theodore J. Lowi, *The End of Liberalism: Ideology, Policy, and the Crisis of Public Authority* (New York: W. W. Norton & Co., 1969), p. 314 (emphasis added).

14 Alexander Bickel, *The Least Dangerous Branch: The Supreme Court at the Bar of Politics* (Indianapolis: Bobbs-Merrill Co., 1962), pp. 32-33.

15 Oliver Wendell Holmes, *Collected Legal Papers* (New York: Harcourt, Brace & Howe, 1920), p. 270.

16 James Bryce, *The American Commonwealth*, 2d ed. rev., 2 vols. (New York: Macmillan Co., 1891), vol. I, p. 348.

17 Robert H. Jackson, *The Supreme Court in the American System of Government* (New York: Harper & Row, 1955), p. 81.

18 Snowiss, "Legacy of Justice Black," p. 248.

19 Oliver Wendell Holmes, "Law and the Court," in *The Occasional Speeches of Justice Oliver Wendell Holmes*, ed. Mark DeWolfe Howe (Cambridge: Harvard University Press, Belknap Press, 1962), p. 172.

20 Holmes, *Collected Legal Papers*, pp. 292-93.

SUGGESTED ADDITIONAL READING

Bickel, Alexander M. *The Morality of Consent.* New Haven, Conn.: Yale University Press, 1975.

Cahn, Edmond, ed. *Supreme Court and Supreme Law.* New York: Simon & Schuster, 1971.

Cox, Archibald. *The Role of the Supreme Court in American Government.* New York: Oxford University Press, 1976.

Ervin, Sam J., Jr., and Ramsey Clark. *Role of the Supreme Court: Policymaker or Adjudicator?* Washington, D.C.: American Enterprise Institute for Public Policy Research, 1970.

Mason, Alpheus T., and William M. Beaney. *The Supreme Court in a Free Society.* New York: W. W. Norton & Co., 1968.

Murphy, Walter F., and Joseph Tanenhaus. *The Study of Public Law.* New York: Random House, 1972.

Rohde, David W., and Harold J. Spaeth. *Supreme Court Decision Making.* San Francisco: W. H. Freeman & Co., 1976.

Schubert, Glendon. *The Judicial Mind Revisited: Psychometric Analysis of Supreme Court Ideology.* New York: Oxford University Press, 1974.

Sheldon, Charles H. *The American Judicial Process: Models and Approaches.* New York: Dodd, Mead & Co., 1974.

Tribe, Laurence H. *American Constitutional Law.* Mineola, N.Y.: Foundation Press, 1978.

Vose, Clement E. *Constitutional Change: Amendment Politics and Supreme Court Litigation since 1900.* Lexington, Mass.: D. C. Heath & Co., 1972.

INDEX

Ableman v. Booth, 146
"absolute" theory of First Amendment, 177-78
Adams, John, 4
Adams, John Quincy, 38
administrative agencies, 100-02
advisory opinions, 23
Allen v. State Board of Elections, 125
Amish, 174, 175
appointment and removal of federal officers, 69-70

"bad tendency" test of First Amendment, 179
Baker v. Carr, 116, 157
"balancing" test of First Amendment, 178
Bank of Augusta v. Earle, 145
Barenblatt v. United States, 106-07
Barr v. Mateo, 131
Beard, Charles A., 11
"benevolent neutrality" theory of First Amendment, 175-76

"benign" racial classifications, 195
Benton v. Maryland, 164
Berger, Victor L., 111-12
bicameralism, 158-61
Bickel, Alexander, 218
Bill of Rights, 79, 161-66, 168, 173-90, 199-201; incorporation of into Fourteenth Amendment, 161-66
Black, Hugo L., 21, 84, 86, 116, 130, 162, 165, 176, 177-78, 198
Brandeis, Louis D., 21, 99, 138, 179
Brennan, William, 116, 124, 157, 160
Bricker Amendment, 74, 155-56
Bricker, John W., 132, 155
Briscoe v. Bank of Kentucky, 145
Brown, Henry, 191
Brown v. Allen, 149, 151
Brown v. Board of Education, 4, 25, 50, 51, 85, 193-95
Brown v. Illinois, 190
Bryan, William Jennings, 36, 40
Burger, Warren E., 87, 88, 150, 161, 183, 215

221

Burnham, Walter Dean, 37, 41
Burton, Harold, 85, 86
business affected with a public interest, doctrine of, 147

Calhoun, John C., 15
capital punishment, 190
Cardozo, Benjamin, 99, 162, 163, 164
Carter v. Carter Coal Co., 22
case and controversy rule, 21-23, 87
Catron, John, 18
Chambers, William Nisbet, 37, 41
Charles River Bridge Co. v. Warren Bridge Co., 145
Chase, Salmon P., 81
Chase, Samuel, 20
"child benefit" theory of First Amendment, 176
Chimel v. California, 185, 186
Chisholm v. Georgia, 132
Civil Rights Act of 1866, 126-27, 131, 132
Civil Rights Act of 1964, 122, 123, 124
Civil Rights Act of 1968, 131-32
Civil Rights Cases, 191, 201
Civil War, American, 39, 76-77, 147, 191
Clark, Tom, 84, 86, 157
"clear and present danger" test of First Amendment, 178-79, 180; "sliding scale" of, 179-80
Cleveland, Grover, 40, 68
Cohens v. Virginia, 141-43
Collector v. Day, 119
commander-in-chief, 75-86
Congress, 96-134; apportionment of, 115-17; civil rights acts passed by, 123-27, 131; commerce power of, 120-23, 133, 146, 147, 148, 167; constitutional restrictions on, 127-30; control over judiciary, 18-19, 20, 132; delegation of powers by, 96-102, 133; immunity of members of, 108-11, 130-31, 133; implied powers of, 117-18; investigatory powers of, 102-08, 133; membership of, 111-17, 133; regulatory powers of, 117-27, 144, 148, 151-55, 167; role vis-à-vis president, 91, 96-97, 130-31, 133-34; taxing powers of, 118-19, 133; treaty power of, 153-56
Constitution of the United States of America, 2-3, 7-10, 14-16, 34, 48, 52-53, 68, 69, 72, 213-17; Article I, section 2, 11; Article I, Section 4, 152; Article I, section 5, 111-15; Article I, section 6, 108-11; Article I, section 8, 11, 117-18, 120-23; Article II, 65; Article III, section 1, 18, 21, 141; Article III, section 2, 7, 21, 142; Article III, section 3, 9-10; Article IV, section 4, 28; Article VI, 7-9, 10, 154; Eighteenth Amendment, 144; Eighth Amendment, 163, 165; Eleventh Amendment, 132, 143; Fifteenth Amendment, 125, 131, 139; Fifth Amendment, 80, 81, 102, 105, 106, 108, 128, 161, 163, 164, 200, 215; First Amendment, 22, 24, 26, 102, 105, 106, 107, 109, 127, 130, 150, 163, 173-83; Fourteenth Amendment, 23, 28, 123, 126, 128, 131, 139, 147, 157, 161-65, 166, 168, 191, 215; Fourth Amendment, 151, 163-64, 165, 184-86, 189, 190, 200; intentions of framers of, 10-12, 64, 75, 97, 111, 112-13, 116, 139, 168, 175, 200, 214; Nineteenth Amendment, 139; Ninth Amendment, 162; Second Amendment, 164; Seventeenth Amendment, 139; Seventh Amendment, 200; Sixteenth Amendment, 132; Sixth Amendment, 80, 81, 163, 164, 165, 166; Tenth Amendment, 118, 121, 139, 144, 147, 150, 151-52, 153, 167; Third Amendment, 164, 200; Thirteenth Amendment, 125-26, 131, 132; Twenty-sixth Amendment, 131, 139, 152
Cooley v. Board of Wardens, 120-21, 146
Coolidge, Calvin, 45
counsel, right to, 164, 165, 187, 189, 190
Crime Control Act of 1968, 132
criminal suspects, rights of, 183-90, 206
Curtis, Benjamin Robbins, 120
custodial interrogation, 186-89, 190

Dahl, Robert, 34-35, 48, 49
Dana, Richard Henry, 76
Dandridge v. Williams, 198, 199, 205-06
Dartmouth College v. Woodward, 145-46
Daugherty, Harry, 103
Davis, David, 80
Debs, Eugene V., 68
delegation of legislative power, 96-102
Democratic Party, 39, 40, 41
Dennis v. United States, 179-80
deviating elections, 36
Dirksen, Everett, 132

Dobbins v. Commissioners of Erie County, 119
Doe v. McMillan, 109, 110-11, 130
Dombrowski v. Pfister, 150, 151
double jeopardy, 163, 164
double standard of constitutional protection, 199-206, 215
Douglas, William O., 78, 84, 86, 123, 158, 175
Dred Scott v. Sandford, 43, 132, 147, 201
due process of law, 23, 101, 106, 108, 128, 147-48, 162-63, 165, 183-90, 196
Duncan v. Kahanamoku, 81

Eastland v. United States Servicemen's Fund, 109
Eisenhower, Dwight D., 20, 70, 77, 156
electoral behavior, 35-37; patterns of, 35-41; relation to judicial review, 41-47, 53-54, 56-57
electronic eavesdropping, 90, 189
Embargo Act of 1809, 98
employment discrimination, 123-24
Endo, Ex parte, 82
equal protection, 128-29, 190-99
Equal Rights Amendment, 197
Espionage Act, 112
Everson v. Board of Education, 175, 176
exclusionary rule, 151, 163
executive agreements, 74-75, 156
executive prerogative theory of presidential power, 65
executive privilege, 86-90
executive theory of presidential power, 65, 66
expression, freedom of, 177-83

Fair Labor Standards Act, 99
federalism, 2, 13, 138-68, 214
Federalist Papers, 10, 111
Federalist Party, 37, 38
Field, Stephen J., 67
Field v. Clark, 98
Flast v. Cohen, 24
Food Stamp Act of 1964, 129
foreign relations, 71-75
Frankfurter, Felix, 21, 34, 84, 86, 105, 162, 178, 202
"free-press—fair trial" problem, 182-83
Frontiero v. Richardson, 128, 197
Frothingham v. Mellon, 23-24

Gaines v. Canada, 192
Gibbons v. Ogden, 120, 143, 149
Gideon, Clarence Earl, 164
Gideon v. Wainwright, 164, 165, 190
Goldberg, Arthur, 123
Grant, Ulysses S., 18
Gravel, Mike, 109
Gravel v. United States, 109-10
Grier, Robert, 18, 76
Griffin v. Illinois, 197, 198
Griggs v. Duke Power Co., 123-24
Gulf of Tonkin Resolution, 77, 78, 100
Gustafson v. Florida, 185-86

habeas corpus, writ of, 79-81, 149-50, 151; suspension of, 79-81
Habeas Corpus Act of 1863, 80
Habeas Corpus Act of 1867, 149
Hamilton, Alexander, 10, 16, 17, 111
Hand, Learned, 180, 200, 201, 202
Harding, Warren G., 45, 103
Harlan, John Marshall, 116, 165-66, 188
Hay, John, 73
Heart of Atlanta Motel v. United States, 122-23
Heren, Louis, 48
Hirabayashi v. United States, 82
Holmes, Oliver Wendell, Jr., 34, 48, 148, 153, 154-55, 161, 178, 218, 219
Hoover, Herbert, 45
House Un-American Activities Committee, 102, 105, 106, 107
Hughes, Charles E., 21
Humphrey's Executor v. United States, 70, 90
Hylton v. United States, 11-12, 22

"impact" studies, 49-52, 188-89
implied powers, 117-18, 144
intergovernmental tax immunities, 119
Interstate Commerce Commission, 98, 101
interstate travel, right to, 130, 198

Jackson, Andrew, 19-20, 38, 39, 42, 63
Jackson, Robert H., 21, 63, 84-85, 86, 174, 201, 204, 218
Japanese-American relocation and internment, 82-83, 201
Jaworski, Leon, 87
Jefferson, Thomas, 4, 6, 9, 38, 42, 63
Jehovah's Witnesses, 174, 175
Johnson, Andrew, 18, 69
Johnson, Lyndon, 77, 100

Jones v. Alfred H. Mayer Co., 125-26, 131-32
judicial activism, 33-34, 130
judicial review, 33-35; defined, 2; constitutional bases of, 7-12; historical precedents for, 12-13; importance of, 2-4; justification of, 14-16; limitations on, 18-29; origin of, 4-14; scope of, 17-30; significance of, 46-57; structural-cultural bases of, 13-14
judicial self-restraint, 21-30, 33-34
Judicial Act of 1789, 5, 6, 141, 142
jury trial, 163, 165-66

Kahn v. Shevin, 197
Katzenbach, Nicholas, 77
Katzenbach v. McClung, 122-23, 129
Katzenbach v. Morgan, 124
Kefauver, Estes, 108
Kennedy, John F., 77
Kilbourn v. Thompson, 103, 111
Korematsu v. United States, 82
Kurland, Philip B., 56

learning theory, 52, 56
legislative apportionment, 115-17, 157-61
legislative investigations, 102-08
legitimacy, 46-48, 52, 56, 217, 218
libel, 181-82
liberty of contract, doctrine of, 148
Lincoln, Abraham, 20, 63, 76, 79, 80
lineups, 189
Little v. Barreme, 90
Lochner v. New York, 161
Locke, John, 65, 91
Lowi, Theodore, 57
Lucas v. Forty-fourth General Assembly of Colorado, 159-60
Luther v. Borden, 27-28

Madison, James, 5, 6, 96
maintaining elections, 36
majority rule, 17, 33, 46, 49, 56, 57, 204, 214, 215, 217, 219
mandamus, writ of, 4-5, 6, 115
Mapp v. Ohio, 163-64
Marbury v. Madison, 4-7, 51, 118, 140
Marshall, John, 5, 6, 7, 8, 9, 10, 19-20, 21, 42, 72, 98, 117-18, 119, 120, 140, 141, 142-43, 145, 146, 161, 201, 215, 218
Martin v. Hunter's Lessee, 140-41
McCardle, Ex parte, 18-19
McCarthy, Joe, 102

McCulloch v. Maryland, 117-19, 144
McGrain v. Daugherty, 104
McKinley, William, 44, 45
McLaurin v. Oklahoma State Regents, 192-93
Merryman, Ex parte, 79
Migratory Bird Act of 1913, 153
Migratory Bird Act of 1918, 154
Miller, Samuel F., 103
Milligan, Ex parte, 80-81, 82, 90
Mills, C. Wright, 203
minority rights, 34, 46, 56, 204-05
Minton, Sherman, 85
Miranda v. Arizona, 186-89, 190, 206, 215, 219
Missouri v. Holland, 153-55
Monroe, James, 38, 143
Mora v. McNamara, 99-100
Myers v. United States, 70

National Industrial Recovery Act, 98, 99
National League of Cities v. Usery, 151-52
Neagle, In re, 66-68, 91
Nebraska Press Ass'n v. Stuart, 183
New York Times v. Sullivan, 182
Nixon, Richard M., 87-90, 91, 132, 186
Non-Intercourse Act, 98
"normal vote," concept of, 36

obscene expression, 181
Opp Cotton Mills v. Administrator, 99
Oregon v. Mitchell, 131, 152

Palko v. Connecticut, 163, 164
Panama Refining Co. v. Ryan, 98-99
parole, 190
party behavior, patterns of, 37-41
Pentagon Papers, 90, 109, 110
Perkins v. Matthews, 125
plea bargaining, 190
Plessy v. Ferguson, 191-92, 201
Poe v. Ullman, 25
"political question" doctrine, 27-29, 87, 112, 115, 157, 160
political theory, 57, 65, 91, 139, 161, 216-17
Pollock v. Farmers' Loan & Trust Co., 132
Pound, Roscoe, 146
Powell, Adam Clayton, 112-15
Powell, Louis F., 90
Powell v. McCormack, 112-15
presidency, 63-92, 214

Prize Cases, 76-77, 91
property, 7, 214; contrasted with "human" rights, 199-206, 215; relationship to freedom, 203; search of, 184-86; seizure of in wartime, 83-86
public accommodations, 122-23, 147

Quirin, Ex parte, 82, 91

racial discrimination, law of, 121-27, 190-95
Rawls, John, 217
realigning elections, 36-37, 38, 39, 40, 41; relation to judicial review, 42-47, 53-54, 56, 214
"redeeming social value" test of First Amendment, 180-81
Reed, Stanley, 85
Reed v. Reed, 197
Reid v. Covert, 156
religion, First Amendment law of, 173-77; establishment of, 175-77; free exercise of, 173-75
remedies, rule of exhaustion of, 25-26
Republican Party, 37, 38, 39, 40, 41
Reynolds v. Sims, 157-59, 160, 161
ripeness, rule of, 25
Roane, Spencer, 141-42
Roberts, Owen J., 3
Roosevelt, Franklin D., 17, 18, 37, 40, 63, 71, 72, 74, 81, 82, 90, 99, 121, 148
Roosevelt, Theodore, 45, 63
Rostow, Eugene, 49
Runyon v. McCrary, 127

San Antonio Independent School Dist. v. Rodriguez, 198, 199
Schechter Bros. Poultry Corp. v. United States, 99
Schenck v. United States, 178-79
Schlesinger v. Ballard, 197
Schlesinger v. Reservists Committee to Stop the War, 24
school prayer cases, 27, 54, 176-77
search and seizure, 184-86
segregation, 191-95
Selective Service, 101, 173
"separate but equal" doctrine, 191-93
separation of powers, 2, 3, 7, 13, 63-64, 96-97
sex-based discrimination, 128, 197
Shapiro v. Thompson, 198
Sheppard v. Maxwell, 183

ShermanAntitrust Act, 121
Slaughter-House Cases, 161, 191
Smith Act, 179
Smith, Al, 36, 40
social science, 49-52, 193
Social Security Act, 128
sovereignty, 140
standing to sue, 23-25
states, police power of, 139
statutory interpretation, 4, 100
stewardship theory of presidential power, 65
Stewart, Potter, 100, 115, 126, 160, 197, 206
Stone, Harlan F., 21, 99, 199, 215
Stone v. Powell, 151
"stop-and-frisk," 189
Story, Joseph, 21, 141
Sullivan v. Little Hunting Park, Inc., 126-27
Supreme Court, 1-2, 16, 29-30, 46-57, 213-19; appellate jurisdiction of, 18-19; appointment to, 20-21, 140-43; composition of, 18, 20-21; docket of, 21-29
Sutherland, George, 70, 72
Sweatt v. Painter, 192, 193
Swift v. Tyson, 146
symbols, 51, 52-54, 218

Taft, William Howard, 45, 65, 70
Taft-Hartley Act, 83, 84, 132
Taney, Roger B., 20, 21, 28, 42-43, 79, 145
Tenure of Office Act, 69
Test Oath Act of 1862, 111
Thayer, James Bradley, 34
Tileston v. Ullman, 23
Tocqueville, Alexis de, 13, 78, 216
treaties, 73-74, 153-56
Truman, Harry S, 83, 84, 85
two-level equal protection analysis, 195-97, 206
two-level theory of free expression, 180-81, 206
Tyler, John, 27, 28

unenumerated rights, 130, 147-48
United Nations, 74, 155
United Public Workers v. Mitchell, 22
United States Dep't of Agriculture v. Moreno, 128-29
United States v. Belmont, 74, 91
United States v. Butler, 3

United States v. Carolene Products Co., 199-200, 215
United States v. Curtiss-Wright Export Corp., 71-72, 91
United States v. Grimaud, 98
United States v. Hale, 190
United States v. Richard M. Nixon, 50, 87-90, 91, 110
United States v. Pink, 74, 91
United States v. Richardson, 24
United States v. Robinson, 185-86
United States v. Rumley, 104-05
United States v. Sisson, 77
United States v. United States District Court, 90, 190

Vietnam, 75, 77, 78, 100
Vinson, Fred, 85, 86
voting rights, 124-25
Voting Rights Act Amendment of 1970, 131
Voting Rights Act of 1965, 124, 125

"wall of separation" theory of First Amendment, 175
war, constitutional law of, 75-86; declarations of, 75, 77; power to make, 75-86; presidential conduct of, 76-79
War Powers Resolution of 1973, 78, 133
Warren, Earl, 21, 106, 108, 112, 114, 130, 132, 158, 160, 161, 164, 166-67, 215
Washington v. Legrant, 130
Watergate, 75, 87, 133
Watkins v. United States, 105-06, 107
wealth-based discrimination, 197-99
Wesberry v. Sanders, 116-17
Whig Party, 39
White, Byron, 188
Wilson, Woodrow, 45, 63, 70, 77, 108, 134
wiretapping, 90, 189, 190
Wyzanski, Charles E., 77

Younger v. Harris, 151
Youngstown Sheet & Tube Co. v. Sawyer, 83-86, 90